The Impact of History?

Driven by the increasing importance of discussions around 'impact' and its meaning and implications for history, *The Impact of History?* brings together established and new voices to raise relevant questions, issues and controversies for debate. The chapters are articulated around the themes of public history, the politics of history, the role of history in the shaping of learning and the situation of history in the changing world of education. While this subject is driven differently by the research bodies and councils of different countries, similar debates about the value and place of the academy in society are taking place in the UK, the USA and continental Europe as well as in other parts of the world.

Chapters cover diverse areas of history from this perspective including:

- public history
- national histories
- new technologies and the natural sciences
- campaigning histories
- the impact agenda.

This collection is a political and intellectual intervention at a time when scholars and readers of history are being asked to explain why history matters; and it seeks to intervene in the debates on 'impact', on education and on the role of the past in the shaping of our future. Bringing together leading authors from a wide range of fields, *The Impact of History?* is an accessible and engaging yet polemical and thought-provoking overview of the role of history in contemporary society.

Pedro Ramos Pinto is Lecturer in International Economic History at the University of Cambridge and Fellow of Trinity Hall. He is the author of *Lisbon Rising: Urban Social Movements in the Portuguese Revolution, 1974–1975* (2013) and is the Director of the Inequality, Social Science and History Network, which brings historians, policymakers and social activists together to understand and combat inequalities.

Bertrand Taithe is Professor of Cultural History at the University of Manchester. He is the founder and Director of the Humanitarian and Conflict Response Institute (HCRI), which brings together academics and practitioners of humanitarian aid; his most recent publications include *The Killer Trail* (2011) and *Evil, Barbarism and Empire* (2011), edited with Tom Crook and Rebecca Gill.

The Impact of History?
Histories at the beginning of the twenty-first century

Edited by
Pedro Ramos Pinto and Bertrand Taithe

LONDON AND NEW YORK

First published 2015
by Routledge
2 Park Square, Milton Park, Abingdon, Oxon OX14 4RN

and by Routledge
711 Third Avenue, New York, NY 10017

Routledge is an imprint of the Taylor & Francis Group, an informa business

© 2015 Pedro Ramos Pinto and Bertrand Taithe

The right of the editors to be identified as authors of the editorial material, and of the authors for their individual chapters, has been asserted in accordance with sections 77 and 78 of the Copyright, Designs and Patents Act 1988.

All rights reserved. No part of this book may be reprinted or reproduced or utilized in any form or by any electronic, mechanical, or other means, now known or hereafter invented, including photocopying and recording, or in any information storage or retrieval system, without permission in writing from the publishers.

Trademark notice: Product or corporate names may be trademarks or registered trademarks, and are used only for identification and explanation without intent to infringe.

British Library Cataloguing-in-Publication Data
A catalogue record for this book is available from the British Library

Library of Congress Cataloging in Publication Data
The impact of history? : histories and the beginning of the 21st century / edited by Pedro Ramos Pinto and Bertrand Taithe.
pages cm
1. Historiography. 2. Historiography--Social aspects. I. Ramos Pinto, Pedro, editor. II. Taithe, Bertrand, editor.
D13.I585 2015
907.2--dc23
2014034291

ISBN: 978-1-138-77509-1 (hbk)
ISBN: 978-1-138-77510-7 (pbk)
ISBN: 978-1-315-72653-3 (ebk)

Typeset in Sabon
by Taylor & Francis Books

To Raphael Samuel

Contents

List of illustrations	ix
Preface and acknowledgements	x
Notes on contributors	xi

1 Doing history in public? Historians in the age of *impact*   1
PEDRO RAMOS PINTO AND BERTRAND TAITHE

2 The genealogy boom: Inheritance, family history
and the popular historical imagination   21
JEROME DE GROOT

3 History 2.0: History, publics and
new technologies   34
TOBY BUTLER

4 The humanities and public service broadcasting:
A history film-maker's view   46
MICHAEL WOOD

5 From Roy Jenkins downwards: The historian/journalist and
journalist/historian in contemporary Britain   70
SCOTT ANTHONY

6 The return of national history   82
STEFAN BERGER

7 History, memory and civic education   95
FRANÇOISE VERGÈS

8 'Different and better times'? History, progress
and inequality   110
EMILY ROBINSON

viii *Contents*

9 Campaigning histories   123
PETER YEANDLE

10 History, science and environment policy   139
PAUL WARDE

11 History and practitioners: The use of history by humanitarians
and potential benefits of history to the humanitarian sector   153
JOHN BORTON AND ELEANOR DAVEY

12 The impact of the state   169
PETER MANDLER

Index   182

List of illustrations

Figures

3.1 The observatory and printing press seen from Jericho meadows, Oxford, *c.* 1810   35

4.1 Michael Wood's location notes at Morebath, Devon, for the fifth programme of *The Great British Story* (2012)   59

4.2 Michael Wood's notes for the editor at Morebath, Devon, for the fifth programme of *The Great British Story* (2012)   60

Tables

4.1 Section of post-production script from *Christina: A Medieval Life* (2009)   52

4.2 Section of post-production script from *Conquistadors* (2000)   56

4.3 Section of post-production script from *The Great British Story* (2012)   57

4.4 Section of post-production script from *The Story of India* (2007)   62

4.5 Section of post-production script from *The Story of England* (2010)   65

Preface and acknowledgements

This project grew from a range of research conversations over the years in Cambridge and Manchester. It also grew from our personal experience in facing a bureaucratic process of 'impact narratives' associated with the British research evaluation process.

This prompt was not in itself sufficient but we had the opportunity to discuss the issues with colleagues and friends during this period at the Institute of Historical Research (IHR) history lab event organized in Manchester by Catherine Feely, and through the Arts and Historical Research Council (AHRC)-funded Inequality, Social Science and History Research Network run by Pedro Ramos Pinto.

We are very grateful to the contributors who have responded so freely to our invitation and to our queries during the year 2013–14.

The universities of Cambridge and Manchester have kindly supported this project – often through the operations of our department and college – rather than through 'impact' related activities!

A number of colleagues have been generous in their advice and friendly guidance and we would like to acknowledge in particular Peter Gatrell, Julie-Marie Strange and Simon Szreter.

Notes on contributors

Scott Anthony has been an historian/journalist at the universities of Cambridge, Oxford and Manchester, and a journalist/historian at Future Publishing, *The Guardian* and *The Times*. He has worked on a number of applied history projects – stretching from exhibitions, talks and film seasons to a set of stamps, corporate speeches and political campaigning – with organizations such as the British Film Institute, the Science Museum and British Airways. He is co-convener of the Public and Popular History seminar at the University of Cambridge and the Institute of Historical Research (IHR)'s Public History seminar. His books include *Public Relations and the Making of Modern Britain* (Manchester University Press, 2012) and *The Projection of Britain: A History of the GPO Film Unit* (co-edited with James Mansell) (BFI, 2011).

Stefan Berger is Director of the Institute for Social Movements, Executive Chair of the Foundation Library of the Ruhr and Professor of Social History at Ruhr-Universität Bochum. He has published widely on historiography, national identity and labour history. His books include a series of edited collections on history and nationalism entitled *Writing the Nation* (2008–2015) which built on his European Science Foundation (ESF) programme entitled 'Representations of the Past: National Histories in Europe'. His most recent monograph *The Past as History: National Histories in Modern Europe* (Palgrave MacMillan, 2015, with Christoph Conrad) followed previous monographs entitled: *Friendly Enemies: Britain and the GDR, 1949–1990* (Berghahn Books, 2010, with Norman LaPorte), *Inventing Germany* (Bloomsbury, 2004), *Social Democracy and the German Working Classes* (Longman, 2000), *The Search for Normality: National Identity and Historical Consciousness in Germany since 1800* (Berghahn Books, 1997, 2nd edn, 2003), *The British Labour Party and the German Social Democrats, 1900–1931* (Oxford University Press, 1994).

John Borton is a freelance consultant who is also a Senior Research Associate at the Humanitarian Policy Group (HPG) of the Overseas Development Institute (ODI) and an Honorary Lecturer at the Humanitarian and Conflict Response Institute (HCRI) at the University of Manchester. He has worked within the international humanitarian sector for thirty-three years in a variety of operational, evaluation, research and capacity development roles.

Notes on contributors

During his eleven years as an ODI Research Fellow (1991–2002) he led the establishment of what is now the Humanitarian Practice Network (HPN), the Study 3 team of the landmark Joint Evaluation of Emergency Assistance to Rwanda and the creation of the Active Learning Network for Accountability and Performance in Humanitarian Action (ALNAP), of which he was coordinator for its first five years. Since moving to a freelance role John has supported the governance and staff of a large non-governmental organization (NGO) programme in Darfur for ten years as well as preparing annual surveys of developments in humanitarian accountability. For the last two years he has been part of the HPG's Global History of Humanitarian Action team and has a particular interest in making the history of humanitarian action more accessible to humanitarian workers.

Toby Butler is a senior lecturer and programme leader for the BA in history and the MA in heritage studies at the University of East London. His research interests include oral history, digital heritage, historical interpretation in museums and the social and cultural history of London. Toby has created several oral history trails that explore place for clients including the Museum of London, Elmbridge Borough Council and Tower Hamlets Council (Victoria Park); see memoryscape.org.uk for details. He has directed and worked on oral history projects in India, the USA, Wales and England, including Royal Docks (www.portsofcall.org.uk). Toby is co-editor of the *History Workshop Journal* and a research associate at Raphael Samuel History Centre and the Scottish Oral History Centre. He is currently writing a book entitled *Memoryscapes: Making Place-based Oral History* for Oxford University Press and directing a project interpreting the history of the 1943 Bethnal Green underground shelter disaster (www.bgmemorial.org.uk).

Eleanor Davey is a Lecturer at the Humanitarian and Conflict Response Institute (HCRI) at the University of Manchester and was formerly a Research Officer in the Humanitarian Policy Group (HPG) at the Overseas Development Institute (ODI). While at HPG she led the project A Global History of Modern Humanitarian Action, promoting the use of history for humanitarian practice and policymaking. Her research on the relationship between third-worldism and contemporary French humanitarianism will be published by Cambridge University Press as *Idealism beyond Borders: The French Revolutionary Left and the Intellectual Origins of Humanitarianism, 1954–1988* (Cambridge University Press, forthcoming). In 2014 she was awarded a British Academy Postdoctoral Fellowship to study the relationship between humanitarianism and national liberation.

Jerome de Groot is a Lecturer at the University of Manchester. He is the author of *Royalist Identities* (Palgrave Macmillan, 2004), *Consuming History: Historians and Heritage in Popular Culture* (Routledge, 2008) and *The Historical Novel* (Routledge, 2009). *Remaking History* will be published in 2015 by Routledge, and a second edition of *Consuming History* is forthcoming.

Notes on contributors xiii

Peter Mandler is Professor of Modern Cultural History at the University of Cambridge and Bailey Fellow in History at Gonville and Caius College. Between 1998 and 2002 he was a member of the Arts and Humanities Research Board (AHRB) History Research Panel; he was also a member of the funding councils' History Panel for the Research Assessment Exercise (RAE) 2008 and Research Excellence Framework (REF) 2014. Between 2009 and 2012 he was Vice-President of the Royal Historical Society with responsibility for education policy; since 2012 he has been President of the Royal Historical Society. In between, and among other things, he is currently researching the history of education policy in twentieth-century Britain.

Pedro Ramos Pinto is Lecturer in International Economic History at the University of Cambridge and Fellow of Trinity Hall. His work has focused on the interaction between citizenship, inequalities and collective action, themes at the heart of his recent book, *Lisbon Rising: Urban Social Movements in the Portuguese Revolution, 1974–1975* (Manchester University Press, 2013). He also directs the Inequality, Social Science and History Research Network, which supports historians engaging with current debates on inequality.

Emily Robinson is Lecturer in Politics at the University of Sussex, where she specializes in modern British political and cultural history. She is the author of *History, Heritage and Tradition in Contemporary British Politics: Past Politics and Present Histories* (Manchester University Press, 2012). She has a PhD from the University of London and has held fellowships at the Universities of East Anglia and Nottingham.

Bertrand Taithe is Professor in Cultural History at the University of Manchester. He founded and directs the Humanitarian and Conflict Response Institute (HCRI) and is a member of Médecins Sans Frontières (MSF)'s CRASH scientific committee. His research is primarily devoted to the history of medicine, war and humanitarian aid in Britain and France, on which he has published widely. He is currently completing a monograph entitled: *Selling Compassion* with Dr Julie-Marie Strange and Dr Sarah Roddy.

Françoise Vergès currently holds the Chair 'Global South(s)/Globalisation et les Suds' at the College of Global Studies in Paris; she is Consulting Professor at Goldsmiths College London and Cultural and Scientific Consultant for the Nantes Memorial of the Abolition of Slavery. She has written extensively on the politics and economy of predation, colonial slavery, Frantz Fanon, Aimé Césaire, and the post-colonial museum; she is the author of films on Maryse Condé, Aimé Césaire and on French post-coloniality and an independent curator.

Paul Warde is a Lecturer in Environmental History at the University of Cambridge, Associate Research Fellow at the Joint Centre for History and Economics in Cambridge and Harvard, and a senior editor at *History and Policy*. He was previously Professor of Environmental History at the University of East Anglia. He has written extensively on the environmental, energy and

xiv *Notes on contributors*

economic history of early modern and modern Europe and Canada. Recent works include *The Future of Nature: Documents of Global Change* (with Libby Robin and Sverker Sörlin, Yale University Press, 2013), and *Power to the People: Energy in Europe over the Last Five Centuries* (with Astrid Kander and Paolo Malanima, Princeton University Press, 2013).

Michael Wood is an English historian and broadcaster whose films have been shown across the world. He has presented numerous highly acclaimed television documentary series, including *In the Footsteps of Alexander the Great* (1998), *Conquistadors* (2000) and *The Story of India* (2007). He has also written a number of best-selling books on English history including *In Search of the Dark Ages* (1981 and later editions), *Domesday* (1986 and later editions), and *The Story of England* (2010). In 2010 he was awarded the Historical Association's Medlicott Medal for outstanding services and current contributions to history. He was appointed Professor of Public History at the University of Manchester in 2013. He is currently working on a history of China for the BBC.

Peter Yeandle is Lecturer in History at the University of Manchester. Part of his research relates to the interrelationships of religion, radical politics and protest between 1880 and 1930. He has published essays on radical theology, Christian Socialist conceptions of 'conscience' and the controversial preacher the Reverend Stewart Duckworth Headlam. He is currently editing a collection of essays, *Politics, Performance and Popular Culture in Nineteenth-Century Britain*, to be published by Manchester University Press (forthcoming, 2015).

1 Doing history in public?

Historians in the age of *impact*

Pedro Ramos Pinto and Bertrand Taithe

Impact: n 'ımpakt

1 The action of one object coming forcibly into contact with another
2 A marked effect or influence

OED

What makes the real historian is not only the sensitivity to the great issues of the past; one also needs to love, like a pleasant intellectual gymnastic, the *bricolage* of research.

Marc Bloch, 'Pour un lecteur curieux de méthode', 22 September 1939[1]

Why are we writing this book?

The last twenty years have seen an unprecedented democratization of history. While there may be questions about which past we now choose to evoke, the public's interest in the past is not novel, nor was the writing and researching of historical subjects ever the exclusive domain of the professional academic. But the dynamics of this growing public engagement with history are clearly a departure from the past. History has become a pervasive cultural commodity, widely and eagerly consumed in the form of heritage, education and entertainment, even explicitly as an aid to the construction of new forms of identity.

This process has, in many ways, reinvigorated the discipline of history by prompting professional historians to think about their audiences, and to seek ways of interacting with publics and historians outside the academy. This imperative was not always present: Fernand Braudel's sense that history had to engage with the contemporary world was framed in 1959 in a very different context from the current debate on the impact of history when he wrote:

> History has to show its virtues, its contemporary usefulness, a little out of a place. I say History because civilisation is more or less History. It is also very nearly, 'global society'.[2]

Then the concern was to anchor historical methods among the social sciences and to present History (with a capital H) as the fundamental interpretative

2 *Pedro Ramos Pinto and Bertrand Taithe*

discipline which might explain the present. The *Annales* school of history and its successor 'New History' were syncretic and brought to bear geographic and economic archival knowledge to articulate an authoritative voice.[3] Though the issue remained implicit throughout most of the historical debates of the 1960s, 1970s and 1980s; historians expected that voice to be heard, its lessons to be heeded, their students to rule through the administrations of nation states. This certainty has all but vanished today. Historians are now immersed in very different societies and their relevance is questioned.

From this condition stems a pervasive sense of unease among history's traditional producers and keepers. The era of the dominance of the official archive as the repository of history, with the academic historian as its interpreter, or the high priest of what Michelet dubbed 'resurrectionism', is over.[4] The myth of the historian as oracle has been challenged by the multiplication of producers, publics, and repositories of historical memory and interpretation. As Toby Butler argues in his essay (Chapter 3 in this book), history is now largely the product of digital archives – digitized or digital native material – lending themselves to the cacophonic interpretations of a wide range of voices. In Samuel's words in his major contribution to the debates on the nature of history, *Theatres of Memory* (1994):

> History is not the prerogative of the historian, nor even, as postmodernism contends, an historian's invention, it is rather a social form of knowledge; the work in any given instance, of a thousand different hands.[5]

The age of demotic and democratic history which Raphael Samuel announced so vigorously in the 1980s and early 1990s is now tangible – though it is less a culture of the material past, the one that Samuel focused on when he considered mock Tudor houses, than one of the virtual past in which conspiracy theories rub shoulders with antiquarian concerns and meticulously documented genealogies.[6] This exponential production outside of academic circles and far from its own debates on the value of history or postmodern theory is offering the most extraordinary Copernican challenge a profession could face.

At the same time as the production of history has broken the banks of academia, universities themselves are undergoing an epochal process of transformation which adds to the pressure for historians to redefine their position. In particular, the relationship between academic historians and the state has been profoundly altered, as Peter Mandler shows well in his contribution (Chapter 12) to this book. Universities are increasingly pushed to adopt an industrial and neoliberal model of knowledge production and distribution,[7] a transformation most apparent in the emerging emphasis on the 'impact' of research as a measure of quality, and the benchmark and justification for universities' claim for public funding, direct or indirect.

The economic idea of impact has come to dominate the economic concerns of British and European funding bodies as well as worldwide academic debates.[8] Through impact narratives – the 'case studies' of public engagement upon

Historians in the age of impact   3

which university departments are assessed – historians have been asked to attempt to tell (if not measure quantitatively) just how relevant history might be to the world. The metaphorical use of impact, an image which evoked the ballistic image of a bullet hitting a target and the idea of concentrated and traceable influence, carries a great amount of baggage. In its more benign version, it sees science as incremental revelation that chips away at the frontiers of knowledge, punctuated by big bangs of discovery that mark epistemological shifts in our understanding of the physical world. In its practice, however, it seeks to identify the individual contribution rather than Samuel's thousand hands, and in doing so reverts to myths about the process of scientific discovery and the role of great men of yesteryear.[9]

Other than in a very limited sense, history is ill-suited to this regime of knowledge production. Historical 'discoveries' lie more in the realm of curiosity than that of epistemological break, from the king's remains found under the parking lot to the occasional forgotten manuscript. As such, history finds itself relegated from the podium of groundbreaking knowledge to the plodding ranks of 'useful' knowledge, or that section of the academy now being restructured as the R&D department of footloose, innovative and 'flexible' industries. The assumption that research was intrinsically good and a common good has given way to the idea of learning and enquiry as a form of private investment which has to fit the logic of the market; the economic and social worlds are no longer synonymous with history as Braudel might have imagined, but with its 'customers', expecting a useful product. History's impact, as with engineering or marketing science, is expected to come through a 'partnership' with industry aimed at creating a successful commodity: the well-visited heritage space, the popular TV series with book tie-in or the serious, yet best-selling historical novel. The question of who is in the driving seat in this 'partnership', and what consequences that has for the nature of the product itself, are left unasked.

Either way, the narrowing of the definition of what the production of history is *for* necessarily entails a loss of academic freedom for the professional historian. At one level this reflects the fact that historians are and were indeed a caste who relied on notions of academic freedom and a university rentier economy facilitated by a consensus on the intrinsic value of knowledge and of the university as an institution for the reproduction of elites imbued with a certain idea of public service – the enlightened and benevolent despotism of the civil servant.[10] The base utilitarian notion that *all* knowledge should be productive, a Dickensian parody taken seriously, has challenged this self-evidence at a time when universities come to define themselves as enterprises of knowledge production rather than sanctuaries for sacred and universal values.

The comfortably bourgeois mode of self-referential history writing that the traditional university supported had already come under attack from the mid-twentieth century by radical historians, Marxists and Feminists and the History Workshop movement, who shared a desire to make history more inclusive, less male and eurocentric.[11] Their challenge continues and when it is combined with the more

4 Pedro Ramos Pinto and Bertrand Taithe

methodological and theoretical critiques of postmodern theorists like Hayden White, it amounts to a serious but also productive unease.[12] Yet it is not these critiques that are fundamentally affecting the academic environment of history production, but rather the transformation of the university into a producer of private goods: the social reproduction of elites which Bourdieu lambasted in the 1960s is no longer the preserve of disciplines such as history but of business studies.[13]

But if there is no golden past of historical production to cling to, there are clearly significant challenges ahead that stand in the way of the creation of a truly democratic, honest and – dare we say it? – relevant model of production of historical knowledge. In order to reflect on this, we draw on the metaphor of production. This does not aim to reduce history to the status of commodity, although as de Groot argues persuasively in his contribution (Chapter 2) to this volume, the commodification of history has greatly expanded its public, for better and for worse. But it does allow us to break down History with a capital H into a series of processes that seem to us critical to reflect on: who produces historical knowledge; where and how it is produced; how is it circulated and consumed. In this way we want to think aloud about what history is meant to achieve as a discipline, how it engages more explicitly with practitioners, with the politics of nationalism and inequality, with the sciences, journalism and the media.

We have gathered in this volume a range of young and more established historians, practitioners and people who have straddled several careers while always referring back to history. The authors were asked to write for a wider audience – a wider audience even than the one we envisage for this introduction. They were asked to present their craft, in the artisanal sense that all historians are indeed workers of a range of materials in their effort to shape a representation of the world that is relevant to their contemporaries. We have asked our authors to be free and not shy away from controversies if these might enrich the debate raging today on the value of historical knowledge. Not every possible theme will be exhausted by such a book. Concerns such as gender and sexuality run throughout the book and are not the object of a single article. The chronological concerns, *longue durée* and event histories are not the focus of this book, and neither do we give precedence to the many subtle subcategories of social, cultural, economic, world, area studies. The controversies around the nature of facts and truth which so divided the historical profession are well documented elsewhere and now belong to the toolbox of all well-trained historians (whether they like it or not).[14] These debates we leave in the background.

In this introduction we deemed it useful, however, to engage with some key themes which might help raise the concerns and hopes that led us to bring together this collection of articles. Our first heading will be to consider the issues arising from the commodification of history; then to consider how history production has changed and is changing today; ending with a reflection on the role of the historian in the era of impact.

History as a commodity

Debates on the nature of history have moved along since the 1980s and 1990s. In that period History Workshop historian Raphael Samuel engaged publicly on the nature of British identity and its relation to history.[15] In particular historians were engaging forcefully with issues relating to the national curriculum, the multiplication of producers and the rampant commercialization of history. The historical turn in television series and identity politics which is evoked in this book (Chapter 2) by Jerome de Groot was in full swing. In the UK Samuel reviewed the rise of demotic forms in the consumption of history. Far from perceiving this as a threat, Samuel highlighted the rich encounter between consumers and micro-producers of history while denigrating the sanitization of the past associated with the rise of so-called 'Victorian values'. In France and on the continent meanwhile, the phenomenal sales of *lieux de mémoires,* which was copied in different guises in Italy or Germany, brought about the complex re-evaluation of how the wider public related to memory and landscapes onto which history had been inscribed.[16] This enabled a political review of the mythologies of the republican tradition which aimed squarely at addressing the populist politics on the far right and their use of old historical language and memorial sites. The bicentenary of 1789 in France, the subsequent anniversaries of Nelson, the First World War or other events ensured that history never ceased to be a successful market.[17]

National Trust and English Heritage, and the wider heritage industry worldwide, have made considerable stock and profit from the sales of popular books, as well as living shows mixing professional and amateur re-enactors, heirs of the experimental archaeology of the 1970s and of a desire to engage with the materiality of history. The televisual liberalization of the 1990s and 2000s facilitated the commissioning of new documentaries and the endless diffusion of old classical ones as shown in this volume by one of Britain's leading documentary makers and broadcast historian, Michael Wood (Chapter 4). Yet the repeats of these documentaries often entailed a gradual distancing from their original cultural production context.

The de-structuring of the history market, as witnessed by the distribution of goods and images, the development of a considerable heritage-themed industry which built on concerns for servants and masters, working villages and factory life (for instance Beamish in the United Kingdom) and shopping experiences, has undoubtedly been a commercial success.[18] The development of film production and the commercial growth of an entire sector amount to a veritable liberation narrative. Professional historians, often limited in their influence over these multimillion industries, barely made an audible impression. The much vaunted return of talking heads presenters on television shows was welcomed; most notable was Simon Schama in the UK, who was equally lionized, derided and criticized when his show intended to create didactic coherence to the national history, as witness a well-known debate in the *American Historical Review.*[19] Arguably the past thirty years have witnessed a considerable marketization

6   Pedro Ramos Pinto and Bertrand Taithe

which has produced new tropes and new commonplace assumptions to the visit of great houses or industrial heritage while leaving many areas of silence around sexuality, violence or race. The private drivers of this mass production of demotic histories (plural) have been to serve discretely each consumer demographic and interest group according to the segregating logic of niche marketing.[20]

If on the one hand the history market allowed a passive consumption of goods labelled as historical and patented as having historical content, on the other history could also be branded as part of the corporate identity of private enterprise.[21] Far from recoiling from evoking *their* history, a multitude of businesses, social and third sector enterprises have seized the blossoming of new technologies of communication such as the World Wide Web (WWW) to broadcast their own *narratives*. From hagiographic or semi-mythical narratives to the vaunting of traditional values, history became part of the corporate identity of many major players who used their prolonged presence in the market as evidence of continuing innovation, and history as the ability to reflect on 'best practice'.[22] In this register history served as a key but not necessarily central element of a communication strategy and branding.

This atomized production of multifarious historical narratives has hardly been the product of historians employed as such. The media undergoing a transformative era towards an ever increasing number of smaller and freelance providers was undoubtedly a participant spectator in this flowering. The community historical production so dear to Samuel undoubtedly generated a supporting infrastructure for the heritage deployment of historical markets or the animation of ruins and heritage building. As the director of English Heritage noted recently, large organizations managing sites of historical importance came to rely on the retired public of the apex of the welfare state, young enough and affluent enough to volunteer.[23] To the pessimists this demographic of support seems unlikely to be sustained on that scale in the coming decades. We may have witnessed therefore a kind of historical heyday during which both the consumers and the suppliers may have benefited from and redistributed the largesse of the welfare state. The historical production pandering to their needs may have been traditional, genealogical and domestic (if not demotic) but it was not necessarily disconnected from the wealth of social, economic and cultural academic research of the previous decades. Local historians often brought the wider patterns of this historical production to bear very effectively on these micro-histories.

The vast hinterland of historical research remains of course the genealogical market which was fostered by churches of the Latter Day Saints; societies of considerable importance and local networks of activists exchanged considerable social and demographic data with which professional historians seldom engage.[24] The worldwide networking of genealogists and their importance in maintaining physical archives alive in times of stringent cuts also relies on a relatively affluent community in search of identity. Corporate actors, on the other hand, seldom employed or respected historical accuracy or scholarship. The use of history sometimes parodied in mock Victorian style by 'period'

Historians in the age of impact   7

brands such as Phileas Fogg or a range of Victoriana,[25] embraced the quaint and sometimes absurd images of the past in order to better assert modern techniques or in a desire to subvert received wisdom.[26]

The ownership of history

As the examples above show, the commodification of history does not necessarily mean the full privatization of its production, nor of its product, and indeed much of the growth of the heritage industry could be seen as an example of extensive public–private partnerships (PPP) in the production of a 'public'. It is within this apparently benign entanglement of economic and cultural interest that the idea of impact finds itself restructuring modes of research and the way professional historians interact with the public. The assumption here is that the commodification of history will lead to a more 'efficient' and 'relevant' product. The public interest and its sustained support for research, it is argued by funding agents and the various levels of academic governance, will best be served by the production of a valuable tailored response to the demands of its various consuming publics. The unspoken implication is that history writing and research that cannot readily find such audiences should be de-invested in, returned to the antiquarian studies whence they originated. This is a restrictive view of the impact of history which, in our view, greatly underestimates the contribution history and historians can make to vibrant, open and democratic societies, as we will argue later in this chapter. But even within the space in which this 'impactful' history is expected to make its mark – through the opening up of history to diverse and hitherto unengaged publics – its democratic/demotic ambitions stumble on the problem that cuts across societies where the collective good is recast solely as the freedom to make choices over what one consumes: the problems of ownership and of inequality.

One of the ambitions of the wider impact agenda is the democratization of 'cultural capital', a term coined by the French sociologist Pierre Bourdieu to explain the creation, maintenance and reproduction of inequalities of power and status.[27] The metaphor of capital is instructive: capital is something to be hoarded, invested, benefited from. Capital is by its very nature exclusive and those who produce historical knowledge are, naturally, well placed to control and 'own' its output. The history of history is bound up with the ambition of the nation state to create a unified, homogeneous historical identity and collective memory in the service of ruling elites and imperial projects.

Such mechanisms were dissected by influential 'new histories' of the late twentieth century, from Benedict Anderson's *Imagined Communities* (1983) to Hobsbawm and Ranger's *The Invention of Tradition* (1992) – books that found audiences well beyond the academy. These critical takes on history exposed the ways in which the ownership of the means of production of historical knowledge could be used as a means to promote anti-democratic and exclusionary projects. Public histories such as those discussed by Françoise Vergès in Chapter 7 in this book are aimed exactly at complicating such memories and engaging

8 *Pedro Ramos Pinto and Bertrand Taithe*

audiences in a more open, pluralistic historical reflection. Yet, as Stefan Berger's Chapter 6 shows, the demise of national(ist) history was celebrated too soon, and the ability to shape and manipulate historical memories and loyalties is a tempting prize for powerful institutions and groups.

One response to this problem is the promotion of alternative and more inclusive national historical narratives. This was the case, for instance, with the view of British history presented by the film director Danny Boyle in his opening ceremony of the 2012 London Olympics. Taking in waves of immigration, rights struggles and the creation of the British welfare state, Boyle's narrative offered an inclusive and progressive version of the national 'our island story'.[28] But this very notion of historical progress, of purpose and of direction is not without its pitfalls, as Emily Robinson shows in her chapter (Chapter 8), since it can present progress towards equality as something that has already been achieved, creating a rift between the empathetic engagement with the victims of social injustices of the past and those of the present.

At first sight the drive towards the production of demotic histories can be a powerful antidote to whiggish and reductive national narratives of both left and right. However, to the extent that this process is driven by the commodification of history, tailoring the product to constituent publics, it carries the danger of creating and reproducing other inequalities to the extent that it generates group-specific, compartmentalized, specialist histories, leading to a segregation of historical identities and reinforcing, rather than diluting, social barriers. 'Impactful' histories have to find their publics and, like successful commodities, nurture in their consumers a sense of loyalty, difference and identification. Then, rather than creating a common pool of widely redistributed 'cultural capital', we run the risk of fomenting a further balkanization of histories,[29] each contributing to the creation of forms of cultural capital and identity exclusive to particular groups.

This is particularly problematic in the context of increasingly multicultural societies, where, like faith-schools, history becomes an aid to the creation of exclusive ethnic identities, each tied to a particularistic genealogy and set of historical markers, contributing to a sense of difference and distance – a type of what Frances Stewart calls 'horizontal inequalities'.[30] It is not that 'Black History' or 'Women's History' are per se a problem: they emerged as a corrective to narrowly focused historical narratives that promoted exclusion on grounds of race and gender. They can, however, foster inequality if they become a product created for, and consumed exclusively by, say citizens of African descent or by women, and ignored by other demographics who are not its target market, thus reinforcing social and cultural boundaries.

We are, therefore, in a bind. Pierre Bourdieu's critique of the uses of cultural capital (including a sense of 'history') as a form of distinction was premised on the idea that 'high culture' should be democratized and made accessible to all.[31] When it comes to history as a form of culture, however, this comes too close for comfort to one-nation stories, be they of the conservative or liberal variety – both are premised on the idea of a unified historical 'truth' emerging from the nation, however broadly defined. The alternative, however, offers us a 'flat'

Historians in the age of impact 9

history whose parts are interchangeable, unconnected, and woven together by the choice of the consumer in ways that contribute to a reinforcement of identity, ethnic, religious and class boundaries.

Commodification and bricolage

Clearly, the manner in which the product of history is consumed matters. But so does the mode of its production. Historical knowledge is not an inert, standardized commodity such as a screw (which give or take differences in quality of the materials and finish, is a screw regardless of where and how it is made and marketed); but rather a malleable product which is itself shaped by these various processes. Recasting the production of historical knowledge in relation to specific publics or 'markets' stacks the incentives towards a narrow specialization. It also demands that historical products themselves have to satisfy the preferences of the consumer. In competition with other historical products, will accounts that challenge or are critically reflexive of their public's assumptions have as much 'impact' as those that go towards meeting their public's expectations? This observation leads us to reflect on how the commodification and modes of consumption of history impact the kind of history that is written – i.e. how the market (and this market is of course not ahistorical) shapes the creation of historical knowledge.

Ultimately, the mode of production that commodification leads to is that of history as '*bricolage*'. This French term reflects well two features of this process worth emphasizing. In its sense of the matching together of disparate parts it refers to the way in which history is now co-produced by publics and historians: the former pick and choose histories that reflect their passions or tastes, which in turn pulls the latter to satisfy such demand by the production of easily digestible, bite-size portions of 'History'. But *bricolage* is also the French term for DIY, 'do-it-yourself', which also points to the way in which the academy has lost the monopoly of the production of history, partly as the result of its commodification. The promise of profit from the sale of historical products has created whole new categories of professional producers of history – in the heritage industry, in the entertainment industry and in the media. Though as Scott Anthony reminds us in his critical review (Chapter 5) of how journalists address historical research, it is far from clear that the researcher sets the agenda when most journalists stand at the bottom of the professional ladder. Yet the commodification of history has also brought history production to the hands of the non-specialist, the DIY-historian, spearheaded by the explosion of interest in family history, but closely followed by community history and other forms of specialist interest. In the same way that the *bricolage* of choice can condition the kind of historical knowledge produced, as we argued above, so does the *bricolage*/DIY history come with its own dangers.

These transformative changes in the mode of production of history towards particularistic idioms specific to a group or subgroup – the fragmentary and individualized narratives of a past often steeped in victimhood – are not

10 Pedro Ramos Pinto and Bertrand Taithe

without profound political consequences. These consequences are compounded by the dominant use of deductive reasoning applied to the past. Deductive reasoning links the premises with the conclusions of any thinking – typically it applies to any closed system of reasoning which uses some historical evidence in order to attain a predetermined objective. The most rampant instances of this tendency are to be found in conspiracy theories which instrumentalize factual historical evidence to 'reveal' often imaginary political plots. This mode of reasoning is ancient and commonplace. The most famous examples, such as the *Protocols of the Elders of Zion* (1903), itself a hoax of conspiratorial origins, are given a breath of life in the new historical market. The legally punishable holocaust revisionist tracts, websites and books proceed from the same technique of extrapolation from isolated elements of accurate information in order to lead to a general denial of facts established through the formidable compilation of available evidence.[32] Deductive reasoning and the rhetorical strength of its biased logic has impacted dramatically on the demotic forms of history writing.

Much of this instrumentalization has made many historical narratives politically reversible. To take folk music as an example is to show how history writing and imagining can be turned on their heads. On the one hand folk music was largely collected and reinvented by individuals seeking the roots of a common race or culture in popular art, while this national endeavour involved tracing complex connections between cultures and groups, which were often breaking racial and social boundaries. On the other hand, the 1960s heirs of the more essentialist Cecil Sharp in the UK or the Lomax father and son in the USA tended to inscribe their 'folk revival' within a political struggle which would give a voice to the voiceless and which simultaneously received and challenged previous folk revivalism.[33] The same concern for traditional folk music, dance and associated attires could nevertheless also give rise, with the same roots, social practices and tools, to ultra-nationalist and ethno-essentialist claims akin to xenophobia or Fascism. The specificity and essential nature of folk traditions – often denied by genuine scholarship which tends to trace change and transmission over excessive or even obsessive claims for origins – lend themselves to being reclaimed by particularistic groups or states. Eastern European socialist regimes, like the Fascist ones before them, sought to use folk as the 'genuine' expression of a race or nation. At the heart of this use of popular history was the reductionist and exclusionary drive to authenticity and mythical origins.

The forms that historical determinism may take are thus legion. Some are close to genealogical accounts and pay some lip service to ancient theories of heredity. While no one adds up and combines pitilessly hereditary traits like Émile Zola once did in the concluding volume of his Rougon-Macquart series of novels, *Docteur Pascal*,[34] the hereditary frame of reference remains part of much racial or ethnic politics. Even nation states which define themselves through their institutions, political boundaries or land as arguably France does (in contrast with a German model of identity) rely on some historical determinism which has also a demotic form.[35] The French public's firm belief in *terroirs* and the influence of climate and land on products is not without its own parochial politics and debates on authenticity, while the claims it makes for goods, wines and cheese are also quasi-mythical. Fernand Braudel himself concluded his career with a poetic homage to the lands that constitute the French territory, under the evocative title of *The Identity of France*.[36]

The historian's craft

What differentiates Braudel's poetic musings on history and identity from rancid exclusionary discourses was, however, more than the themes evoked, a matter of method. There is more to the use of history than is often argued. In the same way that Marc Bloch's notion of *bricolage* in research, cited at the onset of this article, evoked curiosity and an enquiry-led open-mindedness, rather than the bolting together of incongruous fragments of evidence to support a pre-established theory, there is more to the use of history than is often argued. In general usage 'thinking historically' most often refers to using history as a repository of 'usable' past experience. Clearly, there are ways in which the history can be 'useful' in this sense – what Borton and Davey in their chapter (Chapter 11 in this book) call 'strategic' uses of the past – as is the case with disciplines across the humanities.[37]

Yet, usefulness is not without its dangers: evaluating the role of history in shaping decision makers' response to the 2008–9 financial crisis, the economic historian Barry Eichengreen argued that the use of historical analogy – in that case equating the crisis to the Great Depression of the 1920s – overemphasized the similarities between both events. The crash of 1929's salience in collective historical memories militated against the exploration of perhaps more relevant, but less well-known historical cases.[38] In any case, the way in which both the metaphor and the analogy of the Great Depression were used by policymakers was filtered through contending ideological lenses – as were, of course, the historical narratives on which they drew.

More recently the humanitarian lawyer of Doctors Without Borders, Françoise Boucher-Saulnier, warned against projecting onto the Central African Republic (CAR) the approach adopted by non-governmental organizations (NGO) in response to the Rwanda genocide twenty years ago, at the risk of misrepresenting a changing international environment. In her words 'a comparison between CAR [today] and older contexts runs the risk to add to confusion rather than bring solutions'.[39] Where some humanitarians such as John Borton seek to develop deeper analytical methodologies by 'bringing in' historical methods and evidence, lawyers and policymakers are weary of analogical reasoning being taken too far.

The claims we make for the 'impact' of history echo others that have been made by generations of historians. They relate to history not so much as a body of usable knowledge but as a mode of thinking about and questioning the world, both past and present, that is invaluable as part of a wider range of critical faculties and abilities. Reacting to the Rankean call for historians to act as discoverers and cataloguers of fact (the 'Potsdam Guards of learning'), the

12   Pedro Ramos Pinto and Bertrand Taithe

British historian G.M. Trevelyan argued for the importance of the historical imagination as a moral quality to the extent that it could 'train the mind of the citizen'.[40] Trevelyan argued for the role of the historian as an educator of what Mandler has called 'imaginative capabilities'.[41] These are critically important, but we believe we can go even further. As this book emphasizes, it is not just the imparting of history by historians that is important, but also, and perhaps primarily, the democratization of the production of history – and engaging with the new producers and consumers of history (especially its consumer–producers) is for us the battlefield in which to counter the problems arising from the commodification of history and the welcomed demise of the ivory tower.

We are making, therefore, a plea that the 'relevance' or even the 'impact' of history be sought not in its product, nor in a hierarchy of different kinds of producers (academics, non-academics, private, public, corporate) but in a particular mode of producing it. Our metaphor of production echoes what we consider one of the most eloquent outlines of the process of creating historical knowledge, Marc Bloch's *The Historian's Craft*.

The Historian's Craft opens with a question: '*Papa: explique-moi donc à quoi sert l'histoire?*'[42] This interrogation is all the more brutal as it was made in the context of Bloch's internal exile during Nazi Germany's occupation of France, and it is no surprise it pushes the author to consider if 'he has spent his life wisely'.[43] In fact Bloch never finished his book, as he was executed in 1944 for participation in the resistance, and the manuscript was only published by his friend and colleague Lucien Febvre in 1949. Yet, Bloch's answer, far from reflecting the powerlessness of words against coercion, is an elegy for an approach, for an intellectual method, a look into the ever-changing workshop of the historian.

Bloch shifts emphasis of the question in so much as, for him, the legitimacy of the exercise lies not in the end product, but on the virtues of the way it is made. Bloch describes the process of engaging with the 'tracks' of the past, of understanding chronology, and the historian's ever-present awareness of the limits and contingent nature of his/her evidence, and his/her attempts to make it 'speak' – that is, interpret the evidence to reveal something about the past that a given artefact, text or remains was not created to do in the first instance. Such interpretation is done through the methods of historical criticism – the collation, comparison and questioning of the evidence, an almost forensic process Bloch describes with relish – and analysis.

Bloch also uses the term *bricolage* to describe what goes on in the historian's workshop, but this is a methodical and reasoned process. Analysis, in the sense of craft, is more than an adding up of evidence, but a quest to reach an understanding of the past – that is to grasp it in its own terms, rather than to stand in judgement. 'Understanding', writes Bloch, 'is a word pregnant with difficulties, but also with hope'.[44] This hope springs from the act of understanding, or sympathizing with those in the past being studied, an act that can only be underpinned by a belief in our common humanity and an acknowledgement of its diversity. Along the way the historical craftsman needs, of course, tools:

Historians in the age of impact 13

language, abstraction, periodization, even theories of causation. Following this thread – the word *métier* also evokes the weaver's loom – Bloch discusses how to use these with care and in the knowledge that they are the product of our choice, and that its product is never absolute, but always to be itself critically examined.[45]

This stance of open-endedness and reflexivity pre-dates the post-structuralist turn which swept the social and human sciences in the late twentieth century. To be fair, it also pre-dates the post-war triumph of positivistic structuralism that prompted the rebellion. The charge has been levied that post-structuralism and the cultural turn, by blowing apart hierarchies of systems of understanding, have rendered knowledge about the past and the conversation inherent in the concept of historical analysis an impossibility.[46] Ultimately, however, the kind of craft that Bloch describes even when practised by the dyed-in-the-wool cultural historian is not (or rather should not be) a flight of fancy, but an exercise in presenting not a law nor an indisputable fact nor a closed-off certainty, but an explanation that is plausible, or likely. History as a way of thinking is in essence close to what statisticians would call a 'Bayesean' reasoning: the weighing up of probabilities in the face of the limits of the evidence and of human cognition, constantly updated on the basis of new evidence and experience. This contrasts with the preconception that 'scientific knowledge' is characterized by hard fact and certainty – a fiction still dangerously prevalent in parts of economics and policymaking.[47]

Bloch was certainly not the first nor the last to discuss the process of historical research in these terms. Others call what goes on in the historian's workshop 'thinking historically', exercising the 'historical imagination', or even 'thinking with history'.[48] That this approach is shared widely in the community of historians is not a surprise. The vastness of the past and the relative scarcity of its vestiges, and the way in which myriad interpretations fan out from them means that, unlike most other craftsmen and women of knowledge, the historian triangulates and assembles the product from ill-fitting pieces which require both openness to multiple sources of evidence, and – perhaps like few other disciplines – a sense of collective endeavour.[49] This cooperative aspect in the craft of the historian is nowhere more evident, as Bloch points out, than in the humble and misunderstood footnote, where the materials and processes of the historian's work are displayed publicly.[50] This openness is a fundamental part of the process: the historian performs his/her historical criticism and analysis before a public – traditionally that of his/her peers but ideally a much wider audience. This process, which sometimes veers towards pedantic displays of esoteric knowledge, ought to entail the emulation of apprenticeship rather than the enshrining of status. History writing can never be a masterpiece but ought to evoke the craft of the mundane artefacts of daily life.

Bloch's presentation of the historian's craft helps us address the issues we have raised in two ways. First, it emphasizes the relevance of 'thinking historically', not in an instrumentalized, market-driven manner, but rather as an open-ended democratic process. Second, its emphasis on the open, public and accountable

14 *Pedro Ramos Pinto and Bertrand Taithe*

mode of doing the history it describes seems better suited to the challenges we presented than to Trevelyan's view of the historian as teacher (however inspirational).

Bloch's plea for the historian's use of the faculty of understanding as a key tool is a way of thinking that, above and beyond the 'relevance' of the past as a repository of experience or progenitor of the present, can foster an exercise of critical thinking about past, present and future in a way that goes beyond the analytical and argumentative skills gained by scholastic learning.[51] Martha Nussbaum argues in her defence of the humanities that certain abilities are essential for a citizenry that can be the basis of a humane, open democracy: being able to think about and debate political issues 'deferring to neither tradition nor authority'; the ability to see the fellow humanity in others and develop a concern for their lives; and the capacity to imagine contexts and situations other than one's own. As well as requiring critical faculties, Nussbaum emphasizes the need to develop 'moral emotions' to support these abilities: empathy, sympathy and understanding.[52] The imaginative exercise of empathy and sympathy are essential foundations for what the philosopher and economist Amartya Sen (a thinker very much influenced by an historical way of thinking) calls 'open impartiality', that is, the ability to see one's position at a distance, as if viewed by an impartial spectator, and to seek to understand the positions and value systems of others. These in turn are the necessary conditions for a democratic and pluralistic public reasoning.[53]

The issue of distance and position is central to the historian's craft. The trope of 'historical distance' was one of the banners of early twentieth-century ambition to make history detached, scientific and rational, devised in opposition to the emotive engagement (proximity) with the past characteristic of historiography in the romantic period. Distance was, in that sense, premised on the fiction that there are neutral observers and neutral ways of seeing. Today, distance is most often considered by historians in a different way, more akin to Bloch's idea of understanding and one which we would argue is central to the imaginative exercise of 'open impartiality'. Mark Salber Phillips, dissecting the uses and meanings of distance in historical work, sees it as a mediating practice, in that all attempts to narrate the past require the historian to place themselves in relation, i.e. at some distance, to the past. Phillips suggests all historical representations are positioned at different points of distance between the historian and the past along various dimensions.[54] To put it simply, the same past can be seen close up, as through a magnifying glass, as do micro- or family histories; or from afar, in broad panoramic, in the sense of the *longue durée* or the 'deep history' of the interaction between humanity and the environment referenced by Paul Warde (Chapter 10 in this book).

These different distances can also be emotive: the same moment in the past can be made to feel near and familiar, or strange if not entirely alien: it can be grasped both empathetically and sympathetically. Relative distance is also involved in the way that historians link past, present and future. The past can be seen as a bridge to a far-off or near future; for instance in the way that the social movements discussed by Peter Yeandle in his chapter (Chapter 9 in this book) seek to mobilize the past to create a different tomorrow. Yet, practising history can also be an exercise in creating distance to a past that should not be repeated – as with Europe's violent and genocidal past.[55] Finally, the different distances used by historians stem from their use and reflection of distinct modes of understanding change and causality, say cultural and economic historians. What this means is that there is not one 'historical distance' measurable by a yardstick preserved in our most venerable institutions. Rather, the historian's craft is an exercise in navigating between such distances. and productive discussion about the past is often a debate between and across these different positions.

It is in this sense that we see a critical connection between the production of history and broader public reasoning. History then becomes central to a healthy democratic public sphere in at least two important ways. First, the kinds of historical knowledge produced for and by a public that is versed in thinking historically is in itself likely to transcend the limitations of the commoditized and balkanized past we discussed above. Second, history produced in this way and consumed not passively and uncritically, but actively and intelligently, is an exercise that requires the consumer–producer to be aware of these different modalities of distance, to critically reflect on his/her position and those of others around him/her – essentially an exercise in 'open impartiality'.

It is true that the use and fostering of 'imaginative capabilities' are not exclusive to the discipline of history: C. Wright Mills's definition of the sociological imagination as 'the capacity to shift from one perspective to another' points only to the importance of that exercise of distancing for reasoning of all kinds.[56] History is nonetheless distinct not only because of its specialization in the past and dynamics of change, but also for the ecumenicalism of its approach, where the foundational theories of the social sciences are themselves historicized even as they are used to mediate past and present.[57]

Doing history in public

Yet the question remains about how the historian's way of seeing, or his/her craft, is how to spark that approach and imagination in others when the academy has lost its monopoly in the production of history. If we once believed in the supremacy of the historian, probably a myth in itself, it is clear that the genie is out of the bottle and that historians can only make modest claims to the production of historical narratives. Essentialist references to the past are bound to retain their appeal because of their simplicity and, though exclusionary of many 'minorities', comforting inclusiveness. The challenge of diverse historical narratives has rendered these essentialist tropes stronger, albeit for a smaller group and specific demographic. UKIP (UK Independence Party) or National Front electorates may not be representative of the entire population but they aspire to gather considerable groups around simpler historical narratives. Where historians such as Pierre Rosanvallon or Stefan Collini[58] have attempted to provide counter-narratives they have focused on the role of the intellectuals in framing the debates or in elucidating the mechanisms through which groups engage with small and large politics of identity, invariably using an historical idiom to make their points. Although the sociologist Norbert Elias made few references to history writing in his influential *Civilising Process*,[59] historians have relied on the idea that a trickle-down of enlightened ideas may be diffused throughout the land so that our rich and 'textured', 'complex' and 'multilayered' understanding of the past may serve as a dam against the tidal wave of simplistic identity-histories.

The jury is still out on this fundamental gamble, but, should the dam fail, one might evoke a new betrayal of the intellectuals. The original *'trahison des clercs'* was prophetically announced by Julien Benda's 1927 denunciation of the enlistment of intellectuals in the service of populism and nationalism.[60] Benda argued that intellectuals ought to remain at a higher plane and not engage in politics for fear of becoming the instruments of a group; the new betrayal may come from precisely the reverse perspective, if, by being too passive, historians fail to convey their craft, if not their ideals, to the multitude who participate in the writing of history.

Part of the answer lies undoubtedly in the role of the historian as an educator – albeit in a form probably far removed from the way Bloch[61] and Trevelyan conceived it, conditioned by new technologies and new student constituencies and modes of learning. Trevelyan would certainly recognize the second way in which we envisage professional historians – the historian as communicator to the public. But as much as stirring emotions, the public historian must convey a mode of thinking about and approaching problems that can be hard to square with history's more traditional mode of engaging wider audiences – doing history in public means exposing one's craft, opening up the historian's workshop in the same way as the kitchen has moved from the basement or back room to become in many places the heart of the restaurant.[62]

Finally, doing history in public also means being a co-producer of history with those outside the academy. The engagement of historians alongside other producers of history either through public history or as partners in the writing of history entails the acknowledgement that this is a two-way exchange. The rhizome-like distribution of information challenges the educator to focus on method and on craft rather than the imparting of facts. The truth of this approach is to be found in the enriching of historical writing through the dialogue with the public – one that did not escape E.P. Thompson when he wrote his *Making of the English Working Class* while teaching extramural students in Halifax,[63] and which still holds true. The classroom is no longer a simple physical space, usually enriched by recourse to the virtual, but an imagined space which entails new and old forms of exchange and authority. If access to the apprenticeship of history is now more widely open than hitherto, it remains an individual journey – a task akin to learning an instrument – a skill constantly renewed through critical practice and discouraging failure.

Conclusion: Can the impact of history be measured?

But could this participation, this sharing of the tools and idioms of history writing ever be measured? And what would that measure be? Of course the history of measures and the desire to quantify and assess both have a history and imply managerial modes of governance.[64] Attempts to subvert the tools of quantitative measuring notwithstanding, historians may merely trace down the weight of expectations and implicit politics that such measuring attempts carry.[65] The recent debate in British higher education or the new forms generated by European bureaucracy reveal a concern with the measure of research which is neither new nor absent from academic circles – many of which measure themselves against citation indexes as supporting evidence of authority – indexes which merely record how often a name is dropped.

Tracing how historical method and how historians participate in the world is no easy task and if history becomes more intrinsically part of a culture of critique and change, as John Borton and Eleanor Davey argue in Chapter 11 in this book, it will become an unmeasurable fixture of common reasoning. As a fixture of reasoning participants in the writing of history may rightly assume that they can say what they want but not anything they want – that through a shared idiom and a common belief in the value of the techniques and methods of history, history as a thinking process might indeed aspire to shed some light and truth.

Notes

1 Marc Bloch, *L'Histoire, la guerre, la résistance* (Paris: Gallimard, 2006), p. 514.
2 Fernand Braudel, *Écrits sur l'histoire* (Paris: Flammarion, 1959), p. 302.
3 Jacques LeGoff, *La nouvelle histoire* (Brussels: Complexe, 1988 [1978]).
4 Carolyn Steedman, *Dust* (Manchester: Manchester University Press, 2001).
5 Raphael Samuel, *Theatres of Memory* (London: Verso, 1994), p. 8.
6 Samuel, *Theatres of Memory*; Samuel, *Island Stories: Unravelling Britain* (London: Verso, 1998); Samuel, 'Reading the Signs', I and II, *History Workshop Journal* 32 (Autumn 1991): 88–109; 33 (Spring 1992): 220–51.
7 MOOCs (Massive Open Online Courses) for instance share the contradictory politics of the internet. They are both generous vulgarization enterprises and forms of 'introductory' loss leaders which seek to build up an audience or market for higher-level learning.
8 For an overview of the way 'impact' is woven into the assessment of British universities and a critique of this model in relation to the humanities, see Stefan Collini, *What are Universities For?* (London: Penguin, 2012), chap. 9 'Impact'.
9 This is in itself connected to a wider range of transformative processes inspired by business school theories and laboratory science. See Roger Cooter and Claudia Stein, *Writing History in the Age of Biomedicine* (New Haven, CT: Yale University Press, 2014), pp. 35–7.
10 By rentier economy we obviously refer back to the Marxist notion developed in particular by N. Bukharin, including his emphasis on individualism; see N. Bukharin, *L'Économie politique du rentier* (Paris: Études et documentation internationales, 1967), p. 26. For a critical take on the history of the British university system and its entanglement with power, see Patrick Joyce, *The State of Freedom: A Social History*

18   *Pedro Ramos Pinto and Bertrand Taithe*

of the British State since 1800 (Cambridge: Cambridge University Press, 2013), chap. 7, '"The Fathers Govern the Nation": The Public School and the Oxbridge College'.

11 History Workshop footnote; Greg Lanning, 'Television History Workshop Project No 1: The Brixton Tapes', *History Workshop* 12 (1981): 183–8.

12 Roger Chartier, *On the Edge of the Cliff: History, Language and Practices* (Baltimore, MD: Johns Hopkins University Press, 1996); Hayden White, 'The Value of Narrativity in the Representation of Reality', in White, *The Content of the Form. Narrative Discourse and Historical Representation* (Baltimore, MD: Johns Hopkins University Press, 1990); Michel de Certeau, 'History: Science or Fiction?', in de Certeau, *Heterologies: The Discourse on the Other* (Minneapolis, MN: University of Minnesota Press, 1986); A. Dirk Moses, 'Hayden White, Traumatic Nationalism and the Public Role of History', *History and Theory* 44(3) (Oct. 2005): 311–32.

13 Pierre Bourdieu and Jean-Claude Passeron, *Les héritiers: Les étudiants et la culture* (Paris: Éditions de Minuit, 1984).

14 See John Tosh and Sean Lang, *The Pursuit of History* (London: Pearson, 2006, 4th edn); Ludmilla Jordanova, *History in Practice* (London: Hodder, 2006); and Chartier, *Cultural History* (Cambridge: Polity, 1988) for an introduction to these debates.

15 Samuel, *Island Stories*, pp. 3–20.

16 Pierre Nora, 'Between Memory and History: Les Lieux de Mémoire', *Representations* 26, Special Issue: 'Memory and Counter-Memory' (Spring 1989): 7–24; also, on the archives see *History of the Human Sciences* 11(4) (Nov. 1998); 12(1) (Feb. 1999).

17 Holger Hook (ed.), *History, Commemoration and National Preoccupation: Trafalgar 1805–2005*, British Academy (Oxford: Oxford University Press, 2007).

18 See for instance Ben Cowell, *The Heritage Obsession: The Battle for England's Past* (London: History Press, 2008).

19 See the Special Issue of *American Historical Review* 114(3) (2009) on Simon Schama's BBC *A History of Britain*.

20 E.g. Tevfik Dalgic, 'Dissemination of Market Orientation in Europe: A Conceptual and Historical Evaluation', *International Marketing Review* 15(1) (1998): 45–60.

21 For instance see Ian Yeoman, Alastair Durie, Una McMahon-Beattie and Adrian Palmer, 'Capturing the Essence of a Brand from its History: The Case of Scottish Tourism Marketing', *Journal of Brand Management* 13(2) (2005): 134–47.

22 The concept of best practice is primarily one that claims to take stock of historical precedent and evidence, as witness numerous books on the subject, for instance, Carla S. O'Dell and Nilly Essaides, *If Only we Knew What we Know: The Transfer of Internal Knowledge and Best Practice* (London: Simon and Schuster, 1998).

23 http://www.telegraph.co.uk/culture/hay-festival/10866114/Pensions-crisis-could-make-volunteers-a-thing-of-the-past-English-Heritage-boss-warns.html, accessed 1 July 2014.

24 On genealogical studies see Samuel M. Otterstrom, 'Genealogy as Religious Ritual: The Doctrine and Practice of Family History in the Church of Jesus Christ of Latter-Day Saints', in Dallen J. Timothy and Jeanne Kay Guelke (eds), *Geography and Genealogy: Locating Personal Pasts* (Aldershot: Ashgate, 2008), pp. 137–52; Robert M. Taylor, 'Summoning the Wandering Tribes: Genealogy and Family Reunions in American History', *Journal of Social History* (1982): 21–37.

25 On Victoriana see Cora Kaplan, *Victoriana: Histories, Fictions, Criticism* (New York: Columbia University Press, 2007).

26 Jonathan E. Schroeder, 'The Cultural Codes of Branding', *Marketing Theory* 9(1) (2009): 123–6.

27 Pierre Bourdieu, 'The Forms of Capital', in John G. Richardson (ed.), *Handbook of Theory and Research for the Sociology of Education* (New York: Greenwood, 1986).

28 For a sympathetic account of the historical narrative directed by Boyle, see Sunder Katwala, 'Our island story', blog post at *British Future*, 28 July 2012: http://www.britishfuture.org/blog/our-island-story/, accessed 4 August 2014.

Historians in the age of impact 19

29 Unlike the balkanization of esoteric subdisciplines denounced by Samuel, *Theatres of Memory*, p. 3, this one entails the shaping of essentialized groups of exclusive audiences.
30 Frances Stewart, 'Horizontal Inequality: Two Types of Trap', *Journal of Human Development and Capabilities* 10(3) (2009): 315–40.
31 For a review of Bourdieu's position, and subsequent research on cultural capital and its intersection with inequality, see T. Bennett and E.B. Silva, 'Cultural Capital and Inequality: Policy Issues and Contexts', *Cultural Trends* 15(2/3) (2006): 87–106.
32 Saul Friedlander (ed.), *Probing the Limits of Representation: Nazism and the 'Final Solution'* (Cambridge, MA; London: Harvard University Press, 1992).
33 See Georgina Boyes, *The Imagined Village: Culture, Ideology and the English Folk Revival* (Leeds: No Masters Cooperative, 2010, 2nd edn), chaps 2–4.
34 See Daniel Pick, *Faces of Degeneration* (Cambridge: Cambridge University Press, 1989), pp. 79–81.
35 Melissa Aronczyk, *Branding the Nation: The Global Business of National Identity* (Oxford: Oxford University Press, 2013).
36 Braudel, *L'Identité de la France* (Paris: Flammarion, 1986).
37 For a forceful and wide-ranging overview of the contribution from the humanities, see Jonathan Bate (ed.), *The Public Value of the Humanities* (London: Bloomsbury Academic, 2011).
38 Barry Eichengreen, 'Economic History and Economic Policy', *Journal of Economic History* 72(2) (2012): 289–307. For a discussion of alternative, and more considered uses of historical analogy by authors contributing to the British History & Policy website (http://www.historyandpolicy.org, accessed 4 August 2014), see Tosh, *Why History Matters* (Basingstoke: Palgrave Macmillan, 2008), pp. 115–18.
39 Françoise Boucher-Saulnier, 'CAR: MSF should update its position on protection', internal policy document, July 2014.
40 G.M. Trevelyan, *Clio: A Muse* (London: Longmans, 1913), pp. 4, 19.
41 P. Mandler, *History and National Life* (London: Profile Books, 2002), p. 146.
42 The English translation is given as 'Tell me, Daddy. What is the use of History?' but could equally have been the more cutting 'So then, Daddy, what is history good for?' Bloch, *The Historian's Craft* (Manchester: Manchester University Press (2012 [1954]), p. 3.
43 Bloch, *The Historian's Craft*, p. 4.
44 Bloch, *The Historian's Craft*, p. 118
45 Bloch, *The Historian's Craft*, p. 159
46 For overviews and critiques of some of these claims, see Richard J. Evans, *In Defence of History* (London: Granta, 1997), pp. 80–3, 238–48; Geoff Eley, 'Is All the World a Text? From Social History to the History of Society Two Decades Later', in Gabrielle M. Spiegel (ed.), *Practicing History: New Directions in Historical Writing after the Linguistic Turn* (New York: Routledge, 2005).
47 Bloch, *The Historian's Craft*. pp. 104–5; for an approachable introduction to Baysean reasoning see Nate Silver, *The Signal and the Noise: The Art and Science of Prediction* (London: Penguin, 2013), chap. 8 'Less and Less and Less Wrong'.
48 James T. Kloppenberg, 'Thinking Historically: A Manifesto of Pragmatic Hermeneutics', *Modern Intellectual History* 9(1) (2012): 201–16; Carl E. Schorske, *Thinking with History: Explorations in the Passage to Modernism* (Princeton, NJ: Princeton University Press, 1998); R.G. Collingwood, 'The Historical Imagination' in *The Idea of History* (Oxford: Oxford University Press, 1994, rev. edn), pp. 231–49.
49 Bloch, *The Historian's Craft*, pp. 50–7.
50 Bloch, *The Historian's Craft*, pp. 73–4; on the broader history of the footnote, see Anthony Grafton, *The Footnote: A Curious History* (Cambridge, MA: Harvard University Press, 1999).
51 A related point is made in Tosh, *Why History Matters*, pp. 7, 127.
52 Martha Nussbaum, *Not for Profit: Why Democracy Needs the Humanities* (Princeton, NJ: Princeton University Press, 2010), pp. 25–6; 45–6.

20   *Pedro Ramos Pinto and Bertrand Taithe*

53 Amartya Sen, *The Idea of Justice* (London: Allen Lane, 2009), especially chaps 6, 7 and 15.
54 Phillips calls these dimensions of distance those of *form, affect, ideology* and *understanding*. Mark Salber Phillips, 'Rethinking Historical Distance: From Doctrine to Heuristic', *History and Theory* 50 (Dec. 2011): 11–23; 16.
55 See, for instance, Tony Judt, 'The Past is Another Country: Myth and Memory in Post-war Europe', in Jan-Werner Müller (ed.), *Memory and Power in Post-war Europe: Studies in the Presence of the Past* (Cambridge: Cambridge University Press, 2002). The point should be made that Europe's construction of an unrepeatable past was itself mobilized in the creation of a post-war European project. Equally, the engagement with the history of slavery discussed by Françoise Vergès (Chapter 7 in this book) is concerned with the issue of slavery in the present.
56 C. Wright Mills, *The Sociological Imagination* (London: Pelican Books, 1970 [1959]), p. 13. Literature – a related pursuit to history – can also perform the same function as argued by, among others, the literary critic James Wood in *How Fiction Works* (London: Vintage, 2008), chap. 7, 'Sympathy and Complexity'. The role of literature in engendering sympathy historically is explored by Lynn Hunt, who sees in the emergence of the novel in the eighteenth century a precondition for the acceptance of the idea of universal humanity. Lynn Hunt, *Inventing Human Rights: A History* (New York: W.W. Norton, 2008).
57 For an overview of the relationship between history and social theory, see William H. Sewell Jr, *The Logics of History* (Chicago, IL: University of Chicago Press, 2005), esp. chap. 1, 'Theory, History and Social Science'.
58 Collini, *What are Universities For?*; Pierre Ronsanvallon, *Counter-Democracy: Politics in an Age of Distrust* (Cambridge: Cambridge University Press, 2008).
59 Norbert Elias, *The Civilising Process* (Oxford: Wiley-Blackwell, 2000).
60 Julien Benda, *La trahison des clercs* (Paris: Grasset, 1927).
61 Bloch, 'Pour le renouveau de l'enseignement historique, 1937', in *L'Histoire, la guerre, la résistance*, pp. 485–515.
62 Another analogy, and interesting to explore further, is to compare the relationship between 'doing history in public' and the academy, with the relationship between academic literature departments and the creative writing workshop.
63 See E.P. Thompson, 'Preface', in *The Making of the English Working Class*, (London: Vantage, 1966).
64 Gyan Prakash, *Another Reason: Science and the Imagination of Modern India* (Princeton, NJ: Princeton University Press, 1999).
65 Isabelle Bruno, Emmanuel Didier and Julien Prévieux (eds), *Statactivisme: Comment lutter avec des nombres* (Paris: Zones, 2014).

2 The genealogy boom
Inheritance, family history and the popular historical imagination

Jerome de Groot

Looking at the ways that audiences and users engage with the past demonstrates the strange, unaudited ways that 'history' works in contemporary society. If we do not track, engage with and understand such phenomena, we can hardly claim to critique the contemporary historical imagination; furthermore, these modes of historical engagement are happening without the permission of the professional historian. History has happened without historians, and occurs in multiple spaces, sites and locations – the professional's input into which pasts the public gets is minimal. The historical imagination is resourced and supported in multiple ways, and we need to be alert to the principles and epistemological models it is provided with. In particular, we need to look at how certain ideals, concerns, themes or models are becoming key frameworks for historical engagement.

In his post-financial crash polemic *Capitalist Realism* Mark Fisher argues, 'What we are dealing with now is not the incorporation of materials that previously seemed to possess subversive potentials, but instead, the pre-emptive formatting and shaping of desires, aspirations and hopes by capitalist culture'.[1] Fisher's argument concerns the way that capitalism has formed 'a pervasive atmosphere, conditioning not only the production of culture but also the regulation of work and education' (p. 16). An alternative is unimaginable due to the deployment of tropes, aesthetics and images suggesting that this is all there is or ever has been.

In this chapter I discuss the ways that the materials of the past have become part of such a representative nexus, working to construct an imaginative historiography outlining a progress towards the systems of contemporary global capital. If even the materials of the past become part of the narrative towards the capitalist present what does this allow a society to imagine about itself? In particular, I argue, knowledge of the past is increasingly framed within discourses of inheritance, stability through dynastic order, and the comforting explanatory template of genealogy. These governing epistemological models are hardening into a taxonomy. However, I will also suggest ways that these are being resisted by users of the past.

The comments made during a trade mission to China in October 2013 by the British Chancellor of the Exchequer George Osborne demonstrate the way in

22 Jerome de Groot

which heritage is seen as a way of enticing tourism, growing links with emerging economies and developing the UK economy:

> What we want to see is Chinese tourists. Just as a generation ago we had a whole wave of Japanese tourists, the new phenomenon in the world is Chinese tourism. That's fantastic for the British hospitality and tourist industry [...] One hundred and sixty million Chinese are watching *Downton Abbey*, which is more than double the number of people who live in the UK.[2]

Osborne's much publicized observation about the importance of the heritage television series *Downton Abbey* for the strategic positioning of UK PLC in China was greeted with derision and distaste from many commentators. He suggests the cultural–historical television product as part of the solution to long-term post-industrial decline. The historical industries – television, tourism, heritage – might replace heavy industry by creating and marketing a new type of commodity, the past itself. *Downton Abbey* enjoys massive success throughout the world. This 'export' might provide the fictional mainspring for physical, material engagement (through tourism) with the sites of the past found in the UK. His projected economic miracle happily blends the fictional with the actual, the representational with the material. He envisages an imaginative and physical affinity between the material relics of the past that might be visited by tourists and fictional television versions of events. Osborne suggests that these sites of 'history' might be read in terms of product, profit, enticement and brand.

Of course, his comments render more visible the capitalist–realist representational tropes, practices and discourses of the kind that Mark Fisher describes. Culture, and the past, is in thrall to the profit motive. Osborne's words therefore prompt us to think once more about the pros and cons of the commodification of the past. History in the academy has found it difficult to engage with the ways that the past is sold, but it is the case that most people's experience of 'history' is seen through the lens of some kind of financial transaction, from paying a fee to enter a country house to buying a ticket to see a costume drama film. If the past is a product of some kind, how and why does this work, and, most importantly, is it a problem? To understand this we need a commodity–historiography, addressing the effect of for-profit history on the historical imagination. We need to investigate exactly what it means for 'history' to be something that works within a nexus of commodification; we should know how marketing, profit, branding and the bottom line affect what history is made, read and watched. We also need to understand what the commodification of history means for the average (or the casual) user/consumer/customer/purchaser/addict/client of historical product, however we might construct them.

The use of history to make a buck and as nationalist proto-colonial cultural product might be traced back throughout the nineteenth century at least; the use of the past to sell a country through tourism dates back decades, if not centuries. More recently the debates between Raphael Samuel, Patrick Wright, Alison Light, David Lowenthal, Robert Hewison and others during the 1980s revolved around the problematic development of 'heritage' into what Samuel termed 'Thatcherism in period dress'.[3] The rise in interest in heritage, the past, history, during the early 1980s – and a swathe of cultural productions from *Brideshead Revisited* (1981) to the work of Merchant–Ivory – led to an extraordinary flowering of intellectual work. Historians and political intellectuals engaged passionately with the cultural shifts towards explicitly consuming the past.[4] They produced a critique of heritage in multiple contexts: film, clothing, museum, television, political life. For each writer, the idea of 'nostalgia' was key – heritage was a way of monetizing nostalgia and henceforth national identity.

Hewison's book title *The Heritage Industry: Britain in a Climate of Decline* neatly clarified the way that selling the past might replace manufacturing in the UK. The title was tongue-in-cheek in 1987 but in the past two decades the culture, tourist and heritage industries have become clearly defined entities, part of the suite of producers that UK PLC maintains. In his preface to the reissue in 2009 of his 1985 book *On Living in an Old Country* Patrick Wright reflects upon the mix of 'commerce and culture' that he was analysing: 'the argument associating "heritage" with decline has certainly failed to thrive. It has been repeatedly dismissed on the grounds that conservation and heritage values have actually proved to be good for the economy'.[5] The heritage debate was won by the actuality of neoliberal economics. He continues: 'I remember being astonished when I first heard government figures proclaim that heritage and tourism would be developed as an economic alternative to heavy industries like steel-manufacture or coal mining.'[6]

These 'government figures' were proved correct (on their own terms) in many ways. Heritage is a healthy and important contributor to what are now called the 'cultural industries'; the Heritage Lottery fund recently argued that in 2013 heritage-based tourism was worth £26.4 billion to the UK economy.[7] Recent public discussions of history and the public seem largely to revolve around definitions of national identity.[8] The question of how the past is sold to us seems to have been forgotten, ignored or, possibly, reconciled. The post-2000 'history boom' involving Simon Schama, David Starkey and an exponential surge in interest in the past across multiple medias led some professional historians to express concern, but this has not been accompanied with the same intellectually febrile response as that of the early 1980s.

The idea of the past as something that might contribute economically has become increasingly enshrined in institutional policy, from government work on tourism to non-governmental organizations (NGO) such as the Heritage Lottery fund. This is part of a wider social move to adduce the transformative economic impact and effect of culture more generally. This is occurring within a new, complex, inter-embedded system of international capital. The Chinese context for Osborne's comments suggests that *Downton Abbey* works in new financial – globalized – circumstances as a kind of turbo-heritage, history

24 *Jerome de Groot*

without borders, addressing a transcultural audience in a way that early critiques of *A Room with a View* could never have imagined.

Downton Abbey might be seen as participating in the worst caricatures that heritage television can construct, particularly in its concern with inheritance and the urgent need for purity and legitimacy in the bloodline. The concerns with inheritance and genealogy that are the foundations of the series demonstrates how these twin ideas are fundamental in contributing to the contemporary popular historical imagination. From the outset *Downton Abbey* considers the historical events of the twentieth century as challenges to the sanctity and wholeness of the country house estate. The sinking of the *Titanic* – for many commentators the event that 'created' the modern world in 1912 – provides the series' initial dramatic push.[9] It kills the heir presumptive to the estate and brings to Downton the possibility of the loss of the entail. The consequence of this is that the new heir presumptive is from outside of the main family – Matthew Crawley, a solicitor from Manchester. He is possibly the avatar of the middle-class working people who watch the show and who are slowly assimilated into the world of the aristocrats. Most of the first two series is taken up with sorting this 'mess' and making Crawley one of the family. The Great War threatens the house twofold – first by the disappearance of Crawley (now somewhat awkwardly configured in the family) in combat, and second by the use of the house for recuperating wounded men. Thankfully other historical events such as the influenza pandemic of 1918 arise in order to kill off Crawley's non-family bride and leave him open to marry the female heir of the Grantham family, Lady Mary.

Downton endures. As Katherine Byrne has argued, *Downton* is 'post-heritage' insofar as it is self-conscious: 'it does seem apparent that the series is, ideologically speaking, in many ways a return to the more traditional notion of heritage, and the media has tended to agree'.[10] Byrne notes the problematic shift away from intellectual critiques of heritage, but argues that '*Downton* is deliberately, and shamelessly, harking back to the heyday of 1980s and 1990s "classic" heritage'.[11] It has a sense of its own inheritance, therefore, and the show takes its place in a representational genealogy comfortably selling an epistemological and historiographical template.

Downton Abbey suggests that the post-heritage series has little connection with the actuality of rendering the past and much more to do with globalized entertainment tropes. *The Tudors*' much publicized disavowal of historical 'fact' similarly demonstrates how these series are nominally 'historical' but in fact are very unbothered about anything other than the sheen of authenticity. History here becomes part of a fantasy world rather than the relation of anything 'real'; history is an aesthetic trope rather than a driver of content. These shows contribute to a way of knowing the past that is concerned with particular models of authenticity, legitimacy, order, stability and genealogy. The popular phenomenon of *Downton Abbey* as a global historical product is unique, but it is hardly the only show ploughing this particular furrow. The key global historical television series of the past years demonstrate an overriding concern with legitimacy and inheritance: *Mad Men* (the unreality of products sold by advertising; the emptiness of identity in America; the impostor Don Draper embodying the hollowness of the modern man); *Game of Thrones* (pseudo-medieval dynastic drama echoing Shakespeare's history plays with at least four claimants to the legitimate throne duking it out); *The Tudors* (Henry's increasingly shrill attempts to get an heir).

Historical fictions and costume dramas seem to have an underlying anxiety about the sanctity of an institution (the home, the country house, the nation, the family) in their DNA. They betray an obsession with inheritance, linearity, and a particular temporal model. *Downton Abbey*'s epistemology of inheritance, its central concern with genealogy, and the intertwining of these two issues with the development of a popular historiographical road map leading us imaginatively to the contemporary capitalist world, renders it therefore part of a recognizable trend in contemporary popular history.

This obsession with models of inheritance is clearly demonstrated in the biggest growing popular history 'genre' of the past thirty years. This is the area known as family history, or genealogy. As a set of practices and approaches, and as a set of material ways of knowing the past, family history as a phenomenon enables us to begin to discern the complexity of contemporary engagement with the past. It demonstrates, as do the television series, the complexity and diversity of contemporary historical engagement. It shows both sides of the heritage argument – the problematic consequences of unthinking devotion to nostalgic views of the past on the one hand, and the interrogative and independent ways that 'ordinary' people engage with the materials of history to make their own narratives on the other. *Downton Abbey* might seem a retrograde entity in some ways, but family history demonstrates the diversity of contemporary historical engagement globally. When considered alongside the global *Downton* phenomenon it becomes clear that the governing epistemological themes of the early twentieth century relate to legitimacy and inheritance. However, in contrast to *Downton Abbey*'s straightforward inheritance model, family history has sufficient diversity to suggest popular history can both ingest and challenge prevailing discourses through introducing complex epistemological issues to general users.

One of the most prescient arguments made by David Lowenthal's *The Past is a Foreign Country* concerns how '[i]n our time, massive migration and the loss of tangible relics have stimulated interest in genealogy'.[12] He collects genealogy with several other phenomena (preservation, local history, retrochic) as indicators of 'general consensus about past-related benefits ... familiarity and recognition; reaffirmation and validation; individual and group identity; guidance; enrichment; and escape' (p. 38). It is clearly the case that the biggest global historical phenomenon of the past three decades has been family history. The massive rise in investigation of genealogy has been prompted by the development of historical models of 'benefit', as Lowenthal suggests (a kind of humanist sense that we can become better people through an understanding of the past) and through the huge development of database technologies. History is good for us,

26   Jerome de Groot

and can explain us, and can help us to 'become' in the modern world; technology contributes to and to an extent controls this.

Popular culture was relatively slow to catch on to the explosion of interest from the late 1980s onwards in amateur investigation, but has subsequently been at the forefront of the genealogy boom. First broadcast in 2004, the Wall-to-Wall produced BBC genealogical series *Who Do You Think You Are?* (*WDYTYA?*) has proven immensely successful. To date it has gone through ten series and is still being broadcast around the world. Developed initially in conjunction with the National Archives, each episode of the show follows a particular famous figure as they investigate their family history and dig into their genealogy. The show is a way of telling social history stories that accrue around the central narrative of becoming, which moves both towards and away from the celebrity – towards, as all the investigation is about understanding them in the *now*; away, as their research takes them further and further back into the past.

It is also a rumination on Britishness of varying kinds. As Amy Holdsworth argues, 'It attempts to reimagine British identity through the investigations of personal history, memory and identity'.[13] Consequently, *WDYTYA?* demonstrates a wide number of historiographical ideas: social change over time; the mobilization of ethnic groups; the continuing resonance in terms of population of major events such as the world wars, famine, catastrophes and empire; changing attitudes to religion, illness, age, crime, family, gender and education. They are both social history documents and templates for amateur historical investigation. As such they are incredibly diverse documentaries made with little historical agenda. Each documentary explores certain issues by happenstance, coincidence, figuring a mode of historical investigation that is driven by the evidence. The central figure is the celebrity, at once made 'normal' and humanized through their relationship to the past while still reified as being the point and purpose of the programme.

The show demonstrates that investigation of the past through family history had profound consequences for contemporary identity. Where the initial drive of the series was to use the celebrity to uncover issues in social history, the self-actualization element of investigating roots became centrally important to the show's appeal. Celebrities wept, gained understanding, saw the process as therapy and uncovered nasty things about 'themselves'. It became clear that historical investigation of this kind is irrevocably connected to a prevailing sense of how the past might inflect and inform the present, as is demonstrated in the problematic cadences of the title's imperative. Who Do You *Think* You Are? We'll see about that. Alex Graham, CEO of Wall-to-Wall, argues that 'we saw the celebrity as a passive conduit into the broader historical narrative' but the organization was taken aback that they became 'an active participant in a process which is as much about self-realization as about uncovering an external narrative'.[14]

More broadly the series encourages the public audience to in turn undertake their own historical investigation. There are supporting websites and how-to

The genealogy boom   27

guides provided online by the BBC and the National Archives. It is predicated upon the lure of the archive and a sense that with the correct training any amateur can undertake to create a narrative from the materials of the past. The show is an intoxicating blend of celebrity culture, armchair investigation and easy-access reality history. It creates a historiographical sense of change through time while also enshrining an idea that history is a set of trails and trees, a multiplicity of genealogical tables heading towards the now. The show encourages the 'average' viewer to mimic professional research techniques, enabling the pursuit of history outside of the academy. Each show has dead ends, trails which peter out, 'brick walls' that acknowledge the ultimate unknowability of the past. It is often bleak, leaving the celebrity wandering around desperately attempting to imagine into being another piece of evidence. Alternatively it foregrounds the horror of the past, with participants invariably coming up against grim details of everyday life. Famously, various figures – including the combative political journalist Jeremy Paxman – have wept over the various unpleasant fates of their ancestors.

The first series of *WDYTYA?* had an unprecedented success. In 2004 it gained the highest audience share and ratings of any factual show on BBC2 (it is now screened on BBC1). It caused a quantitative increase in interest in family history and genealogy (so, for instance, 475,000 people downloaded the National Archive factsheet from the BBC website; 1.9 million people used the BBC family history website in November 2004; there was an increase of 18 per cent in first-time users of the National Archives website in November 2004). The series' objective was to increase interest in family history, and, particularly, to direct users to the web as a research resource. National events tied to the show were hugely oversubscribed. The success of the British iteration of the show led to a website, a companion magazine, and large conference events around the country over the past decade. The show is now in its tenth series and a staple of BBC programming.

The phenomenon of the show demonstrates a key tension between public service broadcasting as discussed by Michael Wood (Chapter 4 in this book) (the BBC's commitment to innovative documentary making) and the need to develop formats that will be saleable around the world and create multiple profit possibilities. The success of the *WDYTYA?* format has led to its being exported around the world. There have been series in the following countries: Canada (2007, 2012), USA (2010), Australia (2008), Ireland (2008), Poland (2007), Sweden (2009), South Africa (2009), Holland (2010–), Norway (2011-), Germany (2008–), Israel (2010), Russia (2009–12), Finland (2012), Czech Republic (2013) and Portugal (2013–). While the format varies slightly at times, the influence of this model of heritage programming is evident. There are also various programmes mimicking the success of *WDYTYA?*, such as *Genealogy Road-show* (USA, Ireland) and *Finding Your Roots* (USA). The investigation of roots, genealogical investigation more generally, and the use of celebrities to tell social history narratives, is therefore incredibly important in establishing modes of approaching the past in popular culture around the world. The series' influence

28 *Jerome de Groot*

over amateur historical investigation means that it has had a material impact upon the historical and historiographical culture of each country.

On the one hand, then, the format is exportable throughout a globalized television culture. On the other, specific instances of the show demonstrate a local public historical culture thriving within the transcultural information flows of a globalized media culture. The global success of the programme has driven the expansion of genealogical tools and supporting resources from magazines to websites. The show testifies to a burgeoning interest in genealogical research around the world. Family history and genealogical research are hugely important to millions of people, and provide them with hands-on, direct engagement with the evidence of the past.

Is this a problem? What is at stake here?

Family history is amateur, free, with time given voluntarily. It is a leisure pursuit, a private hobby undertaken with public documents. It involves the gathering of information and the development of ideas. The complexity of skills acquired is intense, from codicological to palaeographical. Participants gain skills and also acquire cultural capital, in a manner akin to other 'serious' leisure pursuits that enable the mimicking of professional activities, such as collecting. Its elements include witnessing, archives, conjecture, supposition, educated guesswork, inspiration, diligence, data-mining. Family history involves the application of investigative skills to a body of evidence. It challenges the role of the academic or professional historian as gatekeeper of knowledge by demonstrating that, armed with some few skills and the time to investigate the mass of information, anyone can produce a narrative of the past which explains and textualizes it. Family history is also an intensely modern way of thinking about the past, involving the investigation of the archive through the asking of one particular question or the development of one particular strand or thread. The family is a way through the chaos of the archive, a means of comprehending the vastness of pastness. The family historian is intensely myopic in their approach to the past, insofar as they only seek information relating to a particular bloodline or genealogy; conversely, the family historian is also intensely cosmopolitan, insofar as they will traverse and negotiate class, gender, geography while following their trail.

The participants of *WDYTYA?* demonstrate the breadth of British society at the beginning of the twenty-first century, and the show meditates upon the effects of empire, class mobility, education, health and war on 'ordinary' people. Users of online genealogical tools encounter information and data from around the world. They also celebrate the domestic, the local, the unimportant and unremembered. Family history also resists the overarching narratives of class entitlement and progress advocated by most British fictionalized history – they represent the unremembered servants of Downton Abbey rather than the gentry. Family history is a way of levelling genealogy, taking a pursuit that had previously been antiquarian or about the sustaining of privilege, and popularizing it. The past here might be used to resist the histories of dominant groups, discerning new narratives that disregard the stories told us.

Conversely, we might argue that this globalized family history is deeply problematic. Much of the work is undertaken now outside of the archive. Massive websites such as Ancestry.com, FamilyHistory, GenesReunited and MyHeritage. com allow quick trawling of information but also store and own vast repositories of data. MyHeritage claims to have 25 million family trees and 194 million photographs on its site, for instance. These websites operate on varying types of pay-access membership principles, ranging from free, limited access, to yearly subscriptions. A website such as GenesReunited charges for access to historical databases such as parish records, effectively making money from access to public records. The free version of the site allows access to other users' data, establishing the principle that user-generated information is part of the website product with a premium to pay for actual 'historical' data. Records that have been collected by the state and made publicly available have become the 'product' for these private websites. The websites are hence selling back information that is either publicly collected or created by users; this represents the part-privatizing of formerly public historical space.

The largest, and oldest, of these genealogical websites is FamilySearch.org, run by the Church of Jesus Christ of the Latter-Day Saints, also known as the Mormons. Their proprietary genealogical software GEDCOM is used by most genealogical websites. GEDCOM is a way of coding personal information into a usable genealogical format. There are also many softwares for organizing and writing genealogical information. Apart from the issues inherent in deploying such software to structure the gathering and storing of information, GEDCOM also makes particular assumptions about the structures of families and the importance of certain bits of evidence (mainly factual, such as date of birth, marriage, occupation). The type of information that is collected about individuals, therefore, establishes them within a particular evidentiary nexus that is predicated upon one particular way of constructing the past.

GEDCOM, and the other ways that family history websites organize and store information, suggests an epistemological encoding of individuals within a particular template, connecting them to each other via particular nodes that we might seek to critique. Certainly the principle that historical information might be organized and accessed according to database protocols signals something particular about the construction of the archive. The point here is that the average user is at once enfranchised by the proliferation of information while simultaneously being incorporated (and their families, too, involuntarily) into a set of dominant discourses and problematic structures. Again, retrospectively, our ancestors are forced into a template that finds it problematic to account for difference, or ignores anomalies. The codification of the past that is the consequence of this type of organization is part of a wider problem that mass databases (and hence data-mining) have raised in the past decade. Historical research is now in many ways tied to archiving principles established by coders rather than professionals. The price we pay for the instant access to the wealth

30 *Jerome de Groot*

of information in online resources is this organization. All archives are arranged in particular ways, and establish power relations, but these online genealogical sites are unique insofar as they are user-generated.

The genealogical websites are keen to demonstrate their commitment to privacy (and in doing so encourage their users to have an ethical approach to the evidence of the past). MyHeritage.com reminds users: 'By using this Website and the Service you consent to the collection, use, storage and disclosure of your personal information by us in accordance with this Privacy Policy'.[15] Historical research becomes something to be regulated by a legal policy regarding ownership and disclosure, and the site contributes to the increasing sense that privacy in the contemporary networked world does not exist.[16] Users' ancestors are retrospectively revealed to the world. The privacy policies make uncomfortable distinctions between living and deceased persons. The dead might be revealed on Google; the living are protected. Ancestry.com has Facebook import software that allows a user to merge historical enquiry with contemporary social networking software. If genealogical research has some relationship to a definition of selfhood in the now, a performed online self, then the link with more overt networks makes the relationship of then to now much more complex. It certainly shifts the paradigm when thinking about how and where archival information is accessed, used and maintained.

MyHeritage.com creates 'smart' family trees that allow users to search other users' information, family trees and historical records. Hence, the ease of the modern searchable database is acquired at the cost of the 'privacy' of the past. Historical information is displayed, stored and shared in a way inconceivable a decade ago. It becomes part of a vast social network. The past is formulated according to the templates of a modern organization, in part funded by the venture capitalists behind Skype and Facebook. The websites have diversified and bought various other websites and softwares to support their expansion and brand. Ancestry.com owns RootsWeb.com, a site that began as a listserv in the mid-1990s and which still presents a more independent, scratchy interface for those uncomfortable with the slick corporate quality of the parent company. Ancestry.com also owns Fold3, a proprietary data-mining software that can access 451,483,540 public records (for a price) – so public information such as census data becomes commodified (and monetized) through the software used to navigate it.

These websites raise ethical issues about the investigation of, and display of, the past. They prompt us to ask questions about how we access information about the past, how we store and share our information, and how this pastness inflects our identities in the contemporary moment. As with *WDYTYA?*, the journey is away from the user and towards the user; all information tends to an explanation of the 'now', so the participant becomes inflected by the findings of the research. They allow us to discern the ways that the online self, even in relation to the past, is configured within a financial nexus. Further, we might see how the governing inheritance historiographical model, deployed within this corporate framework, allows people from the past to be colonized in similar

The genealogy boom 31

ways, owned and configured. They are made to do work; they are in some ways a resource; they are cultural capital that is freely shared by the user in order for the website to turn profit.

These sites suppose that 'family' history is somehow 'owned' by the family in question, contributing to a problematic (and deeply Western, capitalist, paternalist) obsession with intellectual ownership and inheritance. The entire process of genealogy is predicated upon models of inheritance, primogeniture (at least in terms of records and manifestation in the archive), hetero-normativity, legitimacy and linearity. The pedagogical and historiographical model that is being pursued is at least linear, if not teleological; rather than, say, analysing via a constellation or a cross-section or a rhizomatic model, the 'tree' structure is resolutely hegemonic. The taxonomical model here is the arrangement of information in a particular order, structuring our understanding of the past. It is an epistemology of formula and order. As social history goes, genealogy is particularly monomaniacal, tribalist even and blithely unbothered about *others* outside the bloodline. Research is based on evidence relating to occupation, property (through wills), family relationships (through census data), family and death. This is the information that social organization has chosen to collect about individuals over the past centuries, and its rendering in a particular template in the present demonstrates both a continuing concern with the mechanics of inheritance and the inescapable inflection of the con-temporary by the archive. Genealogy is just one of a set of areas where the historical imagination has become colonized by a neoliberal, capitalist mindset.

These two seemingly disparate phenomena – Sunday tea-time television and amateur historical investigation – demonstrate an abiding obsession with ancestry, inheritance and legacy. On the one hand this might describe a crisis of legitimacy; on the other an unhealthy obsession with the 'inheritance' of the past. Both are seemingly tied to national identity but hold a dialogue with wider global concerns. How cultures choose to remember, or to represent/stage history is deeply important to the way that those cultures conceptualize them-selves. It is suggestive of the culture's ethics, notions of identity, sense of agency and deepest values. How a society stages its past, engages with the materials of history, and dramatizes the materials of memory, are key ways of compre-hending the ways that society works. This was recognized by the discussants of the 'heritage boom' in the 1980s; it needs to be recognized in the wider global context of the 'Genealogy Boom' of the past two decades. Much recollection of the past is now undertaken within a continuum of commodification, and this needs to be recognized. Most of the materials of memory are now intertwined in an increasingly globalized system, be it that of transcultural media or online networks. We need to account for and audit the opportunities and complexities of this internationalized historical imagination.

Over the past two decades 'History' outwith the academy has grown unchecked and in problematic and eccentric ways. History outside the academy is developing and growing in multiple ways. It is a commodity – and we should worry about this. However, these commercial aspects have led to an incredibly

32 *Jerome de Groot*

protean historical culture unresourced by the academy and not subject to its limiting jurisdiction. Within the broad umbrella of 'inheritance' and genealogy we see the diversity and complexity of contemporary historicity. Examples such as family history are problematic due to incipient commercialization but also demonstrate the complexity of contemporary British and global historical culture outside the university sector. In a sense these examples demonstrate quite how irrelevant scholarship itself is to historical culture and the historical imagination. The commercialization of the past (and 'heritage') is also possibly its enfranchisement, liberation and release from elite centres to more demotic and democratic contexts. In some ways the commodification of history and the 'globalization' of historical information and fictional tropes – the internationalization of public history – has led to an expansion in its reach and influence. By releasing knowledge and developing the historical imagination these phenomena *liberate* the global subject into history in a way professional and academic work has struggled to.

Suggested further reading

Most key readings are clearly identified throughout the text and discussed. See in chronological order the works of:

Patrick Wright, *On Living in an Old Country* (London: Verso, 1985).
David Lowenthal, *The Past is a Foreign Country* (Cambridge: Cambridge University Press, 1985).
Robert Hewison, *The Heritage Industry: Britain in a Climate of Decline* (London: Methuen, 1987).
Raphael Samuel, *Theatres of Memory* (London: Verso, 1994).
Mark Fisher, *Capitalist Realism* (London: Sero Books, 2009).
Amy Holdsworth, *Television, Memory and Nostalgia* (Basingstoke: Palgrave Macmillan, 2011).

Notes

1 Mark Fisher, *Capitalist Realism* (London: Sero Books, 2009), p. 9.
2 *Today*, Radio 4, 14 October 2013, 6–9am. These figures were later contested as erroneous.
3 Raphael Samuel, *Theatres of Memory* (London: Verso, 1994), p. 290.
4 Patrick Wright, *On Living in an Old Country* (London: Verso, 1985); David Lowenthal, *The Past is a Foreign Country* (Cambridge: Cambridge University Press, 1985); Robert Hewison, *The Heritage Industry: Britain in a Climate of Decline* (London: Methuen, 1987); Samuel, *Theatres of Memory*.
5 Wright, *On Living in an Old Country* (Oxford: Oxford University Press, 2009, rev. edn), p. xiv.
6 Wright, *On Living,* p. xiv.
7 'New research reveals heritage tourism boosts UK economy in tough times', Heritage Lottery fund press release, 10 July 2013, http://www.hlf.org.uk/news/Pages/Heritage Tourism2013.aspx#.UtQMFY2LnYw, accessed 13 January 2014.
8 See Richard J. Evans, 'The Wonderfulness of Us: The Tory Interpretation of History', *London Review of Books* 33(6) (17 March 2011): 9–12.

The genealogy boom   33

9 Arguments well digested in Thomas Laqueur, 'Why Name a Ship after a Defeated Race?', *London Review of Books* 35(2) (24 January 2013): 3–10.

10 Katherine Byrne 'Adapting Heritage: Class and Conservatism in *Downton Abbey*', *Rethinking History*, online, DOI: 10.1080/13642529.2013.811811, p. 5.

11 Byrne, 'Adapting Heritage', p. 15.

12 Lowenthal, *The Past is a Foreign Country*, p. 38.

13 Amy Holdsworth, *Television, Memory and Nostalgia* (Basingstoke: Palgrave Macmillan, 2011), p. 94.

14 Email correspondence with author, 5 March 2008.

15 http://www.myheritage.com/FP/Company/popup.php?p=privacy_policy, accessed 8 January 2014.

16 Bobbie Johnson, 'Privacy no longer a social norm, says Facebook founder', *The Guardian*, 11 January 2011, http://www.theguardian.com/technology/2010/jan/11/facebook-privacy, accessed 8 January 2014.

3 History 2.0
History, publics and new technologies

Toby Butler

There is a wonderful picture of nineteenth-century Oxford in which the artist decided to skip the usual views of the dreaming spires and instead look at things from the Jericho side of town, an area of mean terraced houses surrounding a canal, an iron works and the biggest university press in the world, the Oxford University Press. I like the picture because from this vantage point we can catch a glimpse of the working underbelly of the university, the smoking chimney of the press that so rarely features in more romantic views of the city. The coal barge and the chimney are a reminder of the power needed to drive the presses that printed the books that were sent vast distances (by 1925 OUP cover pages boasted that the press had offices in London, Edinburgh, Copenhagen, New York, Toronto, Melbourne, Cape Town, Bombay, Calcutta, Madras and Shanghai); the famous dictionaries, the English language primers, and of course the monographs of countless academics were shipped around the British empire and beyond. The picture (see Figure 3.1) reminds us that the university is not only a place of learning, but a powerhouse of knowledge, a place of production and utility, distributing ideas to the world.

More than a century later I am in the OUP offices on Madison Avenue in New York, discussing an idea for a book with the editorial staff there. In the foyer I notice an old mechanical printing press, doubtless there to remind visitors of the long history of this peculiar organization (it is a department of the university, rather than a business). I ask the staff about printing schedules and get a wry smile from an editorial assistant. 'In two or three years, I wonder if we will be producing paper books at all', she said. At the time it seemed like a throwaway remark, but since then I'm not so sure. After 244 years of printing encyclopaedias, *Encyclopaedia Britannica* gave up printing paper versions in 2012. And of course it is not just books. In the last few years I have seen several journals and trade magazines stop print production and go online only. With discomfort I have noticed that some university libraries, my own included, have done away entirely with a dedicated reading area in which to browse and read journals and newspapers.

How a landscape painter would capture this move from paper to digital is hard to imagine. Perhaps it would feature a warehouse, full of the beige boxes of computer servers, or a man in the foreground peering at a tablet or a smartphone.

Figure 3.1 The observatory and printing press seen from Jericho meadows, Oxford, *c.* 1810
© Oxfordshire County Council – Oxfordshire History Centre

Setting aside my love of paper-based information, it could be argued that fundamentally nothing has changed; universities are still in the business of pumping knowledge around the planet, just in a different format, albeit faster and more prolific. It is more a question of extent than fundamental change – and historians are well placed to explore comparisons with the impact of the printing press on society. They can remind us of challenges that the press represented to authority (the Church, the universities and their scriptoria) and the astonishing multiplicity of ideas that were propelled around society as a result. The digital revolution has simply extended what are fundamentally similar effects – the geographical reach is greater, production is quicker and easier, 'authority' is ever more easily challenged and there is the ever-present debate about what kind of information should be allowed to be in the public domain. Modern examples of this might include things like the role of Facebook and Twitter in the Arab Spring or whether publishing secret material on WikiLeaks might be endangering society. The early modern citizen of any major city would have been familiar with similar concerns surrounding dangerous literature and (printing) press regulation, censorship and licensing.

You might think that universities would be the organizations with the vision and budget, and the willingness to devote huge efforts to digitize and catalogue documents, in a similar way that Oxford University Press compiled national biographies and dictionaries. But major digitization projects focused on ships' manifests or census returns are just as likely to be delivered by online family history companies or search engines. Leaving aside the issue of commodification and the consideration of the type of documents that do and don't make their

36   Toby Butler

way into the public domain, it is hard to argue against the fact that as a result archives are being accessed worldwide by far greater numbers as a result. Those familiar with the history of the printing press would probably argue that this differs little from the commercial printing of the print revolution. But it was not particularly easy to set up as a printer; licences were required and presses were costly. Hyperspace is a very different matter; crowd-sourcing information, personal websites and blog platforms mean that barriers to entry to the researching and production of historical information are surely at their lowest ever; as a result, billions are participating in what might be loosely termed history-related publishing.[1] These key transformations – the move from paper to computer server and the more open access to the means of the production of knowledge – are well known but I think it is worth reminding ourselves of how far we have travelled in the short twenty-first century.

There is much hype surrounding new media, but there *is* more to it than merely an extension in speed and geographical reach. There is the whole issue of the public being given the opportunity to research, write, collaborate and produce their own histories online, which might be usefully seen in the context of Raphael Samuel's conception of history in *Theatres of Memory* as a far broader project than many considered: 'If history was thought of as an activity rather than a profession, then the number of its practitioners would be legion'.[2]

There is a very well-established British example of online publishing in Brighton, a seaside resort and now city in its own right on the south coast of England. The website mybrightonandhove.org.uk was set up in 2000 as part of Brighton's millennium celebrations. It was inspired by a display in Brighton Museum called 'My Brighton', and following seed funding from the museum and Brighton and Hove Council the website is now funded by a not-for-profit community publisher. It is run by volunteers who sort local history-related contributions from the public into categories from allotments and architecture to weather and wartime history. In 2005 a constitution was drawn up to more formally establish the website organization which has a relatively open structure – for example after three months volunteers can become formal members of the organization with voting rights on major decisions. It now has over 8,700 pages of photos, memories, knowledge and views of the city. There are lively 'notes and queries' type discussion boards discussing anything from family history information to identifying buildings in old pictures and postcards. The message boards now contain over a decade of discussion and the site, which has not changed enormously in terms of structure or design, still receives a thousand visits a day. If you think for a second what the readership is for an average academic article or history book, typically in the hundreds, you will appreciate that mybrightonandhove.org.uk is nothing less than an historical blockbuster. The site contains primary source material and several thousand images that would never have made their way into an archive. Computers and the internet have put the 'means of production' of historical publication into the hands of the people in a way that is so revolutionary I do not think we

History, publics and new technologies 37

quite appreciate the enormity of it all; we are just beginning to appreciate the sheer power of the tool at our disposal.

Of course examples like this raise questions about the role of the historian. The tensions between the amateur and the professional historian are as old as the history profession, and the web has doubtless done much to highlight some aspects and dissolve others. For those concerned primarily with writing and producing historical monographs, the web might be regarded as a mixed blessing. Work can more easily be promoted and circulated worldwide; comment and connections with like-minded researchers is effortless; and for good or ill citation indexes can inform us how loved – or hated – our work is in academia and beyond.

But professional work has to compete more than ever before with non-professional work, some well researched, some less so. Online expertise can easily (and occasionally vindictively) be questioned and challenged anonymously (from blogs to forums to Amazon book reviews). But for most historians, the internet has been an astonishingly useful tool, perhaps more useful that we care to admit to our increasingly book-averse students (and perhaps even to ourselves). Web platforms, online archives and crowd-sourced websites have made many historical research and publishing tasks far, far quicker and easier.

The fact is that in many respects we can all be historical doers, and from family history to community history non-professional historians are now able to reach an unprecedented audience through a wide variety of new media. What does this mean for the type of history we engage with, and how is the role of the professional historian changing in this new landscape of history production? In a discussion about the role of the (academic) public historian Jill Liddington argues that the role should not be one of merely producing history for the public.[3] The historian should provide 'expert mediation between the past and its publics' with the 'highest standards of scholarship and academic rigour'. It is hard to argue against preserving high standards, but the issue of expertise and the automatic assumption that academia has this compared to historians outside the academy needs to be considered more carefully. Hilda Kean and Paul Ashton have argued that this is an artificial divide – can the practice of academics with say, genealogists and local historians really be so sharply identified?[4]

Going back to Samuel's idea of history as an activity rather than a profession, the dualism of trying to draw comforting lines of what is and is not professional history rather misses the point. If history is something that we all 'do' in some way or another, the question really becomes one of negotiating how we might cooperate or coalesce our activities for the benefit of humanity, inside and outside the academy. As Hilda Kean and Paul Ashton suggest, a wider view of the work of the public historian (and I think this can very usefully be applied to web-based work) is a much messier, less clear-cut and more complex relationship that must be concerned with issues such as co-creation, sharing authority, negotiating positions and bridging boundaries.

It might be argued that there is nothing particularly new about this – we have had decades of community history projects and oral history ventures, many arising from the social movements of the 1960s and 1970s. But the web has had a kind of multiplier effect, both in terms of reach (a community website is much easier to stumble across than a printed book) and as a collaborative tool which allows the spirit of some of those early projects to emerge again, perhaps with even more scope and vigour.

A key issue here is that in the twenty-first century the printed historical monograph is now just one of a host of possible things that an historian might be expected to produce, and many of the online alternatives make solitary work difficult, if not impossible. In production terms the web-based historian will need to work directly with multimedia practitioners; they will find their work reaches unexpected audiences, and the online ease of communication means that there is much more likelihood of interaction (with readers, specialists and communities) outside the historical sphere. Web material is far more malleable than the printed page; revision and correction is far quicker and easier. Online projects are also more social; as we can see in mybrightonandhove.org.uk, they have far more propensity for sharing and co-creation; comments, reviews, blogs and wikis blur the boundaries between producer and consumer. Compared to print, consider how much online text has no named author, or is labelled with little more than a cryptic username. As a medium, much of the web is designed to work collectively and so often seems to defy ownership.

Another huge issue that historians must get to grips with in terms of online production is the recent geographical turn for location-specific content. At the time of writing (2014) 5 billion smartphones have been sold around the planet that are location aware (via gps chips and mobile phone mast triangulation). Large numbers of applications make use of geo-location, from route finding to dating, and geo-targeted advertising.

Historians are no strangers to geo-locating history of course. W.G. Hoskins's classic *Local History in England*[5] was published more than half a century ago. Hoskins was critical of the Victoria County History fixation with parish histories, which considered little more than the ruling class and the Lord of the Manor. He encouraged generations of historians to consider the economic and social history of other classes. To its credit the Victoria County History project has done just that and continues to work its way around England producing a far more holistic encyclopaedic local history record, much of which is available from British History Online along with gazetteers, travel accounts and historical maps.[6]

British History Online is one of many web-based portals that can locate primary source materials textually by place name, although the site (along with most others) is not particularly user friendly for mobile use. This has its challenges – it might involve major cataloguing tasks such as adding geo-references (coordinates rather than place names) that can work with map-based platforms; or in my own field of oral history creating records with location in mind (for example by asking for the location of the school or workplace an interviewee might be describing). Small steps like designing mobile friendly search pages that can make use of the geo-location capabilities of smartphones can really increase the usability of sites like this – we must remember that for most consumers of historical information, quick access to relevant material is key. Platforms designed solely for serious research use can be a major impediment in terms of accessibility.

Archaeologists and geographers are far more familiar with geographical information systems (GIS) but I believe it is now something that should be a necessary part of the historian's skill set; we desperately need to forge better links with practice in these disciplines because together with history these disciplines are leading the field in applying GIS to the past. It is interesting to note that 'historical GIS' (HGIS) research itself has been increasingly moving from quantitative, social science and technology focused research to what is increasingly being termed as 'spatial history', with more applied uses drawing on qualitative as well quantitative data sets.[7] One organization with a great deal of experience of using GIS systems is English Heritage, which has to provide geo-data to local councils for planning purposes. A happy product of this is that using their data sets sophisticated geographical searches and mapping are possible, from listed buildings to historical photographs. A particularly easy to use example of this is at pastscape.org.uk, which allows a search by postcode, national grid reference and latitude and longitude via a zoomable map.

History is well placed to be at the forefront of spatial applications for history. Recently Ian Gregory and Alistair Geddes observed that the emphasis in HGIS is 'still on technology, data infrastructure, and potential', which they argue is understandable as data bases and usable platforms take a long time to build before applied research can take place. But they see a recent broadening of HGIS to qualitative sources that they argue has the potential to be applied across the humanities. Combining more sophisticated geographical information tools and methods with the kind of historical data sets that you can find on connectedhistories.org (ranging from court records to newspaper articles) could easily be done. Many historical data sets such as the Proceedings of the Old Bailey can already be searched by place name; and conversion of place names to geo-locations on a map could be automated (with adjustments for historical spellings of place names). Gregory and Geddes argue that applying spatial analysis to data sets like this could potentially lead to a whole new field of 'spatial humanities', which Gregory and Geddes describe as 'a field using geographical technologies to develop new knowledge about the geographies of human cultures past and present'.[8]

I think these same geographical technologies have huge potential for providing historical information to the public. I spend much of my working life outside the lecture theatre developing oral history-based content for mobile applications for place-based media. I have developed what I term 'memoryscape' trails, outdoor walking experiences that embed oral history recordings in the landscape (usually through the medium of an mp3 player or smartphone). Over the last decade I have been using this medium as an active and immersive way to understand and map the cultural history of places, and exploring its potential medium for oral historians to use for presenting work to the public.

I began developing these trails along the river Thames with the Museum of London, which has an extensive oral history collection with dock workers; the trails were made available online and in CD format from the museum shops. Since then I have had several commissions from councils and have worked with communities to co-create trails. I first developed the idea working as a cultural geographer and there has been considerable interest in developing trail-based methodology as a way of presenting historical geography. For example the Royal Geographical Society is currently building a national network of trails that are freely available to download; most are academic led but I have worked with them to integrate oral history recordings where possible. Sometimes the subject matter can be profoundly challenging – for example I am currently working on a memoryscape to interpret a major new memorial in East London, commemorating a terrible tragedy in 1943, in which 173 people were crushed or asphyxiated to death on a staircase leading to an underground shelter. Location-based media have allowed us to add spoken testimony from witnesses and survivors of this event to give a personal dimension to the experience of remembering those who died and a very deep, emotional appreciation of how civilians suffer in wartime. Locative technology and spatial history have tremendous potential for historians to return oral history recordings (and pretty much any other historical sources) back to the places that gave rise to them in the first place, and encourage others to consider them in situ.

Of course it doesn't just have to be oral history. In 2013 artist Rachel Lichtenstein released the Diamond Street app – shortly after her book[9] – which featured location-triggered video, text and images as well as sound and voice. The Museum of London's Streetmuseum app superimposes hundreds of historic photographs onto the landscape using the smartphone's camera and location sensing capabilities. The site historypin.com allows anyone to pin images, videos or written material to places; and at the time of writing nearly 364,000 historical items had been posted onto a browsable google map. At the 2014 Museums and Heritage trade show in London I was struck by the numbers of start-up heritage businesses selling app-based historical interpretation platforms, evidence of a rapidly growing sector.

There are tremendous opportunities for historians to help to create exciting and challenging historical work for these kinds of platforms. However, historians need to equip themselves – and new generations of students – with the conceptual, ethical and practical skills necessary to create digital work. As well as all the usual tools in the historian's chest, engagement with a variety of disciplines such as cultural geography, archaeology, museology, architecture, music, IT and art is required. Digital historians are also likely to find they need at least a basic understanding of sound and video recording, editing, webdesign, image manipulation, data mapping, writing succinctly for a broad audience, capturing web statistics, online ethics and copyright issues. If they are not already present, history programmes desperately need to ensure that at least some of these bases are covered; coursework requirements include multimedia tasks for students to learn the ropes.

Many history programmes are taking this on board in terms of their assessment mix. For example Kingston University in London offers an undergraduate

History, publics and new technologies 41

BA history course in history blogging, which demands a very different set of skills from essay writing (even though the student material has to be underpinned by the same standards of academic research and evidence). At the University of East London my students at undergraduate and postgraduate level are expected to create public-facing online projects, for example a multi-media trail, alongside conventional assessments. This is not without its challenges – it involves teaching a greater range of skills and concepts, and colleagues from other departments (such as performing arts and media) have been involved in taking sessions. Equipment is also crucial for students to record professional quality material (we have access to a well-stocked digital equipment lending service at school level). New assessment criteria also have to be considered (consulting colleagues who were used to assessing practice-based work in art, film and photography was particularly useful in this respect). I also think it is important that there is the infrastructure in place to publish the better student work online in a place where it stands a chance of reaching the public (links to student work are published alongside staff work on the trails section of Raphael-samuel.org.uk).

History teachers and lecturers may also need to be much more active in terms of developing students' ability to think in geographical and place-based ways. One of the best ways of doing this is organizing field trips that actively engage students in local research. When I look back over my own history education, I was never once taken outside the history classroom, either at secondary school or as an undergraduate. I think this is astonishing; there was no shortage of historical sites, archives or museums that could have been the focus of this work. It is good to see that this has made the new draft UK subject benchmark statement for history degree programmes (albeit rather non-committal for my liking: 'Fieldwork and field trips may play an integral role within a history module or programme.').

There is no shortage of good practice to learn from – fieldwork is very well developed in geography and archaeology, and at a recent conference on the subject at the Institute of Historical Research, Ian Cawood (head of history at Newman University, Birmingham) pointed out that it was interesting that all the UK history departments with a top National Student Satisfaction Survey score for overall satisfaction had a fieldwork component to their programme. At Newman University students must research and give a guided tour on a chosen aspect of the sites that the whole class visits, and as this work is assessed it is taken seriously by the students and embedded into their learning. Handled well, fieldwork can develop students' visceral ability to read such things as maps, landscape and the built environment in ways that are hard to pick up in a lecture theatre. Students can also be given supported, hands-on experience of using evidence in archives and museum collections that can be forbidding to the uninitiated. For place-focused work, the field trip is where students can best gain an awareness of the complexity of places and the different avenues available to those interested in interpreting them. It is also worth mentioning that the expertise here may well lie outside the academy. Members

42   *Toby Butler*

of local history societies, archivists, curators and family history practitioners may be willing to share their expertise.

Another impediment in the academy to this kind of work is the issue of how this fits in in terms of research assessment. Despite the 'impact' agenda there are still serious issues that need to be addressed in terms of the status given to the considerable academic work that is needed to create applications, online research tools and location-based experiences. As Gregory and Geddes (2014) point out, when historical data sets are made available online they are usually the product of large amounts of scholarly work – but they do not easily fit the traditional idea of presenting academic argument supported by evidence in a journal or monograph. In research assessment exercises, history faculties need to become much more comfortable with accepting, assessing and putting forward online outputs and practice-based work. Public-facing work has another level of complexity when it comes to assessment. When historical data sets are put online for public use, much of the analysis, utility and 'doing' must come from the user exploring them, rather than the author. To what extent are online outputs considered 'academic' publications, and how adequate is the current peer review system to assess their quality? If public collaboration and user experience is important (and in most cases it should be) the experience of the user, as well as the peer reviewer, must be taken into account. Ideally this should be a part of the production process as well as the evaluation phase. Historians are no strangers to working with (and borrowing from) other disciplines, but again they must roam outside the confines of historical studies to learn some of the key skills of user and audience evaluation that are commonly used in practices such as computer games development and museum exhibition development.

If these issues are addressed, history faculties should be very well positioned to make the most of the next phase of the digital revolution, and they have a great deal to offer. Rather than being a threat to the authority of the academy, new media platforms should be embraced for new ways in which they encourage people to research, create and experience historical work. It is very hard to build multimedia work alone; the medium demands interdisciplinary work and collaboration; I think, having worked on digital projects, that they have much resonance with Samuel's more inclusive concept of history. Sensitively handled, the digital platform can be an inclusive, relatively neutral space where contributors can work both inside and outside the academy. In this respect new technology can help us create what Jorma Kalela describes as a 'participatory historical culture' in which historical research and analysis can be a truly collective pursuit.[10]

Suggested further reading

The picture I referred to in the introduction is a scene of Jericho meadows in Oxford around 1850 and can be found at the historic images section of Jericho Community Association website (www.jerichocentre.org.uk/about/historic_images)

and for those who are interested in learning more about this unusual organization (a department of the university rather than a business) will find all they need in an exhaustive three volume *History of the Oxford University Press* (Oxford, OUP, 2013). I touched on a debate about public history and the role of the historian; Jill Liddington, 'What is Public History? Publics and Their Pasts, Meanings and Practices', *Oral History* 30(1) (2002): 83–93, p. 92. See also Paul Ashton and Hilda Kean (eds) *Public History and Heritage Today: People and their Pasts* (Basingstoke: Palgrave Macmillan, 2012). The same authors have also edited *The Public History Reader* (London: Routledge, 2013) which explores the key issues in a very useful introduction alongside some of the key work in this field. Jorma Kalela has also explored the realities of collaborative engagement based on his work with union members in 'research circles' in Finland, and argues that the historian should allow people to approach the past on their own terms, which is not as simple as it might sound in *Making History: The Historian and Uses of the Past* (Basingstoke: Palgrave Macmillan, 2012). The *Public Historian* and *Public History Review* are useful journals for international perspectives and *History Workshop Online* is an interesting online space which is striving to continue the participative philosophy that Raphael Samuel explores in *Theatres of Memory: Past and Present in Contemporary Culture* (London: Verso, 1994).

Despite its central role in much history practice, 'local history' has long been the Cinderella of the history field, often the focus for courses in university extra-mural departments and adult education which have so often been victims of cuts or threatened by unrealistic fee rises, ratcheted up by ill-considered matching to meteoric undergraduate fee levels but without the access to student loans. Ironically these courses often have the deep kind of impact on lifelong learning that universities are now being urged to foster. W.G. Hoskins *Local History in England* (London: Longman, 1984, 3rd edn) is perhaps the best-known guide but there have been numerous more recent examples. C. Dyer, A. Hopper, E. Lord and N. Tringham (eds), *New Directions in Local History Since Hoskins* (Hatfield: University of Hertfordshire Press, 2011) usefully considers the role of local history in more recent times. Tim Cresswell's *Place: A Short Introduction* (Oxford: Blackwell, 2004) is a refreshingly clear and well-written guide to the different theoretical takes on place making and a good starting point for further reading.

Online tools and sources have become prolific. Commercial sites such as ancestry.co.uk have put considerable resources into digitizing records, and their 13 billion records can be accessed for a small fee, or free in partner institutions (like the London Metropolitan Archives). Academic projects tend to have free access although some databases require a university library membership. Project sites are too numerous to list but portal/gateway sites like history. ac.uk have useful lists of web-based projects and lists of digital research tools (history.ac.uk/history-online). It also hosts an array of databases (a little tricky to search geographically; the most thorough approach is to do a full text search by place name). The site connectedhistories.org has a nice overview of many of

44 Toby Butler

the biggest online databases with a single search engine covering over twenty of them, including www.oldbaileyonline.org. English Heritage www.english-heritage.org.uk/professional has links to its own online archive along with pastscape.org.uk and heritagegateway.org.uk, both powerful tools for historic site and spatial history research.

For historians interested in using geographical information systems (GIS) as analytical tools Ian Gregory's work is perhaps the most useful point of access as he has worked extensively applying GIS for historical research; for example I.N. Gregory and P.S. Ell, *Historical GIS: Technologies, Methodologies and Scholarship* (Cambridge: Cambridge University Press, 2007) is a good starting point. Above I refer to the concerns about how web-focused historical work might be under-valued by the academy; these are aired in the conclusion of I.N. Gregory and A. Geddes (eds), *Towards Spatial Humanities: Historical GIS and Spatial History* (Bloomington, IN: Indiana University Press, 2014).

Anyone interested in using oral history in trail making might be interested in my reflections in 'A Walk of Art: The Potential of the Sound Walk as Practice in Cultural Geography', *Social and Cultural Geography* 7(6) (2006): 889–908; 'Memoryscape: Integrating Oral History, Memory and Landscape on the River Thames', in Paul Ashton and Hilda Keen (eds), *People and their Pasts: Public History Today* (Basingstoke: Palgrave Macmillan, 2009), pp. 223–39; 'The Historical Hearing Aid: Located Oral History from the Listener's Perspective', in Shelley Trower (ed.), *Place, Writing, and Voice in Oral History* (Basingstoke: Palgrave Macmillan, 2011).

Examples of my trails can be experienced at memoryscape.org.uk, portsofcall.org.uk and student work can also be found at raphael-samuel.org.uk. Some early ideas about how trails might be used in teaching can be found in 'Memoryscape: How Audio Walks can Deepen our Sense of Place by Integrating Art, Oral History and Cultural Geography', *Geography Compass* 1(3) (2007): 350–72, and an accompanying teaching guide can be found in *Geography Compass* 2(5) (2008): 1750–4. The Royal Geographical Society walk I mention can be found at discoveringbritain.org/walks/region/greater-london/london-woolwich.html; and the Bethnal Green Disaster Memorial Project is at bgmemorial.org.uk. I quote from the *Subject Benchmark Statement for History*, draft for consultation, June 2014, p. 10 (Quality Assurance Agency for Higher Education, Gloucester).

Notes

1 Of course there are still major barriers for many communities in which to participate. Poverty, lack of access to networks and other accessibility issues restrict participation. There is much that can be done to address this, not least maintaining a large network of public libraries with free internet access. We also need tailor-made web authoring tools for different audiences. For example the Rix Centre at the University of East London has designed a web-page building platform (Klick-In) specially designed for use by people with learning difficulties (http://www.rixcentre.org, accessed 8 November 2014).

2 Raphael Samuel, *Theatres of Memory* (London: Verso, 1994), p. 17.

3 Jill Liddington, 'What is Public History? Publics and their Pasts, Meanings and Practices', *Oral History* 30(1) (2002): 83–93.

History, publics and new technologies   45

4 Paul Ashton and Hilda Kean (eds), *Public History and Heritage Today: People and their Pasts* (Palgrave Macmillan, Basingstoke, 2012), p. 10.
5 W.G. Hoskins *Local History in England* (London: Longman, 1984, 3rd edn).
6 See http://www.victoriacountyhistory.ac.uk and http://www.british-history.ac.uk/, both accessed 8 November 2014.
7 Ian N. Gregory and Alistair Geddes (eds), *Towards Spatial Humanities: Historical GIS and Spatial History* (Bloomington, IN: Indiana University Press, 2014), p. xiv.
8 Gregory and Geddes (eds), *Towards Spatial Humanities*, p. xv.
9 Rachel Lichtenstein, *Diamond Street: The Hidden World of Hatton Garden* (London: Hamish Hamilton, 2012).
10 Jorma Kalela, *Making History: The Historian and Uses of the Past* (Basingstoke: Palgrave Macmillan, 2012), chap. 3.

4 The humanities and public service broadcasting

A history film-maker's view

Michael Wood

When I visit Broadcasting House in Portland Place, in the comforting surroundings of the Art Deco foyer and Eric Gill's *Prospero and Ariel*, I often find myself reflecting on the birth of public service broadcasting (PSB), commemorated above the lifts by what one might call the BBC's foundation stone:

> This Temple is dedicated to the Arts and Muses by the first Governors of Broadcasting in the year 1931, Sir John Reith being Director-General. It is their prayer that good seed sown may bring forth a good harvest, that all things hostile to peace or purity may be banished from this house, and that the people, inclining their ear to whatsoever things are beautiful and honest and of good report, may tread the path of wisdom and uprightness.

In our more sceptical and ironical age, many no doubt would find such idealism touchingly quaint. The original Latin is based on Paul's letter to the Philippians (4:8); the seed metaphor, though, is especially apt – it is easy to forget, but in English, broadcasting is a term from open field farming which describes the hand-throwing of seed into the furrow. The year 1931, of course, was a time of political, cultural, social and economic anxiety. By then Britain's imperial mission had become deeply problematized. At home the Great Depression was a time of widespread hardship and unemployment (that year the press made much of Gandhi's visit to the poor mill workers of Lancashire).[1] The loss in just a few years of half of Britain's world trade had dealt a devastating blow, especially to manufacturing and trading cities like Manchester and Liverpool.[2]

But ecumenical ideas were in the air – 'Nation shall speak unto Nation' would after all be the BBC's motto – and paradoxically this was the time to think about using new technology to further cultural and moral progress. The creation of the BBC was one of many cultural projects of the time,[3] and it was then, in the early 1930s, that the future role of PSB was defined. The key figure was not Reith but the brilliant Hilda Matheson who formulated the idea of 'difficult' and important subjects of public interest being discussed on the air-waves.[4] As David Attenborough observed recently in an interview in *The Guardian*, it was not television, but radio, in the shape of Matheson's Radio Talks, which defined the future content of PSB from the 1950s, when TV became a mass medium, till now; broadcasting the sciences, arts and humanities as part of public service 'quality cultural programming'.[5]

This paper is about one small area of that endeavour, namely the making of documentaries, mostly on historical subjects, as seen by a practitioner who has been working since the 1980s; largely but not exclusively for the BBC and its US counterpart, the (US) public broadcasting service (PBS). The last thirty years of course have been another period of great technological change, in which the invention of the World Wide Web, the growth of electronic and digital media and the coming of the multi-channel universe, with iPlayer, Catch-Up TV, Live Streaming and TV On Demand, have altered terrestrial broadcasting forever, not least in the way we all watch TV, if we watch it at all. In this paper TV History is shorthand for a factual documentary on an historical subject seen on screen, and my theme is the making of these documentaries and their public impact. But I write not as a theoretician, as do most of the other contributors in this volume, but as a practitioner, and I should say too at the start, as a viewer/consumer. The 'golden age' of public service TV also shaped my values and interests through the period when the BBC was the dominant public discourse, from *The Great War* and *Seven Up* (1964) through to John Berger's *Ways of Seeing* (1972) and Bronowski's *Ascent of Man* (1973); programmes that influenced my generation of programme makers.

I started as a news and current affairs journalist in ITV, then worked inside the BBC as a freelance documentary maker, and for the last twenty-five years I have worked in a small independent company that makes (among other things) high quality history and cultural documentaries. The company was founded at the beginning of Britain's Channel 4 (C4) with its left of field, cultural diversity and minorities remit to serve 'tastes and interests not generally catered for' by other UK broadcasters[6] and a 'commitment to diversity' which saw C4 make provision in its programming for under-represented groups including ethnic, gender and sexual minorities.[7] So the company I joined was formed at a time of real change and opportunity, when the subject matter of history documentaries on TV rapidly opened up, and the way in which films were made was also challenged and reinvented. Form and content were up for reappraisal in those heady days, though what has become of that early promise is the subject of a different paper.

Beyond C4 of course, over these twenty-five years there have also been many changes in content, style, language and accent, and in ethnic and gender mix; diminishing though not erasing the old patrician, patriarchal, white male middle-class tone of the BBC. But the educational premise of Reith and Matheson still guides the BBC (and C4) in factual programming, and indeed PBS too.

Of course critics will always focus on the 'dumbing down', but I would argue that in factual programmes as well as drama, whether BBC or C4, there has continued to be a consistently rich output of excellent and thought-provoking shows. In my experience today's factual programme makers still think long and hard about how to reach their audience with sometimes complex ideas; how to extend their repertoire; and how to create a bridge between the ideas of the

48   *Michael Wood*

scholars and the viewers 'out there'. Impact and public involvement are now as important to programme makers as they are to the university world; feedback from the audience is taken very seriously by all content providers and gives the programme maker a keen sense of what works for the viewer, and what doesn't. TV may not in the main be a great medium for analysis, but it is very good at telling stories, and inspiring viewers, and countless letters and discussions with audience members in public events over the years reveal interests stimulated by a first encounter with a subject on TV.

Of course people also get many of their ideas about history from novels, cinema films and TV drama. A recent case in point was Maya Vision's D-Day anniversary film made in the summer of 2014 in which the presenter/writer James Holland felt it necessary to point out that Steven Spielberg's *Saving Private Ryan* and *Band of Brothers* and other films and TV shows have created the widespread belief that the US had led the invasion, and 'that D Day was largely an American show'.[8] The same goes for many other Hollywood stories, from the Enigma code breaking to the British role in the emancipation of slaves. *Braveheart*'s fantasy of a woad-streaked Wallace impregnating the icy Longshanks's young French queen follows that old Hollywood practice of portraying the English as villains, on which Roland Barthes has some amusing observations.[9] That said, my impression from countless public question times over the years is that the viewing audience have a good general sense of history; can hold more than one narrative in mind; and generally can distinguish between history and fiction. We may relish Bernard Cornwell on Alfred, but for history we go elsewhere; we may enjoy *Shakespeare in Love* even though we know perfectly well that in its portrayal of the bard's working methods, let alone his love life, it is simply having fun in the absence of historical fact.

History is usually reckoned to be the biggest leisure participation activity in the UK. This is argued from over 100 million annual museum visits, membership of several millions of English Heritage and the National Trust, participation in groups and societies, and so on.[10] But though we get our history from many sources, TV is the most important way *serious* historical ideas (as opposed to popular narratives) reach the general public; especially because TV programmes are used so widely now in the classroom. So TV is a crucial bridge between scholars and public, and when we ask ourselves how to sustain the humanities in public culture, TV must play its part; much more so than cinema or historical fiction (although a work of fiction such as *Wolf Hall* with well over a million UK sales alone, and TV film and stage adaptations, can also seize the public imagination on a wide scale).[11] In history, then, television has a major role as a learning tool and as a public forum for ideas.

This brings us to the ways today's TV history is done on the screen. How does real historical information and interpretation get to the audience? First, it goes without saying that in popular entertainment, with the exigencies of time, pacing, narrative, clarity and entertainment, there are inevitable compromises. In popular history programming there is always a tension (sometimes creative, sometimes not) between Reith's twin goals of instruction and entertainment. In the world of the professional historian, complex multiple narratives and alternative explanations are the name of the game; sometimes no answers are possible, and any reconstruction is tentative. But that's not how TV history works: TV doesn't usually do Either/Or. It doesn't like holding multiple storylines or alternative endings (though drama does: take Danish police thrillers like *The Killing*, or the BBC's *Sherlock*).[12] In historical writing, Gibbon for example might be good TV (his Empress Theodora for one is straight out of the *Game of Thrones!*). Braudel on the other hand is less so – despite the fact that his *Mediterranean* is full of filmic images of landscape and travel: even the lading bills of his Genoese galleys leaving Candia with Cretan wine and olives, conjure up luminous film images. But in TV, narrative, not process, is the key. Lepanto makes good TV; the *longue durée* is not so easy.[13]

A very different animal is the 'How we used to live' school of TV. The last few years have seen a big rise in TV shows about experiential history; a kind of historical DIY: *The Medieval Farm, The Tudor Farm, Victorian Farm, The 1930s House*, and so on (going back to their path-breaking precursor, *Living in the Past*, which in 1978 pioneered a fly-on-the-wall 'obs doc' on an Iron Age farm). There has been well-founded criticism of that approach recently by Tristram Hunt,[14] but there is surely room for both. 'How we used to live' is fine entertainment so long as balanced by Reith's 'inform and educate': that is, so long as we also get more searching forms of historical analysis to go with it.

The fact is, entertainment is central to any form of public arts or discourse; especially if it is publicly funded. A story badly told is a story not heard or remembered; in TV it is a switch off, or a switch over. Popular 'how we used to live' TV history may be criticized as folksy, or 'touchy-feely', but it is still history. And empathy after all is one of the core qualities needed by an historian – or any reader of history. Sympathy for the people of the past is at the heart of our response to history; the willingness to place oneself in their shoes; to sympathize with their ideas, beliefs and cultures, no matter how alien. I would add that it also embodies what I like to call history's reality principle, because through it we also see our own values tested – for example seeing what is universal to humanity, and what is merely local, regional or cultural idiosyncrasy.[15] Sympathy for people not like ourselves, and for other cultures, then is essential to the teaching and practice of history, as it is to our lives as human beings, and seems to me at the centre of any discussion of the value of history's place in the humanities and in the school curriculum, even more than the critical judgement it helps foster.

A case in point is one of the big developments since the late 1960s, namely the growth of alternative histories and especially Women's History. It is chastening to think that little over forty years ago Women's History did not exist as a course, or even a paper, let alone a university department. Its development has led to a transformation in our view of history as a whole, which has in recent years come into TV History too. In Maya Vision we have made a number of films on women in history, including among others a Saxon queen, Aethelflaed of Mercia;[16] a medieval peasant, Christina Cok;[17] and an eighteenth-century

50   *Michael Wood*

poet and feminist, Anna Laetitia Barbauld.[18] Identification with such women, high and low, invites us to contemplate our own life and culture too, as we see the often conscious erasure of women's history through all periods, and with it too recognize what Amanda Vickery recently called 'the deep-seated belief in the impossibility of female genius'.[19]

We are wrestling with this at the moment in looking at women's history in China, bringing in the eleventh-century poet Li Qingzhao, subject of Ronald Egan's aptly titled *The Burden of Female Talent*.[20] Egan, a distinguished Sinologist, offers a fresh account of Qingzhao's contested life, her marriages and literary career, and a close reading of her poetry. In the nature of things his study will be read by a small circle of scholars, students and Sinophiles. But the attraction to the film-maker is to air these ideas – and the poet's powerful and exemplary story – to millions.

Another forgotten history where the dialogue between academics and film-makers has produced rich new insights is Black History. British TV again was a latecomer in this field, although C4 led the way from the 1980s, more recently linking up with the UK's annual Black History Month. When we made our BBC2 films about Shakespeare and his age in 2003[21] many of the audience were still surprised to learn of black people living and working freely in Elizabethan London. Since then we have looked again at that history in *The Great British Story* (BBC2, 2012).[22] Brief as the scenes are in these films, they can literally open the eyes of millions to unknown histories which can inspire and empower in our very mixed heritage society with the discovery of shared histories. They can also help teachers map new themes for teaching.[23] In the case of black history in Britain of course, we are dealing with the fallout of centuries of colonial racism which denied civilization and culture to black Africans: it is notable that the slave trade still awaits an extended treatment on British TV.[24]

Gay and lesbian history is another important area in this dialogue between TV and academe. Again C4 led the way in the 1980s, with a big presence of gay and lesbian film, much of which had a strong historical element. Maya Vision played a part in this, for example in the films of the late Stewart Marshall such as *Comrades in Arms* (on gays in the services in the Second World War), and *Desire* (about sexual politics and the persecution of homosexuals under the Nazis).[25] A huge amount of material has followed since, but TV still needs to catch up with the incredibly rich scholarship in this field over the last generation or so, on gender, masculinity, and the social construction of sexual identity. Great historical issues about same-sex love now being explored by scholars are still to be treated in the media:[26] same-sex love in the Middle Ages,[27] in the Renaissance[28] and its persecution in the eighteenth century, still await any kind of TV treatment. Stories of same-sex love between medieval knights or Oxford scholars, of Tudor gentlemen, of Anne Lister or John Newman,[29] are all about ethics and humanity in the broadest sense. The dilemmas of Lister and Newman are not the preserve of a minority: they tell us all about universal humanity, and that is something TV history at its best can do powerfully.

As a small independent film-maker over the last thirty years, our work then has touched on many of these themes, and in the remainder of this paper I shall give a few examples to try to show from the film-maker's perspective how the dialogue works in practice. TV of course is a simple medium. Factual programming has not changed much from its beginnings, despite all today's digital wizardry; for example much greater flexibility in the use of graphics to convey additional layers of information, making more complex what can be said on screen. Every film is still a combination of pictures, words, sounds, music. The pressure of a one-hour film, say, mid-evening on BBC2, is to draw the audience in, to excite and entertain, to create narrative, and to have some kind of resolution. Narrative therefore is vitally important. TV has a relentless imperative for narrative. Historians by contrast will have many explanations, economic, social, short-term and long-term; interweaving factors which can often never be satisfactorily pinned down. A TV film of one hour, on the other hand, demands the clarity and simplification of a simple medium.

So here are a few examples from our own work to show the programme-making process and its relationship to academic discourse. I hope they give a sense of how we put our films together. They are illustrated with sections of the post-production scripts, the record of what was actually transmitted:

Biography: *Christina: A Medieval Life* (2009)

First, biography. The arc of someone's life is made for TV: especially if the life can be a mirror of the times. TV biography in history documentary has tended to be about the famous or the royal, but among Maya Vision's many biographical films is a portrait of one of the poorest people in pre-Black Death English society, a medieval villein called Christina Cok who lived in Codicote in Hertfordshire from the 1270s to 1348.[30] Shot and edited in fewer than ten weeks, the film has had over a dozen repeats on BBC4 and is widely used in schools. Expert interviews included those with the scholars Chris Thornton and Miri Rubin and the osteoarchaeologist Simon Mayes, but also re-enactors who were experts in medieval food, cooking and peasant cultivation.[31]

The core document was the St Albans Court Book in the British Library:[32] the Codicote Local History Society kindly provided their own draft translation from the 1330s; for the earlier part we were dependent on our own reading of the manuscript: so far as original research went this film was pretty hard-core! Locations were around Codicote and St Albans and at the Weald and Downland Open Air Museum. Those elements were all part of conventional history film-making, but to create a more atmospheric filmic style, in an effort to suggest the 'feel' of time, we used modern news footage of floods and cattle epidemic over which fragments of BBC Radio + TV broadcasts drifted in and out of contemporary accounts of the environmental disasters of the early fourteenth century. The section of the post-production script reproduced in Table 4.1 is from the Great Famine of 1314–18.

Table 4.1 Section of post-production script from *Christina: A Medieval Life* (2009)

TC	Picture	Synch/Dialogue	Music
10:39:25:00	MW PTC in helicopter Archive: *Aerials of Devastation* and *Island of Tewkesbury* and *Flooding* and *Severe Flooding in Western England* (Source: BBC News)	MW Synch: If you'd been able to take this bird's-eye view in the worst time of the Great Famine, through the summer of 1315 or 1316, you would have seen below you flooded valleys, flattened fields and ruined crops. And in places the food distribution system simply broke down. Merchants from as far away as Yorkshire were travelling through the home counties desperately trying to buy up the last precious supplies of grain.	
10:40:07:00	Archive: *Aerials of Devastation* and *Island of Tewkesbury* and *Flooding* and *Severe Flooding in Western England* (Source: BBC News) Caption: 'Poem of the Great Famine 1319'	Diana VO: *sorowespradde over all urelonde Anthusent winter there bifore... com nevere non so strong.* *To binde all the mene men in mourning and in care...* *And urecatel died al togedir, and maden the lond al bare* *-so faste* *Com never wrecche into Engelond that made men more agaste*	
10:40:37:00	Archive: *Aerials of Devastation* and *Island of Tewkesbury* and *Flooding* and *Severe Flooding in Western England* (Source: BBC News) Caption: Gloucestershire 2007	BBC News VO: 'Swathes of central England are under water tonight. In the last few minutes it's been confirmed that 150,000 homes in Gloucestershire are now without ...'	

Table 4.1 (continued)

TC	Picture	Synch/Dialogue	Music
10:41:00:00	GVs of a Farm Interview with David Mead, farmer, near Codicote, Herts:	MW Synch: What would it be like for a farmer in the 14th century? You know, you've got two years of total destruction of the crops and everything, I mean, can you put yourself in that position?	
10:41:10:00	Caption: David Mead, farmer	David Synch: Well, almost certainly we'd be tenant farmers, certainly wouldn't own the farm. Rents would have to be paid, so it's a desperate situation of finding enough money to pay the rent otherwise landlord comes along and says you're out. So that's the first thing. And then of course feeding the family and keeping the farm running and trying to get the next crop in. Any cattle he'd have to be forced to sell because he couldn't feed. If you're forced to sell you always get a lower price, so you'd suffer that way, he wouldn't be able to recoup the money by selling his cattle, and once the cattle are sold, he can't produce milk. That really sounds absolutely appalling	Music 'Floods' Out 10:41:19:24 Music 'Storm2' In 10:41:48:00
10:42:02:00	Graphic: Graph of farm repossessions Caption: 'Great Famine Farm Repossessions' (Source: Ian Kershaw, Past and Present 1973)	MW VO: The landlords' repossessions from Christina's neighbours are entered in the Codicote Court Book. Up from an average of half a dozen to 38 surrendered tenancies in 1316 …	

Table 4.1 (continued)

TC	Picture	Synch/Dialogue	Music
10:42:18:00	GVs snowy countryside GVs Codicote Source: Codicote Court Book Int. Cottage, Weald and Downland Open Air Museum	MW VO: The Great Famine was accompanied by a virulent pestilence of cattle and by a human epidemic, maybe typhoid? About 10% of the population died: over half a million people. Among the dead was Christina's brother John; and her husband William also disappears, probably dead in the epidemic of 1319. So Christina is left with her mother Agnes, her two small children John and Alice, in her little house, with its precious garden.	
10:42:56:00	Ext. Cottage, looking at map of a garden Caption: Bob Holman, Gardener CU Hangleton medieval garden map Caption: 'Excavation by Dr Sylvia Landsberg'	Bob Synch: Starvation was always a possibility and you would grow whatever you possibly could and this is where your edible weeds came in. If your crops failed at least you'd have something to put in the pottage. Things like: fat hen and borage and bitter cress, even things like bristly ox-tongue which is like eating cardboard. I mean you boil it and it goes into a horrible green wad, but at least it fills the belly.	

The *longue durée: Conquistadors* (2000)

By contrast, here is an example of grand sweep narrative history from *Conquistadors* (BBC2, 2000) a series on the Spanish Conquest of the Americas. This series used the key Spanish sources, Bernal Diaz, Zarate, Orellana, etc., but also native sources: Aztec poetry, Sahagun's huge compilation using native Mexican informants (one of the world's greatest works of historiography),[33] Waman Poma on Peru (whose original manuscript we filmed in Copenhagen). To this we added a strong element shot among surviving Central American and Andean cultures where memory of the Conquista is still current in poetry, song and stories, in the ancient languages of Quechua, Nahuatl, Quiche, etc. On the ground journeys added a further filmic dynamic 'experiential' element – we trekked to Espiritu Pampa in the headwaters of the Peruvian Amazon, and with Orellana down the Coca in Equador (just as in *The Footsteps of Alexander the Great* we went on foot over the Hindu Kush – there is nothing like interrogating historical texts on the ground to make them come alive!) The result was one of the widest viewed history series ever made by the BBC, so far seen in over 150 countries and territories.

The brief scene in the post-production script (see Table 4.2) is one I particularly like (wearing both hats – as historian and film-maker!) After days in the jungle following Manco Inca in 1578, we were taken out by helicopter and used the moment to take the ideas of Braudel on the *longue durée* – in his case the world of the old Mediterranean[34] – and apply them to the pre-Spanish cultures of the Andes; a scene which led into one of the most remarkable sequences we have ever shot: the pilgrimage onto the glaciers of Ausangate, where a pre-Spanish cult survives with an overlay of gaudy and raucous Catholicism ... an amazing visual demonstration of the tenacity of culture which Braudel describes.

For a different kind of historiography, next is a scene from *The Great British Story* (BBC2, 2012), a series of eight films made in one year across Britain and Northern Ireland with community involvement and a special focus on regional and local history. The scene I have chosen concerns the Reformation in the Devon village of Morebath on the edge of Exmoor. Our historiographical inspiration was the work of Eamon Duffy.[35] It is salutary to recall that as late as the 1960s, our sixth form textbooks presented the English Protestant Reformation as an inevitable and consensual rejection of a corrupt, venal, superstitious Catholic Church; in other words an establishment Church of England (CE) view. Duffy's *Stripping of the Altars* portrayed instead the Old Faith's vitality in the early Tudor period. Along with Keith Thomas, Christopher Haigh, Patrick Collinson and Susan Brigden, Duffy has transformed our understanding of the pre-Reformation past and provided essential reading for anyone interested in British history – not least of course, schoolteachers. Duffy's work had already informed our approach to the Warwickshire background in our biographical series on Shakespeare for BBC2 in 2003; and we went back to him as a portkey (to borrow a phrase from J.K. Rowling!) to the Reformation

56   *Michael Wood*

Table 4.2 Section of post-production script from *Conquistadors* (2000)

Time	Picture	Dialogue/synch	Music
51:39	Moody skies over the High Andes Mountainscapes Helicopter POVs	V/O: Manco had been the one Inca who offered hope of long-term resistance	
52:03	Helicopter int: MW – PTC	Sync: So the Inca empire ended, the political order was destroyed. But things exist at different levels in history, and empires are just on the surface of history ... and below them is a much deeper structure that lasts much longer. A long lasting, tenacious, deep rooted culture of the people of the region was shaped by their landscape and their climate, and up here in the Andes the Inca people survived and the beliefs survived. Just as Manco Inca had said, the people themselves did not forget.	52:10 Music ends
52:54	Quoyllur Riti glacier	Nearly 500 years on the people of the Andes still revere the ancestral spirits of the Incas ...	
53:11	Night in Quoyllur Riti Rituals by pilgrims at the edge Of the ice	Every year in June they go up in their thousands onto the glaciers of the sacred mountains: And just before dawn, at a breathless 16,000 feet, they worship the ice of Quoyllur Riti ... The Lord of the Snow Star ...	
53:42	Dawn/Sunshine Quoyllur Riti: people on the ice	And afterwards, like their Inca ancestors, the people greet the rising Sun.	
54:05	Pilgrims dance	And then they sing the lilting song they sang to Atahuallpa all those years ago:	54:08–54:49 Festival Music at Quoyllur Riti
54:26		'When the last Inca is dead,' said old Francisco Pizarro, 'the people will weary of resistance and take our path'. But the Conquest is not over. Yet.	54:49 End Credits Music starts

© Michael Wood/Maya Vision International.

in Kibworth in our series on an English village (discussed further on pp. 64–66; see Table 4.3, Figure 4.1, Figure 4.2). Duffy's scholarship it seems to me is remarkable not only for its sensitivity to the lives of real people undergoing often traumatic shifts of spiritual and cultural allegiance, but also because it showed how a generation of gifted historians can make us see our national

Table 4.3 Section of post-production script from *The Great British Story* (2012)

Time	Synch/Dialogue	Pics/Caps	Music
10:23:01:10	MW VO: In such country communities, old-fashioned country religion was simply the way things had always been. The saints, the feasts, the festivals. And so it was in the little village of Morebath under Exmoor. The vicar here from 1520 to 1574 was the wonderfully named Christopher Trichay. It would be Trichay's task to steer his village through four changes of religion in twenty years, and his notes in the churchwarden's book tell the story, starting in the last days of the Old Faith.	Morebath Church exts Caption: St George's, Morebath.	Acoustic in: Nation Solo Cello piece 10:23:19:03 Dur 00:00:01:29 Out: 10:24:08:20
10:23:47:00	Lynne: 'William Potter gave his hive of bees to maintain a lamp …' (Reading from churchwarden's book)	People crowded round churchwarden's book inside church.	
10:23:53:20	Reader: 'Burning before the figure of Jesus. And before St Sidwell, every principle feast in the year …'	Caption: 'Morebath Churchwarden accounts'.	
10:24:02:15	Reader: 'And to St Sidwell a ring of silver. Which did help make St Sidwell's shoes …'		
10:24:10:14	Lynne: I think one of the things that fascinates people is the fact that it is just ordinary people. Just everyday ordinary people, nobody special. But because they've kept these wonderful records, that story, that voice of those ordinary people, can come out. I think that's what attracts people	Caption: Rev Lynne Burgon	
10:24:29:09	MW: What about Trichay himself, do you get any impression of what he was like as a bloke?		
10:24:34:04	Paul: I think he must have been an incredibly, tough, resilient man. There must have been times when he really didn't like what was going on, but he still stuck it out. He didn't leave or do the sort of modern thing. He actually just stuck it out and took care of the community in the way in which he did.	Caption: Paul Tuck.	10:24:50:18, Nation Solo Cello piece-10.L in. Dur 00:00:44:00

Table 4.3 (continued)

Time	Synch/Dialogue	Pics/Caps	Music
10:24:55:09	Reader: 'Anno Domini 1548. The warden of the church was Lucy Scelly and in her time the church was sold away. And no gift was given to the church. But all taken from the church …'	Caption: 'Morebath Churchwarden accounts, 1548'	10:25:03:07, Cello Sanctus-06.L in. Dur 00:00:34:05
10:25:18:03	Reader: '1551 paid to John Flossmoor for taking away the altars and the rood loft. 3 Shillings …'	Caption: 'Morebath Churchwarden accounts, 1551'.	
10:25:30:22	MW: These are things that involve the most basic human feelings aren't they? About family and the hereafter, and how you bury your mum and dad, or your child that's died. All these things were being in some sense attacked, weren't they, by the new rules?	MW talking to village people in church	10:25:34:19, Nation Solo Cello piece-10.L out. 10:25:37:13, Cello Sanctus-06.L out.
10:25:48:06	Paul: It definitely changed things to this day: particularly within the church. How this man ever managed the change that they went through is astounding. You know, we have a slight change now and you know – it takes counselling!		
10:26:09:07	MW GO: So across the country Edward's government pushed through the destruction of the medieval Christian heritage. From Morebath to Lancarfan and from Long Melford to Halesowen. Popular support for Edward was strongest among the middle classes in London and the south-east, where Lollard beliefs had been found the century before. Loyalty to the Old Faith was strongest in the north and the west. And there the changes were bitterly resisted. Especially down here in Cornwall and Devon, where opposition burst out in open warfare …	Graphic: Spinning map. London and south-east coloured blue. North and west go red. Caption: Saltash, Cornwall.	Strings in 10:26:06:01 Dur 00:00:50 Out 10:26:56:11

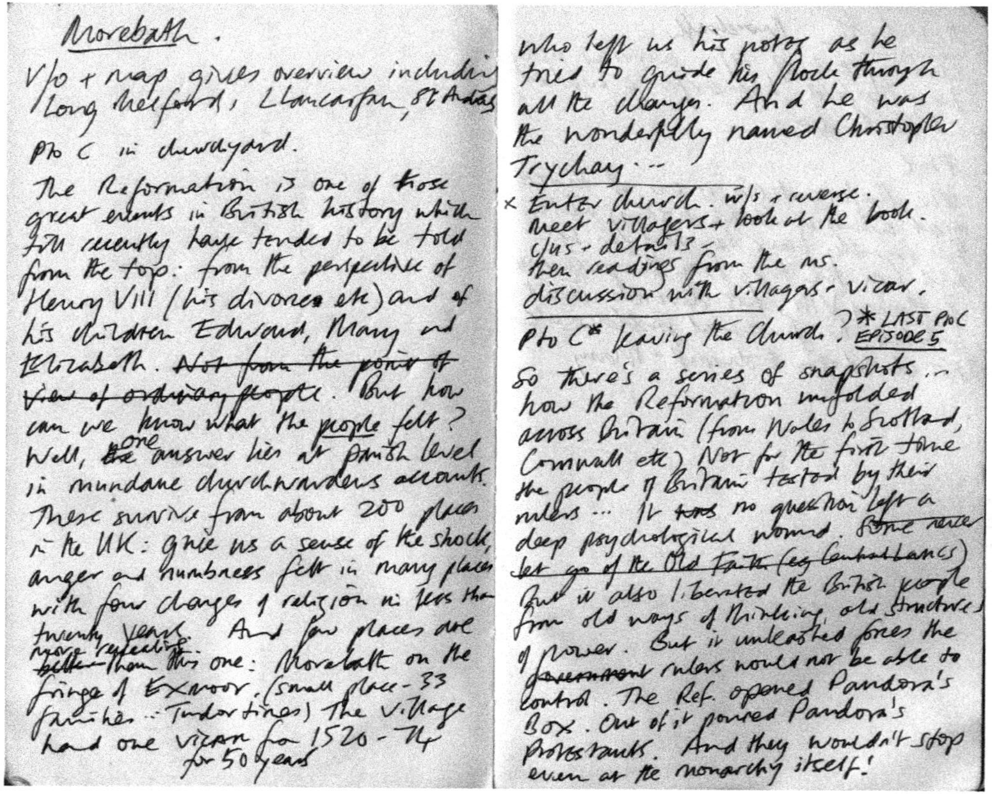

Morebath.

V/O + map gives overview including Long Melford, Llancarfan, St Andrews

PTC C in churchyard.

The Reformation is one of those great events in British history which till recently have tended to be told from the top: from the perspective of Henry VIII (his divorces etc) and of his children Edward, Mary and Elizabeth. ~~Not from the point of view of ordinary people.~~ But how can we know what the people felt? Well, ~~the~~ one answer lies at parish level in mundane churchwardens accounts. These survive from about 200 places in the UK: give us a sense of the shock, anger and numbness felt in many places with four changes of religion in less than twenty years. And few places are ~~better~~ more revealing than this one: Morebath on the fringe of Exmoor. (small place – 33 families .. Tudor times) The village had one vicar from 1520–74 for 50 years

who left us his notes as he tried to guide his flock through all the changes. And he was the wonderfully named Christopher Trychay ...

× Enter church. w/s + reverse. Meet villagers + look at the book. c/us + details – then readings from the ms. discussion with villagers + vicar.

PTC C* leaving the church? * LAST PTC EPISODE 5

So there's a series of snapshots .. how the Reformation unfolded across Britain (from Wales to Scotland, Cornwall etc) Not for the first time the people of Britain tested by their rulers ... It ~~was~~ no question left a deep psychological wound. ~~Some never let go of the Old Faith (eg Lancs)~~ But it also liberated the British people from old ways of thinking, old structures of power. But it unleashed forces the ~~government~~ rulers would not be able to control. The Ref. opened Pandora's Box. Out of it poured Pandora's Protestants. And they wouldn't stop even at the monarchy itself!

Figure 4.1 Michael Wood's location notes at Morebath, Devon, for the fifth programme of *The Great British Story* (2012) © Michael Wood

DEVON/LANDSCAPES/BAMPTON FAIR *← *Exmoor wide shots from Sampford Ctay;*
— plus wide shots from the Cheriton Bishop sequence?

Mid 16th century England outside the towns was a traditional rural
Catholic society: where most of the people lived and worked;
Their life marked by the rhythms of the farming year; by fairs like
Bampton fair here on the edge of Exmoor

I/Vs *Norman (the guy with the fez!) is good + the auctioneer on Devon traditions.*

In such country communities religion was simply the way things had
always been:

WALK: In the little village of Morebath, the vicar for the whole period
1520- 1574 was the wonderfully named Christopher Trychay... With
four changes of state religion in twenty years he had to be.....
✱ CUT THE P TO C outside the church which introduces Trychay? – works better without it.
(Enter Church: we open the manuscript.)
To See what happened at grass roots theres a new kind of source in our
story: churchwardens books ...mundane day to day stuff but rich in
detail about ordinary peoples lives.
(c/us manuscript)
Written up by Trychay himself, its laconic notes take us through the
whole story, starting in the last days of the Old Faith.. *1551? altars?*

READINGS + I/Vs with villagers *– use the St Sidwell readings plus the 1548 stripping of the altars – 'all was taken from the Church'? ??*

So across the country Edward's government pushed thru the destruction
of England's Catholic heritage *(+ I like Paul's joke about counselling!!)*

Popular Support for Edward's reformation was strongest among the
middle classes in London the SE and East Anglia, — *could ref Lollards from start of show?*
(ONTO MAP)
Loyalty to traditional Catholic Religion was strongest ...In the North and
West, , and there the changes were bitterly resisted:
.......Especially down here in Devon and Cornwall
/ first take of first p to c ('a different race with their own language – own religion)
FERRY P TO C
To the people here, Edward's introduction of a Prot Prayer book in
English was the last straw: For people who spoke Cornish and prayed in
Latin... it was seen as an attack on their identity ...

Figure 4.2 Michael Wood's notes for the editor at Morebath, Devon, for the fifth programme
of *The Great British Story* (2012)
© Michael Wood

history in a very different light. TV history is great if it can bring that sense of discovery to the audience at home.

Dramatizing the past: *The Story of India* (2007)

Great events of course are the staple of TV history. But going back before the era of film, how are we to convey their scale and drama without recourse to dramatization, which on the small screen will inevitably fall short? This next example concerns the Indian 'Mutiny' of 1857, one of the most astonishing events in history. *The Story of India* was a grand sweep series on India from prehistory until independence: a great deal to pack into six hours, needless to say, and I must confess a film-maker's perennial frustration that twice as many films were not available to tell a tale which perforce had to be brutally compressed. And then there were the issues of content and selection. Anyone handling Indian history faces major – and perhaps irreconcilable – questions of historical interpretation; especially recently, since the Nehruvian secularist vision espoused by Congress since 1947 has been challenged by the BJP's Hindu nationalism which triumphed conclusively in the 2014 election.[36]

Since 1949 Indian history has been a very contentious area: the origins of Indo-Europeans, the so-called 'Aryans'; the history of Islam in the subcontinent and its sometimes bitter relationship with the Hindu majority; the role of the British empire, for good and ill – these are only three of the most contentious, on all of which the Bharatiya Janata Party (BJP) is in fundamental disagreement with the Congress vision. Obviously, as a writer, a middle-aged, middle-class white Briton, I came with many received ideas – not least a temperamental as well as intellectual attachment to the Nehruvian narrative with which I grew up. Nonetheless the series was welcomed in India and is widely used in schools as a teaching aid, though it is less certain whether it will continue to be so under the new BJP government who have already promised to rewrite school history textbooks as they did in 2002.[37]

The scene in the following post-production script excerpt (see Table 4.4) was shot at Bareh near Etawah in the Jumna plain, epicentre of some of the severest fighting in 1857, where resistance was led by the charismatic Rani of Jhansi. Interviewees are the historian of Congress, Professor Sriram Mehrotra, and Himruda Singh, descended from the minor Raja of Bareh whose ancestors sided with the rebels in 1857 and later joined the Salt March with Gandhi. It seemed to me emblematic – the three of us in the heat of summer in the Jumna Plain – a tale of terrible cruelty, suffering and savage retribution which to Indian people is still living history. (All text in italics appeared as subtitles.)

As I have said above, process in history is a most difficult thing to convey on television. TV doesn't do process; except perhaps by visual metaphor. But there were moments in *Story of India* when the combination of stills camera time lapse sequences, archive footage and the haunting music by A.R. Rahman and Howard Davidson, evoked just that to some viewers: 'I can't explain how music, words and pictures affected my heart', said one UK viewer of Indian

Table 4.4 Section of post-production script from *The Story of India* (2007)

Time	Picture	Speaker	Synch/Dialogue/ Commentary	Music
10:29:06:00	Climb rocky path	VO	An hour or so out into the countryside we reached Bareh: the descendants of the collaborator and the resister and the oppressor.	(Music specially composed by Howard Davidson)
10:29:18:00	View of the fort	MIKE	Wow, that's impressive, isn't it? What was this here?	
10:29:23:00	View of the fort	HIMRUDRA	The ladies' apartment	
10:29:24:00	View of the fort	MIKE	The ladies' apartment? Fantastic, isn't it?	
10:29:31:00	View from atop the fort: village	VO	And this was what they were fighting for …	
10:29:38:00	View from the fort: River Chambal	SRIRAM	That's the India which you can call eternal, the unchanging.	
10:30:05:00	Mike and Himrudra Singh in ruined fort	MIKE	So what happened here in 1857?	
10:30:07:00	IV with Himrudra (Subtitles)	HIMRUDRA	*In 1857 we went against the British.*	
10:30:10:00	IV	MIKE	You were the rebels.	
10:30:11:00	IV	HIMRUDRA	*yes of course …*	
10:30:12:00	IV	MIKE	The First War of Independence, they call it now, don't they?	
10:30:17:00	IV	HIMRUDRA	*and we joined Jhansi Rani*	
10:30:19:00	IV with Himrudra contd	MIKE	These were the local rebel commanders?	
10:30:20:00	IV	HIMRUDRA	*The Rani of Jhansi*	
10:30:22:00	IV	MIKE	Oh, Jhansi? She was the great heroine, the Joan of Arc of the Resistance.	Music Out P6 M14 10:30:23:00
10:30:28:00	IV	HIMRUDRA	*and Tatya Tope and Nana Sahib who you feared so much.*	
10:30:33:00	IV	MIKE	'Nana's coming! Nana's coming!' It was Nana who attacked Lucknow.	
10:30:37:00	IV with Himrudra	HIMRUDRA	*Lucknow and the massacre at Satichaura Ghat.*	

Table 4.4 (continued)

Time	Picture	Speaker	Synch/Dialogue/ Commentary	Music
10:30:40:00	IV with Himrudra	MIKE	So these were the greatest of the rebel leaders. So your family were committed to fighting against the British? And what happened here?	
10:30:51:00	IV	HIMRUDRA	*The British destroyed it ... With a 16 pounder gun.*	Music In P6 M15 10:30:56:00
10:31:06:00	Mike, Himrudra and Sriram ascend steep steps to temple. They survey the view	VO	And here in Bareh, in the baking summer heat of the Jumna plain, a long way into my journey in search of the story of India, I felt enveloped by the greatness of India's history. By those terrible events 150 years ago that seemed to have only happened yesterday.	
10:31:42:00	IV with Himrudra and Sriram Mehrotra	MIKE	The two of you maybe represent two different Indian views of all these great events, these great events.	Music Out P6 M15 10:31:44:00
10:31:51:00	IV with Himrudra and Sriram	SRIRAM	I am not ashamed of the fact that my ancestors cooperated with the British. Situated as they were, and being educated, they knew the might and the resources of the British.	
10:32:02:00	IV with Sriram and Himrudra	MIKE	Your view is different?	
10:32:04:00		HIMRUDRA	*We became agitated because of Jhansi Rani They had taken everything from us ... ... so what did we have? We had to fight – nothing else.*	

© Michael Wood/Maya Vision International.

64   *Michael Wood*

descent, 'and stirred memories and feelings about what it means to be Indian that I had not formulated in my mind, or didn't know I had, or had forgotten'.[38]

That of course is what the film-maker hopes to achieve when going beyond the straightforwardly didactic. In this case what was seen on screen probably went a long way beyond what a buttoned-up Scot like Reith would have conceived of as 'informing', but I hope and think it is still on that path charted out by Hilda Matheson and her colleagues down to our generation of film-makers.

Micro-history: *The Story of England* (2010)

My final example of how ideas in the humanities can work in TV history is from *The Story of England* (BBC4 and BBC2, 2010). We had long mulled over the idea of taking one village through history; an idea you could say which in a broad sense was Hoskins-inspired.[39] The idea was history from the bottom up, not top down; the people, not the rulers; the provinces, not the south-east and London. Grand sweep history then, but viewed from close up. The series was set in Kibworth in Leicestershire, not the classic English village – Ambridge or a Hovis advert – with the A6, a council estate, Chinese and Indian takeaways, and workers' terraces. But that was what appealed to us. Kibworth was one of the East Midlands' villages that formed the setting for E.P. Thompson's *Making of the English Working Class*,[40] in which he famously set out to 'rescue the poor stockinger, the Luddite cropper the "obsolete" hand loom weaver ... from the enormous condescension of posterity'.[41] With its unrivalled manorial records Kibworth had been the subject of a path-breaking academic work, Cicely Howell's 1983 study of land tenure and inheritance.[42]

But the key for us was Rodney Hilton's essay on Kibworth from 1949.[43] A Marxist alumnus of Manchester Grammar School (MGS), Hilton spoke of historians' generalizations about the great movements in history, such as 'the transition from feudalism to capitalism', and turned to Kibworth to ask what actually had happened at grass roots. In the vast archive in Merton with its rolls and rentals from the 1260s to today – Hilton with unrivalled expertise sampled for example the rent strikes of the 1420s to show how the villagers negotiated their way out of customary labour dues and into contract money; a close-up picture of the beginnings of capitalism.

Kibworth's later story, of canals and railways, framework knitters and suffragettes, all made fascinating stuff too: and the involvement of today's community with their primary and secondary schools' researching and bringing their own past back to life gave the films a great sense of fun, empowerment and immediacy – of communal history as lived experience – and it has received great feedback from teachers in schools and universities.[44] *The Independent* called it 'the most innovative history series ever on TV'. The following post-production script (see Table 4.5) is a very simple piece of narrative running out of a village concert as momentum begins to gather ominously towards the First World War:

Table 4.5 Section of post-production script from *The Story of England* (2010)

Time	Picture	(Song Lyrics)	Synch/Dialogue/Voice Over	Music
10:30:21	Photographs plus song from village concert	Claire Synch: *And be just as happy as the birds in the trees.* *The boy I love is up in the gallery, The boy I love is looking down at me,* *There he is, can't you see, waving his handkerchief,* *As merry as a robin that sings on a tree.*	MW VO: When they celebrated Queen Victoria's 60th Jubilee in 1897, the people of Kibworth, as those of England – at least most of them – had shared in the material benefits of industry and Empire. And by good luck and good judgement England had avoided revolution ... but other trials lay ahead	
10:30:55	MW enters town hall		MW Synch to cam: The village celebrated the 1897 Jubilee that June in the streets and in the church and here in the village hall	Music 17 in: 10:31:16:13
10:30:18	Image of Victorian advances in travel		MW Synch: Tremendous things had been achieved over the 60 years of Victoria's reign and a justifiable pride in all that comes leaping out of the pages of the local newspapers ...	
10:31:32	MW in town hall		MW to cam: But with it, a shadow on the horizon: an unlocalized anxiety. The century was coming to an end, the reign clearly coming to an end soon, and a sense that progress, perhaps, was no longer assured	

Table 4.5 (continued)

Time	Picture	(Song Lyrics)	Synch/Dialogue/Voice Over	Music
10:31:49	Photographs: Leicester unemployed march		MW VO: In 1905 a march for the unemployed from Leicester to London came through Kibworth. The working people of England had found their own voice now and they had their own heroes.	Music 18 in: 10:31:48:24 Music 17 out: 10:31:56:08
10:32:11	Votes for Women		And none more so than the proletariat of the proletariat WOMEN: half the workforce in the industrial age, as they had been in the 14th century.	
10:32:14	Suffragette rallies			
10:32:21	London		In 1905 still less than half of men had the vote, and still no women. The response was the Women's Suffrage movement: the Suffragettes.	
10:32:23	MW approaching Women's Library			
10:32:26	Sign: The Women's Library		The Women's Library in London, the greatest collection of women's history in the world, holds many of their records.	
10:32:29	MW entering library		The Suffragettes united middle-class and working women all over the country.	
10:32:35	MW and Suzanne Keyte			
10:32:43	Rogue's Gallery Caption: 'Surveillance photos of Suffragettes 1912'		MW VO: And they even drew women from our village, like Nellie Taylor who lived in Smeeton Westerby.	
			Jess Synch I/V: Nelly was from a very respectable background, her father had been Mayor of Leicester twice, but somehow she was drawn into the women's movement in Leicester. Probably swept in because there were so many meetings in Leicester …	

© Michael Wood/Maya Vision International.

Conclusion

So here are a few examples of how film-makers in mainstream TV think about popular history broadcasting in relation to the academic practice of history and humanities and its impact. I hope they give a sense of how we work, how we engage with the work of academic specialists on which we depend. None of these films in any sense is framed as academic discourse, but all are underpinned by academic ideas: even for example when Chris Dyer shared his knowledge with primary school children in Kibworth about farm houses and manuring in the open fields! This is not so didactic as say Simon Schama's *History of Britain* which was a purely presenter-led series; rather it is film-making using landscape, people, living cultures, buildings and texts; history as now – the current product of our imaginations, not fixed, and certainly not definitive. Our job is still to be entertaining and informative, but it is also to search for meaning and explanation. History on TV then should have life and energy, and it may be experiential; but as Forster urged, it must 'only connect'.

This collection is about the role of history including public history and its impact. As a simple practitioner in broadcasting I have tried to give a sense of what we do. Factual TV is today connected with the academe as never before: we depend on each other for ideas, audience and impact; so the more academics understand the medium, the more effective the message, which I think we all agree is still what it says on the BBC's foundation stone. To conclude let me extend Reith's 1931 metaphor: broadcasting throws out many seeds from the world of scholarship, in the arts, sciences and humanities. Not all of them sprout; some fall on fallow ground; but many grow and bear fruit, who knows where or when, long after they have left the hands of the broadcasters, nurtured in the imaginations of the people themselves.

Notes

1 http://www.bbc.co.uk/radio4/history/making_history/makhist10_prog2f.shtml, accessed 14 August 2014.
2 See Charlotte Wildman 'Urban Transformation in Liverpool and Manchester 1918–39', *The Historical Journal* 55(1) (2012): 119–43.
3 Manchester Central Library (1931–4) among them: a consciously 'pioneer experimental work' in education for 'all classes in the community', Wildman, *Historical Journal,* 136–7.
4 On Matheson see her biography in the *Dictionary of National Biography*: http://www.oxforddnb.com/templates/article.jsp?articleid=49198&back=,35902,35903, accessed 14 August 2014.
5 Charlotte Higgins 'What Can the Origins of the BBC Tell Us about its Future?', http://www.theguardian.com/media/2014/apr/15/bbc-origins-future, accessed 14 August 2014. For the whole series of Higgins's articles see http://www.theguardian.com/media/series/the-bbc-report, accessed 14 August 2014.
6 Georgina Born, 'Strategy, Positioning and Projection in Digital Television: Channel 4 and the Commercialisation of Public Service Broadcasting in the UK', *Media, Culture & Society* 25(6) (2003): 778.

68   *Michael Wood*

7 Channel Four Television Company Limited, *Reports and Accounts for Year Ended 31st March 1985* (London: 1985), 8. On C4's Public Service Remit in General: http://www.channel4.com/info/corporate/, accessed 14 August 2014.

8 'Normandy 44: The Battle beyond D-Day' dir Aaron Young: TX BBC 2 6.6.2014; two-thirds of the men, three-quarters of the ships, and two-thirds of the aircraft were British. My thanks to James Holland: http://www.bbc.co.uk/programmes/p01zcvp7, accessed 14 August 2014.

9 Roland Barthes, 'The Romans in Film', in *Mythologies* (London: Paladin, 1972 [1957]).

10 See e.g. http://www.museumsassociation.org/about/frequently-asked-questions#.U8Fe43 hlosE, accessed 14 August 2014.

11 As indeed can a work of drama, such as Jez Butterworth's *Jerusalem;* but this lies outside the scope of this paper.

12 For an interesting exception, see the 2013 BBC2 film, *The Last Days of Anne Boleyn*, http://www.bbc.co.uk/programmes/p015vhp1, accessed 14 August 2014, where the director played with alternative scenarios based on conflicting sources, each defended by a specialist in the period; but helped by the audience's familiarity with the story, given the popularity of the Tudors on TV.

13 Though for Fernand Braudel's ideas on the long term in TV history, see pp. 55 (see also n. 34).

14 Tristram Hunt, 'Reality, Identity and Empathy: The Changing Face of Social History Television', *Journal of Social History* 39(3) (2006): 843–58; also discussed by Emily Robinson (Chapter 8 in this volume).

15 See for example on Western historiography on China, the essays in Simon Leys, *The Burning Forest* (London: Paladin, 1988).

16 *The Lady of the Mercians*, BBC4 2013.

17 *Christina: A Medieval Life*, BBC4 2009.

18 *The Story of England*, BBC4 and BBC2 2010, episode 5.

19 Amanda Vickery, 'Bring Female Artists out of Storage', *The Guardian*, 16 May 2014, http://www.theguardian.com/artanddesign/2014/may/16/bring-women-artists-out-of-storage, accessed 14 August 2014.

20 Ronald C. Egan, *The Burden of Female Talent* (Cambridge MA: Harvard University Press, 2014).

21 *In Search of Shakespeare*, BBC2 2003; cf. my book of the same name, Michael Wood, *In Search of Shakespeare* (BBC, 2003) pp. 251–4.

22 http://www.bbc.co.uk/news/magazine-18903391, accessed 18 August 2014. Other projects in this area including *African Rome* (2007) on the role of black people in the Roman Empire were turned down by the commissioners.

23 For another story in the Shakespeare series which led to the development of a play by Bradford Museums as an educational tool for schools, see: http://www.mylearning. org/tudor-drama–the-strangers-case/p-569/, accessed 14 August 2014.

24 See my recent article 'Why have we refused to accept the possibility of female genius?', *BBC History Magazine* 15(7, July 2014): 21, http://www.historyextra.com/?, accessed 18 August 2014.

25 Stuart Marshall, *Comrades in Arms,* and the feature-length *Desire* (both C4, 1990). On Marshall: http://lux.org.uk/blog/what-was-british-independent-film-part-5-stuart-marshall *BBC History Magazine*, accessed 14 August 2014.

26 Maya Vision has a history of homosexuality and same-sex love in preparation.

27 See Mark Jordan, *The Invention of Sodomy in Christian Theology* (Chicago, IL: Chicago University Press, 1997); and Alan Bray, *The Friend* (Chicago, IL: Chicago University Press, 2002).

28 Bray, *Homosexuality in Renaissance England* (New York: Columbia University Press, 1996).

A history film-maker's view 69

29 Lister has been treated in drama recently, with Maxine Peake as Lister in *The Secret Diaries of Miss Anne Lister* (BBC2, 2010); and in the documentary: *Revealing Anne Lister* (BBC, 2010).

30 *Christina: A Medieval life* (BBC4 and BBC2, 2009). The inspiration came from Ada Elizabeth Levett, *Studies in Manorial History*, ed. Helen M. Cam, M. Coate and L.S. Sutherland (Oxford: Oxford University Press, 1938), which prints excerpts from the Codicote court book involving Christina's father Hugh.

31 Using for example data from the excavation of a small peasant's cottage at Hangelton Sussex, http://www.wealddown.co.uk/Buildings/Medieval-cottage-from-Hangelton, accessed 14 August 2014.

32 BL ms Stowe 849, along with the survey of 1332, printed by Levett, *Studies in Manorial History*, pp. 338–68.

33 Bernadino de Sahagun, *Florentine Codex: General History of the Things of New Spain*, ed. A.J. Anderson and C.E. Dibble, 12 vols (Salt Lake City, UT: Utah University Press, 1950–82).

34 Braudel, *The Mediterranean in the Age of Philip II* (London: Collins, 1973, 2nd edn), I, pp. 20–2; II, 1238–44.

35 Eamon Duffy, *The Stripping of the Altars* (New Haven, CT: Yale University Press, 1992); Duffy, *The Voices of Morebath* (New Haven, CT: Yale University Press, 2001) for which the key source is J.E. Binney, *Accounts of the Wardens of the Parish of Morebath, Devon, 1520–1573* (Exeter: James G. Commin, 1904). Thanks to the Devon Record Office, we were able to bring the manuscript back to the church where it was written.

36 For a brief summary, see my *The Story of India* (London: Basic Books, 2007), pp. 37–40, 163–6, 241–2; for detailed discussion, see Romila Thapar, *Cultural Pasts* (Oxford: Oxford University Press, 2000), pp. 963–1140; for the classic statement influenced by British imperial historiography, see Jawarharlal Nehru, *The Discovery of India* (Calcutta: Signet Press, 1946).

37 See *Times Higher Education Supplement*, 15 March 2002, http://www.timeshigher education.co.uk/15-march-2002/10083.issue?, accessed 18 August 2014; and *Times Education Supplement* 18 June 2002.

38 Family of the Calcutta printer Dilip Kumar Gupta at the Cheltenham Literary Festival, 2007.

39 W.G. Hoskins, *The Making of the English Landscape* (London: Collins, 1955 and later editions); on the BBC *Landscapes of England* (1976) and *One Man's England* (1978), see Charles Phythian-Adams, 'Hoskins's England: A Local Historian of Genius and the Realisation of his Theme', *Transactions of the Leicester Archaeological and Historical Society* 66 (1992): 143–59.

40 E.P. Thompson, *The Making of the English Working Class* (London: Vintage, 1966).

41 Thompson, *The Making of the English Working Class* (London: Gollancz, 1980, rev edn), p. 12.

42 Cicely Howell, *Land, Family and Inheritance: Kibworth Harcourt 1280–1700* (Cambridge: Cambridge University Press, 1983).

43 Rodney Hilton, 'Kibworth Harcourt: A Merton Manor in the 13th and 14th Centuries', in Hoskins (ed.), *Studies in Leicestershire Agrarian History* (Leicester: Leicestershire Archaeological Society, 1949), pp. 17–40; reprinted in Hilton, *Class Conflict and the Crisis of Feudalism* (London: Continuum, 1985).

44 'The *Story of England* has been immensely helpful in raising the profile of local history and archaeology in the county ... ' Dr Julie Attard, School of History at the University of Leicester, VCH Leicestershire Project, by email 19 July 2014.

5 From Roy Jenkins downwards

The historian/journalist and journalist/ historian in contemporary Britain

Scott Anthony

In the UK stellar careers in journalism tend to be crowned by the writing of a history book. The mould is Roy Jenkins. Recent examplers include the likes of Max Hastings as well as by figures such as Andrew Marr and Jeremy Paxman. These books, it must be said, tend to adorn a very masculine type of career. They are usually bestrode by great men and tend to address 'big' aspects of the twentieth century like war and ideology, rather than the other sort of important developments such as the communications revolution, mass transportation or the history of modern medicine (which, among other things, provide different ways of talking about war and ideology). These figures (journalists turned occasional historians) also play an important role policing the boundaries of historical authority from university-based historians turned occasional journalists; the recent past, which is usually synonymous with the recent political past, tends to be marked as the natural terrain of the journalist/historian rather than the historian/journalist.

Other than inciting a degree of jealousy, it has never been obvious to me why this irritates many historians based in universities. It's an old tradition. The books are seldom very exciting. There is a degree of dutiful school assembly about the whole enterprise. Academics often disparage this lack of imagination even though university faculties rarely market themselves any differently. Stitch together the landing pages of the top ten history faculties in the UK and you get images of monarchs, old maps, politicians (male), parchment, flags, battles and Big Ben (or a photo of the exterior of the Elizabeth Tower, to be pedantically exact). The older universities also like to show off images of their buildings though rarely the ones where history students are actually taught. It has been argued that there is both an opportunity and a need for historians and 'history' to engage with the news media, but universities do not present themselves as obvious places to which to turn for guidance.

Now this is not in any way whatsoever to cast any kind of aspersion on the reality of life in those institutions or university departments (several of which I am extremely proud to have, or have had, some connection); it is simply to point out that because scholars themselves tend to be highly motivated enthusiasts they are perhaps not always alive to the fact that, institutionally, scholarly history does not project itself as particularly alert or outward-looking. As things are it is far from obvious (as many appear to imagine) that historical

The historian/journalist in contemporary Britain 71

knowledge flows – as if in a pipe – from academics to journalists; it seems more likely that successive generations of media practitioners simply learn things (in public) that they did not previously know. Journalists are not generally breaking historical news previously unknown to scholars.

These cross purposes are illustrative. There can be an expectation that because both journalism and scholarly work involve researching, writing and disseminating, the trades are related, if not closely aligned. But they are not. At the risk of stating the obvious: journalism and academia are two very different kinds of industries with different kinds of priorities. Offering any kind of generalization about varied scholarly practices is a fraught business, but purely for rhetorical purposes let us take two contemporary offerings from university-based historians. At one end of the academic spectrum we could take *The Undivided Past*, a recent book by Sir David Cannadine (2014), which argues 'to write about our past no less than to live in the present, we need to see beyond our differences, our sectional interests, our identity politics, and our parochial concerns to embrace and to celebrate the common humanity that has always bound us together'.[1] At another, we could examine the first working paper from the Modern British Studies group at the University of Birmingham, which proposes 'cultures of democracy' as a focal point for framing an historical understanding of 'pressing questions about inclusion and exclusion, but also about the complex nature of participation across different forms of everyday cultural, social and political life, elucidating the ways in which individuals could be simultaneously franchised and disenfranchised'.[2]

With my scholarly hat on, both strike me as rich and interesting ventures; I most reverently take my hat off to them. With my journalistic hat on, I cannot help but wonder what they mean in practice; to a news editor they would sound like a licence to be nebulous.[3] That is not to say that news editors are uninterested in history. It is to stress that news editors are interested only as far as 'history' can illuminate something about today. Journalists' need to make now extraordinary: history is a fantastic prop for the unenviable task of framing today's news because it brings into play the dramatic parallel. In their quest for sensation and revelation, journalists understand that the past is there to be plundered.

Having said all that, it would be foolish to pretend university-based historians are entirely free from similar pressures. Academics may be primarily interested in historical knowledge for its own sake, but in practice extremely few are prepared to completely ignore prevailing cultural and institutional trends, even if the degree of freedom to shape their own agenda is ultimately higher. They may not have to rubbish up 850 words by three o'clock on why the Tessa Jowell–David Mills scandal is just like the Profumo affair, but many are prepared to spend several months drafting research plans that flatter potential referees and speculate at great length about the importance of their research in the context of current funding priorities. Last year an influential academic spoke at an event I co-organized; for me it was a truly inspirational session, but for other attendees it was less impressive. 'What have they actually published?'

72   Scott Anthony

they muttered. It is a depressing equation: interesting and influential public figure < REF (Research Excellence Framework) submission.

Max Hastings once wrote that the media audience was one of the major limitations he faced as a journalist/historian. 'The most that can be said of it', Hastings wrote, 'is that it distributes modest crumbs of historical knowledge at tables where otherwise the past remains a very misty, remote place.'[4] In terms of attitude to audience it is a revealing metaphor, but he does nevertheless raise a key issue. On the average weekday a reader of *The Times* spends twenty-seven minutes with the entire paper (fifty-four minutes at the weekend). In news media terms this is a geological period: online studies show that only around 50 per cent of people get even halfway through a news article. There also seems to be no correlation between time spent with an article and how often it is tweeted; in other words most people who are forwarding, recommending and liking electronic media have not actually read that thing in its entirety. (On the other hand nearly everyone who opens an article will look at all the pictures in it.) This is not to make an 'end of days' point about news in an age of digital media, it is simply to explain that the taut narrative structures of the mass media (Jowell = Profumo) reflect both the impatience of a large general audience and also the lack of journalistic self-confidence in breaking stories about people, places and events that are not already familiar. Just as blockbuster films are now dominated by reboots, remakes and 'franchises', the news media presently demand Google optimized stories about the US President, the royal baby and the Premier League.

At the same time, commercially significant popular history faces very similar pressures: the two world wars, the monarchy and subjects studied at school dominate, if not entirely define, the popular appetite for history. School is especially important, as what interests children (Romans, Henry VIII, Nazis) tends to act as a 'trigger', renewing the enthusiasms of parents whose interest in the past has waned.

The argument so far has been that the news media and academia are fundamentally different industries, although practitioners in both do share some common challenges. For the more evangelically minded popular historians, one fundamental challenge to be squared up to, or perhaps just to be accepted, is that the market for popular historical knowledge tends to be extremely conservative. In news media terms, the *Daily Mail* is the historian's best friend: it delivers an enormous global audience and devotes more space (paid at a healthy word rate) than any comparable UK media outlet. That's always a sentiment guaranteed to silence a seminar room. A valid reason for the disapproval is that the journalistic use of history in the *Daily Mail* is nearly always to excoriate the present: it specializes in inverted whiggery; although it must be said that even enthusiast magazines – such as *BBC History* or *History Today* – rarely go against the grain of their readers' assumed expectations.

The cover lines of the current issue of *History Today* address the anniversary of the First World War, the history of the world cup and the last decade of Elizabeth I's reign. When the boundaries of history's own 'specialist' commercial

The historian/journalist in contemporary Britain 73

media are so delineated, expectations of mainstream news editors probably need to be lowered: a good rule of thumb is that editors basically want to sell 'topical' historical stories that are already known to the majority of people. The question is how might journalist/historians and historian/journalists negotiate this (if it is even possible)?

***

Dominic Sandbrook is probably the most prominent historian in the UK's contemporary news media. Critically acclaimed, commercially successful and expertly promoted by Andrew 'The Jackal' Wylie, Sandbrook's career as a freelance historian has blossomed since leaving his post at the University of Sheffield. His articles can currently be found in the pages of many national newspapers and magazines including the *Daily Mail* and the *Sunday Times*.

Sandbrook made his name with a series of books about the recent past including *Never Had It So Good*, *White Heat* and *State of Emergency*. The model for the books was American; Sandbrook has spoken of wanting to write the broad best-selling histories that he saw 'stacked up in Barnes & Noble' when visiting the United States. Editorially the books are rather cautious. They tend to hang off the high politics of the period and it is striking that large sections of the analysis feel like they could have been written at the time – the material is summarized as much as sorted, with the result that the books tend to reinforce the existing narratives of the period being written about. It is a conservative enterprise in as much as the books' integrity comes from stripping away the hyperbole of popular memory, detoxing the obvious excesses rather than arguing the toss. The results can be peculiar. Large sections of *Seasons in the Sun*, which covers the period 1974–9, are dedicated to building up a familiar picture of the UK's industrial problems and the threat of national bankruptcy.[5] Another section covers an ageing Harold Wilson's increasingly odd behaviour, where the Labour Prime Minister takes people who want a private discussion into a lavatory where he turns on the taps before beginning to whisper. However, because Sandbrook is a diligent historian he also acknowledges in passing that during this period the UK lost fewer days to industrial unrest than much of Europe and the US and that Harold Wilson was actually being bugged by the security services. Such asides are illustrative of the fact that a very different (and less familiar) story about the 1970s could be written. Now it might be that the volume of writing that Sandbrook has to do (three door-stopping books in three years, some 2,732 pages) prevents him from reformulating understandings of the recent past, but it might also be that familiar historical narratives are fundamental to guaranteeing a minimum level of commercial success.

As a university-based historian Sandbrook found himself frustrated by the lack of engagement with wider public debates, and this is the space that his newspaper articles now fill. He speaks with real pride about the variety of letters he gets from readers across the social spectrum and the ways in which they inform his work as an historian. Climbing the media parapet is, he reflects, nevertheless a risky strategy. 'When you write a piece of work of scholarship,

74   *Scott Anthony*

you have at the back of your mind a fantasy that in decades to come it will be on the shelves and so you try to write it as enduringly sensibly and judiciously as possible', he says.[6] This is the polar opposite of writing for a newspaper, where you are only really writing for tomorrow. 'You are writing often deliberately to be provocative', he explains, 'to tease them, provoke them to make them laugh, cry, be angry, outraged whatever and you may bring in history but you do so in the service of your argument rather than an exercise in disinterring the reality of the past'.

Over the long term one possible outcome of this is that the journalist/historian may start to drift into the altogether more predictable realm of the professional controversialist. 'If you want a bigger platform then you have to accept that there are risks involved', he admits, 'you will end up doing and saying things that your colleagues won't necessarily agree with and which are based on different principles than their own. There is always that risk of tarnishing your brand.' None of these pressures, as Sandbrook well knows, is particularly new. 'If you look at A.J.P. Taylor's work for ITV and the *Sunday Express* then my columns look positively feeble and mealy-mouthed by comparison', he reflects, 'but then Taylor basically decided that he would rather have (a) the money or (b) the fame and the big audience than the undiluted respect of his nearest colleagues. I think there always is a bit of a trade off.'

When you are working as a freelance journalist, the closer you get to the politics pages the more you come to understand that you are essentially employed as a subcontractor; your job is to flesh out a pre-formulated story. You either accept the gig or you don't, you're either comfortable with the argument or you're not. Keeping that context in mind, here are the headlines of three recent columns by Sandbrook: 'A political giant, yes. But if he'd got his way, we'd have been like North Korea' (on the death of Labour politician Tony Benn);[7] 'Pygmies, selfies and why democracy in Britain is dying thanks to our pathetic politicians' (on David Cameron's apparent fondness for selfies);[8] and 'Another boat packed with migrants heads for Europe as it's revealed Britain's population has grown by 5 million in 12 years: This human tide will be the crisis of the century' (on immigration).[9] It must be said that the actual substance of the articles is not well represented by the headlines partly because, as a sub's paper, the packaging of the *Daily Mail*'s editorial is too important to leave to the writer.

To my mind, Sandbrook's matter-of-factness about the journalistic work he does is appealingly straightforward. 'I once read an interview with Matthew Parris where they asked him "do you believe everything that you write?"', explains Sandbrook, 'and he said "not many of my beliefs can really be summarised in 700 words but I have to write 700 words anyway and of course the me in the column is not necessarily *me*."' This is worth remembering. Not only do Sandbrook's articles have more subtlety than the headlines imply (admittedly it's not often easy to see how they could have less) but there is also a clear distinction between the articles he writes and the books he publishes. Dominic Sandbrook the journalist/historian is a very different beast from Dominic

The historian/journalist in contemporary Britain 75

Sandbrook the historian/journalist. The same is also true for figures like Niall Ferguson. 'If you take someone like Richard Evans at Cambridge, he doesn't really write that much for the papers, he's not on telly, he's not a public figure in the same way David Starkey or Simon Schama are but he is nevertheless a top class historian', concludes Sandbrook, 'Chris Clark is not a media figure, but is a first class historian at the top of his game. If suddenly they pitched up and started to write a column in the *Daily Star* I don't think it would make them better historians.'

While Dominic Sandbrook has become perhaps *the* historian in the UK news media, he does have a generational rival to that throne in *The Guardian*'s Andy Beckett. Like Sandbrook, Beckett studied history at Balliol. Like Sandbrook he has written about the 1970s. However, Beckett's book, *When the Lights Went Out: Britain in the Seventies*, is a beast of a tangibly different stripe.[10] It mixes reflective interviews and research; the method is more obviously hybridized; half-journalistic and half-'historical'. 'There's a lot of people writing contemporary history books and a lot of people writing contemporary political journalism but there's not so many people doing both', he says, 'I suppose I'm nibbling away at the same subject, which is what's happened to Britain over the last 40 years, but from different ends.' The distinction that Sandbrook makes between the production of his history books and his historically informed journalism does not really apply to Beckett.

In both *When the Lights Went Out* and in his journalism, Beckett's writing is animated by the idea that lots of important contextual knowledge about the recent past vanishes into thin air. People might know about the world wars, or be able to name prime ministers, but even extremely educated people may be completely unaware of the longer trajectory of apparently contemporary issues. Such an approach draws Beckett's journalism (extended features are the preferred form) towards less familiar tales, such as the house price booms of the 1960s or the strength of support for Thatcher in Scotland. 'I don't want to sound pompous but sometimes in work that I am doing', he says, 'I'm trying to find out new things. I like to write, and I like to read, work where the sort of evidence being presented and the things being discovered might even be cutting against the argument being made. Where there is complexity, rather than all the evidence being streamlined into a kind of polemic which, from Roy Jenkins downwards, I think is a very common British mode.'[11]

It must be said that, by eschewing polemics, Beckett has probably limited his audience. He himself admits, 'I'm writing for *The Guardian* and by British standards I would see that as an intellectual, upmarket paper and I feel I am very much writing for the chewier end of that.' Beckett's work is discursive in a media that is increasingly impatient. Or as he puts it, 'why would you spend 25 minutes on a Tuesday morning reading Andy Beckett's article when you normally spend 20 minutes consuming your entire news media for the day?'

In terms of influence, approach and aesthetics, Beckett has taken a slightly tangential road to Sandbrook. At university, a course on post-colonial history proved formative. 'We had this quite charismatic young guy [Peter Carey] and

76   *Scott Anthony*

we were talking about Indonesia in the Dutch colonial era and what came after. In the summer he had been with some anti-government rebels, literally sitting in a ditch being shot at, and I remember finding that very exciting.' In an era where contemporary history was rarely taught at university, finding a live link to the past captured the attention. In terms of other important historians he mentions Ginzberg, Braudel and Febvre. 'What these historians have in common', he argues, 'is that they draw a tremendous amount out of a particular detail, which was always more appealing to me than academic historians who have gone through the archives for years and rather judiciously accept what they have found.'

In addition to illustrating the unchanging nature of the historiographical paper at Oxford (what Beckett studied more than twenty years ago is still on the reading list today) Beckett's enthusiasms also point to a more self-consciously literary mode. He most admires writers such as Ian Sinclair, Jonathan Meades and Owen Hatherley and admits to being bored by a great deal of 'history': he would rather read a novel by David Peace. This is a textual point; it's the rough edges (as well as the contestability) of those figures' writings that make them both compelling and aesthetically interesting. It's also a matter of aim and approach. The internal logics of academic research exert a stronger pull than is usually admitted on both what is researched and how it is researched. 'In academia or outside academia a lot of things seem too obvious to be examined', says Beckett, 'you look at what Patrick Keiller did about the architecture of retail parks, warehouses and so on, things that are really quite significant to changes in Britain in the last 30, 40 years (but) it took someone like him, an outsider, probably not a trained historian, to do it.'

The 'personalized' parts of Beckett's books have been those subject to most criticism. Here reviews in academic journals have not always been very astute. There's little recognition that Beckett is not trying to write a scholarly monograph: only the very faintest understanding that he is trying to address different methodological and interpretative issues. 'I've been thinking about (historical evidence) in the book I'm writing now', he says, 'I'm doing '81, '82 and this is a period only just before you are getting colossal amounts of video evidence, such a glut of testimony, eye witness stuff, whatever. It does make me think when people want to write good history books about the 90s it's going to be a very different business'.

If Dominic Sandbrook represents the dominant mode of history in the news media, with Andy Beckett's approach as its half-competing shadow, Patrick Wright represents Beckett's more avant-garde predecessor. Wright wrote features for *The Guardian* for several years in the early 1990s while completing *The Village That Died for England*.[12] Wright was an outsider in exactly the sense that Beckett describes. He was not formally trained as an historian, indeed he cheerfully admits to not even having an O-level in the subject; but the fraught political environment of the 1980s had made him increasingly interested in utilizing the historical method. 'There was this GLC kind of political atmosphere', he says. 'In some perspectives, you know, the idea that a man

The historian/journalist in contemporary Britain 77

would even describe a woman was seen as a kind of dangerous act and an aggressive act. So part of what I was trying to do was kick open that possibility of just talking in the concrete again.'[13]

The historical method offered a way back at a time when there was an excess of theory. 'It's not anti-intelligence or anti-critical theory, but it's just', he remembers, 'you know, there was a period in which people went round just doing deconstruction in one form or another that just got very tedious'. The ultimate start point of this interest was studying as an undergraduate at the recently opened University of Kent where, even before the heyday of the *New Universities Quarterly*, the syllabus was focused on experimenting with new ways of approaching the humanities. This was about formal reach and analytical curiosity, an empirical method but one less confident of, and more philosophically curious about, 'disinterring the reality of the past'.

Having tried and failed to get into journalism through the front door, Wright eventually ended up being offered a feature-writing contract by Alan Rusbridger (now editor of *The Guardian*) thanks to the series of controversies unleashed by the publication of *A Journey Through Ruins* coinciding with the need for more content to fill a new broadsheet supplement.[14] 'There's this "thousand words on anything" school of journalism where a journalist can write a story about anything in two or three hours with the help of a phone and two interviews', Wright explains, 'but in that broadsheet age they had lots of space to fill and for someone like me 4000, even 5000 words, was not a problem; for me it was much harder to write a 1000 word piece'.

During his time at *The Guardian* Wright took on everything from Richard Littlejohn to privatized phone boxes. 'I mean there were all these big heavyweight series doing the Will Hutton thing, going on about macro-political level change', remembers Wright, 'but, you know, the truth about privatization was it was also about the transformation of little things, it was about the transformation of taken for granted attitudes and public amenities too'. No matter what the article was supposed to be about, his subject was exploring the notion of the past as the cultural present. Although he adds, 'I was also pleased to get the chance to take apart *The Modern Review*'.

In addition to making a political contribution, and earning the money to write books, Wright believes the experience of writing historically informed commentaries was a beneficial one. 'I learned a lot from doing journalism', he admits, 'I learned if you want to know what somebody like Enoch Powell thinks you can do the academic route and spend five months in the library going through old newspapers and books or you can pick up a phone and talk to him'.

He also enjoyed the privilege and the prospect of a large audience. 'To me the idea of writing for an academic journal was about as depressing a prospect as death', he says. 'In my freelance days, of course, this may have been because you couldn't expect to be paid. But you also knew that nobody would read it except for some students who wanted to pinch the best ideas or one-up you; you don't feel like you're participating in any sort of wider debate.'

78   *Scott Anthony*

Like politicians, like footballers, perhaps like everything, all journalistic careers end in failure, and Wright eventually fell out of favour following the appointment of a new section editor. The launch of a tabloid-sized *G2* further reduced the space for discursive essays and instead encouraged editorial commissioning to shift towards greater 'political' positioning. Wright came under pressure to judge his subjects, to state that certain views were appalling, to take sides and underline issues in what he considered an editorially intrusive way. In his estimation, this marked the start of the paper's '*Daily Mail*-ization', but it also illustrated a deeper truth about the operation of the media. 'I always say to students, "look there's one thing you should know about the world of the media"', says Wright, 'it's that it functions according to the principle of mimetic desire; people want what other people want, there's a kind of crisis of value'. 'It's exhausting keeping up', he continues, 'and you meet people who do this for years and they fall out and end up with barely the energy to run a B&B in the West Country'.

The answer for Wright was to leave the media world behind and with it some of the pressure for repetition, some of the continual need to mirror currents of fashion, and the constant jockeying for position that animated the small 'p' politics of the media world. The same pressures exist in the trade press, of course, and are far from absent in academia. 'Trade publishers seem to favour a summarising approach which offers the reader a way of understanding carefully packaged periods, or perhaps a decade,' Wright suggests. 'I came out of the University of Kent with a sense that the book trade's distinction between fiction and non-fiction was too crudely drawn and that modern experience demanded more subtly differentiated forms of prose and all sorts of new ways of handling archival and documentary material too.'

***

It is worth remembering that, when the idea of 'news' was being invented in the fifteenth century, journalists were (at best) marginal to the whole enterprise. The eighteenth century marked the watershed; it saw the creation of a newspaper-reading public and the valorization of that public, a process that fused growing literacy and demands for greater democracy with the idea of a free press. News in the format of a printed newspaper written by journalists could at last claim that it had a valuable role in a modern society. 'It is not only right to strike while the iron is hot', as Benjamin Franklin put it, speaking as a politician but recalling his days as a printer, 'but it may be very practicable to heat it by continually striking'.[15] The historical contingency of both the press and the journalism we take for granted now is worth recalling because journalism as has been is currently in the process of disaggregation and realignment.

Developments in the digital landscape mean that serious newspapers increasingly utilize the moving image, sound recordings and interactive graphics to do more and more of the work that the printed word used to do. We appear, in part, to be returning to the more formally eclectic world of 'news' before the

The historian/journalist in contemporary Britain 79

eighteenth century: the coverage of news stories is now accompanied by archival film, historic photographs and the reproduction of historic key speeches and texts. On the seventieth anniversary of D-Day the actor Benedict Cumberbatch read original news bulletins from the day at the same time of their original transmission on the BBC, while the *Daily Telegraph* used live reporting and social media to recreate the experience of the landings in hour-by-hour updates. News organizations are finding, a bit like Patrick Wright, that the distinction between fiction and non-fiction can be very crude and that modern experience demands all sorts of new ways of handling archival and documentary material. Journalists are faced with the challenge of how best to reshape their terrain.

News organizations are also changing. *The Guardian* has been developing an MA in journalism and recently opened a 'cultural and educational institution' in the old Midland Goods Shed at Kings Cross. News International (as was) not only acquired a series of educational companies producing digital educational content, it actually planned to open an academy school in East London. The *Daily Mail* is acquiring financial interests in specialist educational companies. The *Financial Times*, part of the Pearson Group, in 2013 launched an executive diploma. Private citizens may be ever less inclined to pay for news, but the liberalization of the education sector means that media companies are well placed to benefit from the state's willingness to stump up for education and training.

By contrast, while the idea of what a news organization does and how it does it is expanding, public universities in the UK are in a process of retrenchment. The waves of university expansions, which produced the kind of experimentation that Wright described at Kent, are for the moment over. The demographic structure of the post-war period made some retrenchment inevitable and the state of public finances has increased that pressure. History increasingly 'competes' with other humanities; at some universities history is used to generate profits which are to be reinvested elsewhere. Even historians based in 'elite' Russell Group universities need to keep an eye on student numbers and pay attention to student satisfaction surveys. While institutions like The Tate, as well as various media organizations, may be developing new kinds of public educational programmes it makes obvious sense, as a commercial strategy, for history faculties to focus on their core, traditional strengths rather than attempt to compete with these more innovative offerings; especially when even the most successful attempts to break out of the academy, such as History & Policy, have only been successful in very modest terms. Whether university historians are ultimately well served by the longer-term consequences of this commercial strategy is another matter. It would be a shame if the parameters of historical research produced in public universities began to narrow.

This chapter was commissioned as an extended think piece, accordingly any insights it offers are far from scientific; it's an attempt to highlight some of the frictions that characterize the relationship between academic historians and the news media in a intelligent but readable fashion, rather than an attempt to tell it 'how it is'. Nevertheless, from the point of view of the university-based

80 *Scott Anthony*

historian/journalist the public culture of historical knowledge is about to change in potentially interesting ways. We are poised to enter the era of the open access journal. There is one vision of this future that sees open access as a way of positioning public sector scholars as providing the grist for all manner of profitable mills. There are some academics who appear to welcome this – and are already aligning future research projects with the dreariest political anniversaries in mind. You feel like pointing out that in media companies, unlike universities, a 'researcher's' place is at the bottom of the institutional hierarchy. They are what you do for work experience.

An alternative model, a 'niche busting' model, might see scholars work in a wide array of formats that are curious and welcoming about different forms of historical expression and understanding – works that avoid the straightjacket of stultifying scholarly politics and the ever-diminishing returns offered by chasing commercial success, to provide a platform for astonishing and unexpected historical vistas that create their own audiences. Perhaps practical encouragement for the creative development of such formulations will work their way into REF2020, perhaps not. Like journalists, scholars are faced with the challenge of how best to reshape their terrain, and also of keeping their footing while it is reshaped beneath them.

Suggested further reading

Andy Beckett tells the story of the Blairs' homes and the reshaping of London's political geography: 'Move on Up', *The Guardian*, 9 December 2004, http://www.theguardian.com/politics/2004/dec/09/property.britishidentity, accessed 18 August 2014.

Clare Makepeace uncovers the officially sanctioned brothels of the First World War: 'Sex and the Somme: The Officially Sanctioned Brothels on the Front Line Laid Bare for the First Time', http://www.dailymail.co.uk/news/article-2054914/Sex-Somme-Officially-sanctioned-WWI-brothels-line.html, accessed 18 August 2014.

Patrick Wright on telephone boxes: 'How the Red Telephone Box Became Part of Britain's National Heritage', http://www.patrickwright.net/1988/08/05/how-the-red-tephone-box-became-part-of-britains-national-heritage/, accessed 18 August 2014.

Dominic Sandbrook on Ed Miliband's borrowings from Disraeli: 'Red Ed's One Nation Hero … ' *Mail Online*, 6 October 2012, http://www.dailymail.co.uk/debate/article-2213607/Red-Ed-s-One-Nation-hero-vacuous-egotistical-hypocrite-sent-British-soldiers-die-needlessly-foreign-wars–Remind-anyone.html, accessed 18 August 2014.

Andy Beckett on the forgotten story of Chile's socialist internet: 'Santiago Dreaming', *The Guardian*, 8 September 2003, http://www.theguardian.com/technology/2003/sep/08/sciencenews.chile, accessed 18 August 2014.

Notes

My thanks to the editors and Dr Bernhard Fulda for their ideas, suggestions and amendments, which helped improve this essay immeasurably. My apologies to them for ignoring some of their other ideas, which might have improved the essay further.

The historian/journalist in contemporary Britain 81

1 See David Cannadine, *The Undivided Past: History Beyond our Differences* (London: Allen Lane, 2013).
2 http://www.birmingham.ac.uk/Documents/college-artslaw/history/mbs/MBS-Birmingham-Working-Paper-1.pdf, accessed 10 August 2014.
3 With my academic hat back on, shouldn't academics be celebrating that licence to be nebulous?
4 See Max Hastings, 'Hacks and Scholars: Allies of a Kind', in Cannadine (ed.), *History and the Media* (London: Palgrave, 2004).
5 See Dominic Sandbrook, *Seasons in the Sun: The Battle for Britain, 1974–1979* (London: Allen Lane, 2012).
6 Interview with Sandbrook, 30 May 2014.
7 Sandbrook, *Daily Mail,* 14 March 2014.
8 Sandbrook, *Daily Mail,* 7 March 2014.
9 Sandbrook, *Daily Mail,* 27 June 2014.
10 Andy Beckett, *When the Lights Went Out: What Really Happened to Britain in the Seventies* (London: Faber and Faber, 2010).
11 Interview with Beckett, 4 June 2014.
12 Patrick Wright, *The Village That Died for England* (London: Jonathan Cape, 1995).
13 Interview with Wright, 17 June 2014.
14 Wright, *A Journey through Ruins: The Last Days of London* (London: Radius, 1991).
15 Benjamin Franklin, *Memoirs of the Life of Benjamin Franklin,* vol. 1 (London: Henry Colburn, 1818), p. 344.

6 The return of national history[1]

Stefan Berger

> The very fact that historians are at least beginning to make some progress in the study and analysis of nations and nationalism suggest[s] that, as so often, the phenomenon is past its peak. The owl of Minerva which brings wisdom, said Hegel, flies out at dusk. It is a good sign that it is now circling around nations and nationalism.[2]

Historians are poor prophets and even Eric Hobsbawm was no exception. He wrote these lines in 1990, when a new dawn for nations and nationalism in Europe was just about to begin. And historians played an important role in the revival of national(ist) narratives in the 1990s and 2000s – both in Eastern and Western Europe. In fact, Hobsbawm had realized the central role of history in nationalist narratives. Writing about nationalism, ethnocentrism and fundamentalism he had this to say: 'the past is an essential element, perhaps the essential element in these ideologies.'[3] And there are many passages in his work where he is highly critical of historiographical nationalism. In his introduction to *Nations and Nationalism* for example he indicts historians who fail to leave their 'convictions behind when entering the study or the library'.[4]

And yet, if we look around Europe during the last twenty-five years, it is striking to what an extent historians are still engaged in the forging of national master narratives. However, in almost every case there have also been opposing voices of historians, warning of the construction of such master narratives. Professional history writing has witnessed a decisive move towards global and transnational history – with many efforts to transcend national horizons and storylines. Thus, the picture that presents itself with regard to national history is complex and manifold. Nevertheless, the post-cold war world has seen a return to national history. What this return amounts to will be the subject of this brief essay. We shall start off by reviewing some of the post-cold war debates on national history, both in Eastern and Western Europe, before we conclude by asking how historians as public intellectuals in many parts of Europe should position themselves vis-à-vis the revival of national and nationalist storylines.

The end of communism in Eastern Europe and the revival of historiographical nationalism

With the end of communism, the post-communist nation states of Eastern Europe had to position themselves vis-à-vis their recent pasts. As Stefan Troebst has pointed out, four positions can be distinguished: first, national histories rejected the communist period as imposed by a foreign power (as was argued in the Baltic states, but also Slovakia and Croatia). Second, there was more or less intensive contestation in national histories about how to interpret the communist past in national history (for instance in Hungary, Poland, Czech Republic, Ukraine). Third, national histories were self-consciously ambivalent about communism but hastened to add that not everything was bad under communism (as argued in Serbia, Bulgaria, Romania, Macedonia, Albania). Finally, we find in some cases the complete absence of any attempts to distance national history from the communist period (Russia, Moldova and many other post-Soviet states which have continued with authoritarian structures going back to the Soviet period).[5]

In the light of this it is intriguing to observe that all of these options could go hand-in-hand with the revival of historiographical nationalism. In the first case, the denunciation of communism allowed the new national master narratives to write the communist period out of national history as a system of foreign, i.e. Soviet occupation. Older national narratives, which had often been repressed under communism, returned and promptly caused controversy, as they frequently had problematic legacies. So for example they were tainted by collaboration with the National Socialists in the Second World War; they were linked to authoritarian right-wing regimes in the interwar period and they had anti-Semitic overtones, to mention but a few of the problems that older national narratives in Eastern and East-Central Europe opened up.

In the second case, there was greater contestation over re-emerging national narratives after 1990. However, those political forces judging the communist past more positively also often adopted strong national master narratives. They could in many cases hark back to the 1980s which had already witnessed a revival of national narratives which, behind the Iron Curtain, were still then painted red. In the third variant those positive national narratives from the communist period were emphasized even more and in the fourth variant there was simply no critical distance at all, although it is noticeable that, very selectively, the continuation narratives from the communist period could also adapt and adopt more traditional national narratives, thereby continuing the process of nationalization of communist national narrative that had already started under communism.

In communist East Germany, for example, traditional nationalist elements in their national historiography included a routine referral to the wars of 1813/14 as 'wars of liberation', and a portrayal of the Bismarckian solution to the German question as unavoidable and progressive. Sometimes one could even read the argument that the war against France in 1870/1 had been a defensive war.[6]

84   *Stefan Berger*

Bulgarian national history during the 1980s increasingly shed the pretensions of Marxist class analysis to return to traditional forms of often nationalist historical narrative, focusing on the Bulgarian national revival and the national question. During the 1980s a specially created research group on the national liberation movement employed twenty-one researchers and sought to cover all aspects of the Bulgarian national question.[7] Many communist national historiographies divided nationalism neatly into a progressive and reactionary variant. They could build on Stalin's classical formula for historiography – 'socialist in content and national in its form'.[8] One of the worst cases of historiographical communist hyper-nationalism could be found in Romania, where Romanian-ness was promoted as the key to the communist development of the fatherland.[9] Nationalist communism was also strong in Albania, where, under the leadership of Aleks Buda (1911–93) and Stefanaq Pollo (b.1923) historians were busy in constructing a canon of national heroes and glorifying the national 'renaissance' of the nineteenth and early twentieth centuries.[10]

If the return of national and nationalist history in Eastern Europe could build on groundwork completed under communism, a strong anti-communism, present in some Eastern European countries, exacerbated historiographical nationalism after 1990. In Estonia, history played a crucial role in the late 1980s and early 1990s in re-establishing the national master narrative. Many historians became leading members of the movement for independence, and historical institutes, such as the Rahvastikuloo Uurimise Laboratoorium (Laboratory for Historical and Demographic Research), set up at Tartu University in 1991, began denouncing what they perceived as the Soviet occupation of their homeland. The Society for National Heritage became a mass member organization, and historical journals such as *Kleio* (since 1998 published as *Ajalooline Ajakiri*) fostered the national turn of Estonian historiography.[11] In Hungary, centre right-wing governments since the 1990s have persistently been promoting nationalist history whenever they have been in power. Historians associated with the centre right, such as Mária Schmidt (b.1953) and László Tőkéczki (b.1951), presented the Hungarian past in glorious terms and argued that all the tragic events of Hungary's history were the result of foreign "intervention". Authoritarian political leaders, such as István Tisza, were suddenly presented as models having already promoted economic modernism and political nationalism.[12] In Yugoslavia the revival of nationalist historiographies directly contributed to a bloody civil war. The Serbian Academy of Sciences was a hotbed of Serbian nationalism and historians were in the forefront of those academics who sought to construct notions of an eternal Serbian victimhood that was historical justification for Serbian aggression in the Yugoslav civil war.[13]

For the new states in post-communist Eastern Europe, it was important to construct continuities which demonstrated the historicity of their nation states. History everywhere became intensely politicized. Thus, in Belarus, the new national narrative after 1990 celebrated the short-lived independent Belarus which existed immediately after the Russian revolution; it rediscovered the Belarusian national movement, whose tentative beginnings were traced back to

The return of national history   85

the nineteenth century. It also took over all the key arguments of late nineteenth- and early twentieth-century Belarusian historians, such as the Polish–Lithuanian Commonwealth as first Belarusian–Lithuanian state, the special mission of Belarus as mediating between Russia and the West and the creation of a Belarusian pantheon of famous Belarusians. It is a sign of the strong overlap between national histories in Eastern Europe that among the Belarusian national heroes are also key figures from the Polish pantheon, including Adam Mickiewicz (1798–1855) and Tadeusz Kościuszko (1746–1817), who were born into Belarusian families of Polish culture.[14]

In many post-communist states after 1990, the denunciation of the communist past was an integral part of the revival of national histories. Communism was depicted as an oppressive force and routinely associated with an occupying power, the Soviet Union. The Instytut Pamięci Narodowej (Institute of National Remembrance), set up in Poland in 2001, can serve as a good example of the vilification of the communist past. As an archive of the communist secret political police files, it makes those files available to the community of historians. But as a research institute it contributes to a narrative of communist Poland as anti-national Poland; in other words a Poland led by national traitors doing the Soviets' bidding. This was particularly marked after the elections of 2005, when the government turned the institute into its political tool.[15]

In Slovakia, Slovenia, Croatia and Romania, some professional historians even sought to rehabilitate those who had collaborated with National Socialist Germany in the Second World War – often stressing the collaborators' justified anti-communism. In Hungary, the rehabilitation of a number of Catholic-conservative and right-wing historians from the late 1980s onwards saw the most protracted and bitter debates surrounding the medieval historian and long-time minister for religion and education Bálint Hóman (1885–1951). There was little doubt about the scholarly merits of his work on medieval political and economic history, but questions were raised whether someone who had shown clear sympathies for fascism in the 1940s should be re-introduced into the historiographical canon. In Romania, the historian Gheorge Buzatu (b.1939), a main apologist for nationalist communism under Ceauşescu, has been in the vanguard of an Antonescu cult, which has been seeking to rehabilitate Ion Antonescu, the extreme right-wing war-time leader of Romania, as an anti-communist patriot, when others have been denouncing him as a war criminal. Overall then, there is a clear correlation between the end of communism in Eastern Europe and the return of national and often nationalist history to post-communist spaces.

Historiographical nationalism in multinational states in Western Europe

A mixture of anxieties over a perceived crisis of national solidarities and fears over the increasing powers of the European Union sometimes also encouraged a return to more traditional national histories in Western Europe from the 1980s onwards. They were meant to strengthen "national feeling", maintain national

86 *Stefan Berger*

sovereignty and mobilize national sentiment against a perceived threat of national crises and increased Europeanization. The two tendencies were not necessarily interconnected, but both trends contributed to a rise of national and sometimes nationalist history.

Before we look at the emasculation of national historical narratives in core European countries from the 1980s onwards, it is worthwhile pointing out that in some cases Europeanization also encouraged the writing of national master narratives. Especially in multinational states such as Spain, Belgium and Britain, Europe raised the aspirations of 'regions' to turn themselves into fully fledged nations. Again, this tendency can be traced back to the 1980s.[16] The leader of the Nieuw-Vlaamse Alliantie (New Flemish Coalition), the largest political party in Flanders in September 2011, Bart de Wever, who has a history degree from the Catholic University of Leuven, champions the writing of an autonomous national history of Flanders rather than a history of Belgium.[17] Scotland is another example of this development. A collection on Scottish history from 1992, aimed not just at an academic audience, starts: 'Scotland's history is important. It gives us as individuals and as members of Scottish society a vital sense of where we are and how we got here.'[18]

If we look towards the more established nation states of Europe we can observe trends to return to national history. In 1986, Fernand Braudel, the undisputed post-war leader of the *Annales*, who had championed transnational forms of history writing and had made them famous with his book on the Mediterranean,[19] at the end of his life published a two-volume national history of France entitled *L'identité de la France* (The Identity of France), which surprised more than a few of his admirers.[20] If one needed confirmation that national history writing in Western Europe was back in vogue, here it was. And Braudel's history was in fact only the tip of the iceberg of often multi-volume histories of France which had been pouring out of the French publishing houses in the 1980s. Where did such a revival of national history writing come from? It is perhaps not unreasonable to assume that, in France, as in many other places in Europe, it was deeply connected to a sense of crisis – crisis of the nation state and its meaning in an Europeanizing Europe and a globalizing world.

The French story is multiplied across Western Europe. In Italy and Germany debates surrounding the fascist past were central to attempts to renationalize historical writing and use history to strengthen national identity. In Italy, as more and more historians came to doubt the simplistic story of heroic resistance between 1943 and 1945, the archive-based studies of Renzo de Felice (1929–96) put forward a revisionist interpretation of Italian fascism, which distanced it from German national socialism and emphasized its genuinely revolutionary characteristics and popular appeal. For Felice and his followers, Italy had undergone a civil war between 1943 and 1945, in which the forces of anti-communism aligned themselves against communism. In the course of the 1980s and throughout the 1990s the myths of the resistance, which had underpinned Italian post-war identity to a large extent, were increasingly undermined by historical research. This in turn contributed to a much commented-on national identity crisis exacerbated by the threat of Northern separatism. Historians, by and large, rallied to the defence of the Italian nation against the forces of separatism, especially the Lega Nord (Northern League). Some national histories sought to reclaim specifically the Risorgimento in an attempt to marginalize the legitimacy of the Lega Nord.[21]

In the Federal Republic of Germany (FRG), the historians' controversy erupted in 1985 and focused on the singularity of the Holocaust and the need to renationalize German identity. Conservative–liberal historians, such as Michael Stürmer (b.1938), who acted as a political advisor to Chancellor Helmut Kohl during the 1980s, accentuated the more positive elements of German national history and argued that it was necessary to go beyond the, in his view, almost exclusive attention given to the twelve years of national socialism in German history. Fellow historians such as Ernst Nolte (b.1923) and Andreas Hillgruber (1925–89) relativized the Holocaust by comparing it to the Gulag (in Nolte's case) and the destruction of the 'German east' (in Hillgruber's case). By contrast, critical left-liberal historians, led by the philosopher Jürgen Habermas (b.1929), argued against any renationalization of German national identity and against the apologetic use of history. Instead they championed ideas of constitutional patriotism and post-nationalism.[22] By 1987 it looked as if the left-liberal critical historians, many of whom had initiated the critical turn of national history in the 1960s, had won the day.

However, the historians' controversy had a second instalment after the unexpected reunification of Germany in 1990. Although radical right-wing attempts to re-establish a nationalist paradigm in German historical discourse came to nothing in the first five years after 1990, many of those historians who had warned against renationalizing German historical consciousness in the mid-1980s now changed their tune and sought ways of championing a 'normal' national identity among Germans. Their former conservative–liberal adversaries concluded triumphantly that they had been right all along. Epitomizing the new national consensus in historical writing that emerged in the reunified Germany during the 1990s is Heinrich August Winkler's (b.1938) two-volume national history of modern Germany entitled *Der lange Weg nach Westen* (The Long Road West) which argued that Germans had travelled a tortuous path to bring German national identity into line with 'normal' Western national identity. While both the history of Germany before 1945 and the histories of the divided Germany before 1990 represent deviations from Western 'normality', reunification in 1990 presented the Germans with a unique opportunity to develop 'normal' national identity built on Western understandings of the nation state.[23]

Britain did not escape the trend towards renationalization in the 1980s. Conservative historians in Britain had for some time established a conservative interpretation of Britain's past which had been remarkably successful in permeating British national consciousness.[24] Margaret Thatcher, who had no great interest in history per se, encouraged the heritage mania of the 1980s by making frequent positive references to 'Victorian values' and empire. The epic national historian Arthur Bryant (1899–1985) was a staunch supporter of Thatcher. He

88   *Stefan Berger*

reached mass audiences with his pleas to save the unique national character from the allegedly all-devouring, all-flattening European Union. He depicted the EU as a Brussels monster that was about to extinguish a British national identity. The latter, he argued, had grown organically in centuries.[25] In line with the political mood of the times, Geoffrey Elton (1921–94), Regius Professor of History at Cambridge University, denounced unpatriotic historians and called for a renewed commitment to teaching the glories of English political history.[26] Historians such as Jonathan Charles Douglas Clark (b.1951), Norman Stone (b.1941) and Maurice Cowling (1926–2005) gave the historical profession a distinctly conservative imprint during the 1980s. Corelli Barnett's (b.1927) revisionist histories of war and post war put the emphasis on Britain gambling away its world-power status in return for a flawed welfare state. Ruinous and burdensome, it stood as symbol of the post-war Labour government's failure to modernize Britain and halt the decline of a once great and powerful nation.[27]

Yet the return to national history in Britain was not an exclusively conservative phenomenon. Left-liberal historians, taken by surprise by the strength of popular nationalism in the context of the Falklands war, began to research nationalism and national identity. The History Workshop Movement organized major symposia to explore the phenomenon of patriotism.[28] And in the pages of *Past and Present* David Cannadine (b.1950) started a debate on the meaning of Britishness which was to set the direction of research on British national identity up to today.[29] Linda Colley's (b.1949) publication of *Britons* in 1989 fanned the flames,[30] and ever since, research on questions of British, English, Scottish and Welsh national identity has been going strong.

Much of this research is intent on deconstructing rather than constructing national identity insofar as Britain is concerned. The 'four nations' approach, first championed by Hugh Kearney (b.1924),[31] undermined the British national story rather than strengthening it. Some, like Norman Davies (b.1939), have even gone as far as predicting the imminent break-up of Britain.[32]

The British example demonstrates well the ambivalences of national history writing in Western Europe since the 1980s. On the one hand we observe an attempted renationalization of historical narratives, but on the other we also witness the continuation of a critique of historical national master narratives. It indicates that what has been returning from the 1980s onwards is not the same national history that had been dominant in many national historiographies up until the 1950s. The 1950s was the tail end of a self-confident and homogeneous construction of a proud national history, to which almost every national historian in a given nation state subscribed. From the 1980s, some historians were controversially returning to national history as a possible response to a deepseated feeling of crisis of national identity. Almost everywhere their attempted return was contested by alternative viewpoints continuing the more critical perspectives on national history that developed during the 1960s and 1970s. In Britain, the History Workshop Movement problematized the attempted renationalization. In West Germany, the left-liberal mainstream comprehensively refuted conservatives like Ernst Nolte, Andreas Hillgruber and Klaus Hildebrand (b.1941), even if they subsequently embarked on the search for 'national normality' in the face of German unification in 1990. And in Italy, de Felice's controversial debunking of the resistance was met by the much more measured and differentiated reassessment of the resistance by Claudio Pavone (b.1920).[33]

What national narratives for the twenty-first century?

From what we have said so far, it might appear as though national histories have been on the rise in contemporary Europe and that efforts to counter the renewed success of national histories look forlorn by comparison. However, such a conclusion would wilfully ignore the fact that many of the national histories are no longer nationalist; in fact, many are self-reflective and playful about identity, and they avoid homogenizing tendencies. Irish national history for example has witnessed vigorous debates since the 1970s – with Irish historians questioning the extent of Irish suffering, the levels of British oppression and the effectiveness of Irish resistance to the British, all topics which have been of totemic significance for Irish nationalist narratives.[34] We already referred above to the diverse ways in which the British national narrative has been deconstructed at the same time as other historians revived notions of Britishness. German national history is yet another good example of an historical profession returning to a good deal of national history, but doing so, for good measure, in a highly self-reflexive and self-critical manner.

Other examples of such self-critical and self-reflective forms of national history writing include the French desire to come to terms with the war in Algeria,[35] and the tentative beginnings of problematizing the Francoist past in Spain.[36] Even in Eastern Europe, many of the renationalizing historiographies found it difficult to produce homogeneous national master narratives. Instead, plurality has emerged out of very different attempts to narrate the national history under post-communist conditions. Amid all the nationalist history writing of post-communist Romania, Lucian Boia's (b.1944) work attempted to blur the line between fact and fiction in Romanian national history, thereby calling into doubt the very scientific nature of national history writing on which its authority and political influence was based. His study on the relationship between myth and Romanian national history shows that, depending on place and context, the debunking of national myths remains controversial.[37]

If national history was in large parts more self-critical, it was also challenged by a variety of other histories that concentrated on spaces other than the national ones. Local and regional history had long been in a symbiotic relationship with national history in many parts of Europe. And yet, under the influence of history-from-below approaches and historical anthropology, local history and the history of everyday life have tended increasingly to ignore the national; or rather, these approaches demonstrated how unimportant the national framework, let alone national identity debates, often were for the lives of ordinary people. This new history movement not only sidelined the national; it also shared an understanding as an explicitly transnational movement. Its key

90 *Stefan Berger*

representatives had a strong international orientation and the networks they built were transnational in character.

European history as a form of transnational history also became more and more popular. It was not just the prospect of EU money that led historians to European history; it was also an attempt to understand the history of the 'dark continent'.[38] Especially, the first half of the twentieth century with the two world wars, the Armenian genocide, the Holocaust and ethnic cleansing on an unprecedented scale needed explanation in a European framework, as did the division of the continent and the rise of a peaceful and prosperous Western Europe in the second half of the century. European histories of the twentieth century have as central ingredients notions of breakdown, rebirth and progress, all of them hinged on the date of 1945. The Second World War thus becomes the vanishing point of twentieth century European history, as is immediately evident from the title of Tony Judt's popular *Postwar*.[39] Following Stuart Woolf, many European historians seem to be intent on exploring themes structuring comparative European history from above and from below that would be more than its national histories writ large.[40] Initiatives such as Eustory or Euroclio also are motivated by the attempt to use history to bring Europeans together, prevent conflict and build a common European home on a common understanding of the past – or at least an acceptance of different understandings of the past.[41]

Global and universal historians have been criticizing the Eurocentric perspectives of European historians. Rising to prominence since the 1990s, they questioned traditional spatial entities, such as nations or Europe. Arif Dirlik (b.1940) for example points out that global history is, above all, about showing up the 'historicity, boundary instabilities and internal differences – if not fragmentations – of nations, civilizations, and continents'. Such a global history is problematizing spatial entities as 'products of efforts to bring political or conceptual order to the world – political and conceptual strategies of containment, so to speak'.[42]

World history, by focusing on such themes as migration, mobility, trade, diaspora, travelling and communication has highlighted the hybridity, nomadism and cultural transfer which mark out a good part of the modern human existence. Ideas of homogeneous and stable national cultures have been increasingly undermined by these perspectives. Whereas, during previous eras of globalization, the nation state had been remarkably adept at managing global linkages and accommodating global processes within national storylines, at the beginning of the twenty-first century we are, in the words of Michael Geyer (b.1947) and Charles Bright (b.1943)

> losing our capacity for narrating our histories in conventional ways, outward from one region, but gaining the ability to think world history, pragmatically and realistically, as the interstices of integrating circuits of globalising networks of power and proliferating sites of localising politics.[43]

The current popularity of transnational forms of history writing coincided with major methodological changes in European historiographies. Comparative history, seen as a panacea to the woes of narrow national history ever since Max Weber (1864–1920) and Marc Bloch (1886–1944), increasingly captured the imagination of younger historians.[44] At long last a growing number of historians seemed willing to practise what some of them had preached for a considerable time.

If the return of national history has to be juxtaposed with a range of developments that point away from a national focus of history writing, what is the role of national histories in a twenty-first-century Europe? It is indeed noticeable that many professional historians in Europe today are no longer willing to endorse methodological nationalism. More and more historians turn to comparative and transnational forms of history writing, precisely because they want to overcome such constraints of the national frame. Professional historiography has moved towards a greater concern with distancing the past from identitarian projects.[45] However, historiographical nationalism is far from being a spent force in Europe today. There is no shortage of national histories anywhere, and in many parts of Europe at least some of those national histories still espouse a nationalist message. Even where they do not, the pervasiveness of national history guarantees the propping up of collective national identities and national master narratives.

Therefore it seems all the more necessary to ask ourselves: Can new national history be written in a more subtle, tolerant and self-reflexive form? Can we, in other words, find benign narratives that are a solution to the problem of violent, aggressive and xenophobic narratives? In this respect we find helpful Konrad Jarausch's (b.1941) and Michael Geyer's description of (German) history as a 'broken mirror'.[46] Of course, the image of the 'broken mirror' always carries overtones of nostalgia – nostalgia for the broken parts becoming whole again. Far from being nostalgic about the fact that the mirror is broken, however, we would argue that historical writing about the nation should indeed contribute to the breaking of mirrors. The broken pieces of the mirror provide very different reflections depending on which way the observer looks into the mirror. It is an image which tries to capture positionality and perspectivity and tells the reader that there always are several and contested national histories.

Writing national history in this way is an important step in weakening the link between grand narratives and identity construction. This kind of national history would allow readers (or students in a school class or visitors to a museum exhibition) to see how national narratives are constructed and invites them to reflect which histories they are choosing and why they are doing so. It will produce more heterogeneous, less exclusive and more playful forms of national history, allowing for plurality and even incommensurability of the many stories. In fact, historiography with such a high degree of self-reflexivity would to all intents and purposes fit into and interact easily with more cosmopolitan and transnational perspectives.

Suggested further reading

Key readings are clearly identified throughout the text and discussed: for an introduction, see, in alphabetical order:

92 Stefan Berger

Sorin Antohi, Balazs Trencsényi and Peter Apor (eds), *Narratives Unbound: Historical Studies in Post-communist Eastern Europe* (Budapest: Central European University Press, 2007).

Stefan Berger, *The Past as History: National Histories and National Identities in Modern Europe* (Basingstoke: Palgrave Macmillan, forthcoming 2015).

Stefan Berger and Chris Lorenz (eds), *Nationalizing the Past: Historians as Nation Builders in Modern Europe* (Basingstoke: Palgrave Macmillan, 2010).

David Cannadine, 'British History: Past, Present and Future', *Past and Present* 116 (1987): 169–91.

Eric Hobsbawm, *Nations and Nationalism* (Cambridge: Cambridge University Press, 1990).

Raphael Samuel, *Patriotism – the Making and Unmaking of British National Identity*, 3 vols (London: Routledge, 1989).

Notes

1 This article is based on arguments that I explicate more fully in Chapters 6 and 7 of my book *The Past as History: National Histories and National Identities in Modern Europe* (Basingstoke: Palgrave Macmillan, forthcoming 2015).

2 Eric Hobsbawm, *Nations and Nationalism* (Cambridge: Cambridge University Press, 1990), p. 192.

3 Hobsbawm, *On History* (Cambridge: Cambridge University Press, 1997), p. 5.

4 Hobsbawm, *Nations*, p. 13.

5 Stefan Troebst, '"Budapest" oder "Batak"? Varietäten südosteuropäischer Erinnerungskulturen. Eine Einführung', in Ulf Brunnbauer and Stefan Troebst (eds), *Zwischen Amnesie und Nostalgie. Die Erinnerung an den Kommunismus in Südosteuropa* (Cologne: Böhlau-Verlag, 2007), p. 24 f.

6 Georg G. Iggers, 'New Directions in Historical Studies in the German Democratic Republic', *History and Theory* 28 (1989): 69.

7 Ivan Elenkov, 'The Science of History in Bulgaria in the Age of Socialism: The Problematic Mapping of its Institutional Boundaries', *CAS Working Paper* (2003), p. 12.

8 Árpád von Klimó, 'Helden, Völker, Freiheitskämpfe. Zur Ästhetik stalinistischer Geschichtsschreibung in der Sowjetunion, der Volksrepublik Ungarn und der DDR', *Storia della Storiografia* 52 (2007): 83–112.

9 Catherine Durandin, 'La fonction de l'histoire et le statut de l'historien à l'époque du national-communisme en Roumanie', in Marie-Élizabeth Ducreux and Antoine Marès (eds), *Enjeux de l'histoire en Europe Centrale* (Paris: L'Harmattan, 2002), pp. 103–12.

10 Oliver Schmitt, 'Genosse Aleks und seine Partei oder: Zu Politik und Geschichtswissenschaft im kommunistischen Albanien (1945–91)', in Markus Krzoska and Hans-Christian Maner (eds), *Beruf und Berufung: Geschichtswissenschaft und Nationsbildung in Ostmittel-und Südosteuropa im 19. und 20. Jahrhundert* (Münster: LIT, 2005), pp. 143–66.

11 Aadu Must, '*Estonia*', in Iliana Porciani and Lutz Raphael (eds), *Atlas of European Historiography: The Making of a Profession, 1800–2005* (Basingstoke: Palgrave, 2010), p. 81.

12 Balázs Trencsényi and Péter Apor, 'Fine-Tuning the Polyphonic Past: Hungarian Historical Writing in the 1990s', in Sorin Antohi, Balazs Trencsényi and Peter Apor (eds), *Narratives Unbound: Historical Studies in Post-communist Eastern Europe* (Budapest: Central European University Press, 2007), p. 45.

13 Nenad Stefanov, *Wissenschaft als nationaler Beruf. Die Serbische Akademie der Wissenschaften 1944–1992: Tradierung und Modifizierung nationaler Ideologie*

(Wiesbaden: Harassowitz Verlag, 2011); specifically on Serb suffering and nationalist mobilization see also Florian Bieber, 'Nationalist Mobilisation and Stories of Serb Suffering: The Kosovo Myth from 600th Anniversary to the Present', *Rethinking History* 6 (2002): 95–110.

14 Rainer Lindner, *Historiker und Herrschaft Nationsbildung und Geschichtspolitik in Weißrußland im 19. und 20. Jahrhundert* (Bielefeld: Oldenbourg Wissenschaftsverlag, 1999), pp. 400 ff.

15 Maciej Górny, 'From the Splendid Past into the Unknown Future: Historical Studies in Poland after 1989', in Sorin Antohi, Peter Apor and Balazs Trencsenyi (eds), *Narratives Unbound: Historical Studies in Post-communism Eastern Europe* (Budapest: Central European University Press, 2007), p. 102 f.

16 Xosé Manoel Núñez Seixas, *Historiographical Approaches to Nationalism in Spain* (Fort Lauderdale, FL: Breitenbach, 1993).

17 I am grateful to Jo Tollebeek for pointing this out to me.

18 Ian Donnachie and Christopher Whatley, 'Introduction', in Donnachie and Whatley (eds), *The Manufacture of Scottish History* (Edinburgh: Edinburgh University Press, 1992), p. 1.

19 Fernand Braudel, *The Mediterranean and the Mediterranean World in the Age of Philip II*, 2 vols (Berkeley, CA: University of California Press, 1949; reprint Paris: Armand Colin, 1995).

20 Braudel, *L'Identité de la France*, 2 vols (Paris: Flammarion, 1986).

21 Saverio Battente, 'Nation and State Building in Italy: Recent Historiographical Interpretations', *Journal of Modern Italian Studies* 5 (2000): 310–21 and 6 (2001): 94–105; Silvana Patriarca, 'Italian Neopatriotism: Debating National Identity in the 1990s', *Modern Italy* 6 (2001): 21–34.

22 Richard J. Evans, *In Hitler's Shadow: West German Historians and the Attempt to Escape from the Nazi Past* (London: Pantheon Books, 1989).

23 Stefan Berger, 'Rising Like a Phoenix: The Renaissance of National History Writing in Britain and Germany since the 1980s', in Stefan Berger and Chris Lorenz (eds) *Nationalizing the Past: Historians as Nation Builders in Modern Europe* (Basingstoke: Palgrave Macmillan, 2010), pp. 426–51. For the renationalization of historical consciousness in Germany generally, see Berger, *The Search for Normality: National Identity and Historical Consciousness in Germany since 1800* (Oxford: Berghahn Books, 2007, 2nd edn).

24 Reba Soffer, *History, Historians, and Conservatism in Britain and America: From the Great War to Thatcher and Reagan* (Oxford: Oxford University Press, 2009).

25 Julia Stapleton, *Sir Arthur Bryant and National History in Twentieth-century Britain* (Lanham, MD: Lexington Books, 2006).

26 G.R. Elton, 'The Historian's Social Function', *Transactions of the Royal Historical Society*, 5(27) (1977): 197–211; Elton, *The Future of the Past* (Cambridge: Cambridge University Press, 1984).

27 Corelli Barnett, *The Audit of War: The Illusion and Reality of Britain as a Great Nation* (London: Papermac, 1987); Barnett, *The Lost Victory: British Dreams, British Reality 1945–1950* (London: Macmillan, 1995).

28 Raphael Samuel, *Patriotism – The Making and Unmaking of British National Identity*, 3 vols (London: Routledge, 1989).

29 David Cannadine, 'British History: Past, Present and Future', *Past and Present* 116 (1987): 169–91.

30 Linda Colley, *Britons: Forging the Nation, 1707–1837* (London: Yale University Press, 1994).

31 Hugh Kearney, *The British Isles: A History of Four Nations* (Cambridge: Cambridge University Press, 1989).

32 Norman Davies, *The Isles: A History* (London: Papermac, 2000); a prediction that was, of course, made a long time ago by Tom Nairn, *The Breakup of Britain*

94 *Stefan Berger*

(London: NLB, 1977). See also Nairn, *After Britain: New Labour and the Return of Scotland* (London: Granta, 2000).

33 Claudio Pavone, 'A Civil War', in Stanislao G. Pugliese (ed.), *Fascism, Anti-fascism and the Resistance in Italy, 1919 to the Present* (Lanham, MD: Rowman & Littlefield, 2004), pp. 253–8.

34 Roy Foster, *The Irish Story: Telling Tales and Making it up in Ireland* (Oxford: Oxford University Press, 2002).

35 Benjamin Stora, *Le transfert d'une mémoire. De l'Algérie française au racisme anti-arabe* (Paris: La Découverte, 1999).

36 Nicolás Sartorius and Javir Alfaya, *La Memoria Insumisa* (Madrid: Editorial Critica, 1999).

37 Lucian Boia, *History and Myth in Romanian Consciousness* (Budapest: Central European University Press, 2001).

38 Mark Mazower, *Dark Continent: Europe's Twentieth Century* (Harmondsworth: Penguin, 1998).

39 Tony Judt, *Postwar: A History of Europe since 1945* (Harmondsworth: Penguin, 2005); for a close reading of recent European histories see Jan Ifversen, 'Myths in Writing European History', in S. Berger and C. Lorenz (eds), *Nationalizing the Past: Historians as Nation Builders in Modern Europe* (Basingstoke; New York: Palgrave Macmillan, 2010), pp. 452–79.

40 Stuart Woolf, 'Europe and its Historians', *Contemporary European History* 12 (2003): 323–37.

41 On Eustory see http://www.eustory.eu; on Euroclio see http://www.euroclio.eu, both accessed 15 October 2010.

42 Arif Dirlik, 'Performing the World: Reality and Representation in the Making of World History(ies)', *Bulletin of the German Historical Institute* (Washington, DC) 37 (2005): 9–27, quote from p. 18 f.

43 Michael Geyer and Charles Bright, 'World History in a Global Age', *American Historical Review* 100 (1995): 1058.

44 Berger, 'Comparative History', in Stefan Berger, Heiko Feldner and Kevin Passmore (eds), *Writing History* (London: Bloomsbury, 2009), pp. 187–208.

45 Aleida Assmann, *Geschichte im Gedächtnis. Von der individuellen Erfahrung zur öffentlichen Inszenierung* (Munich: Beck, 2007), p. 185.

46 Konrad H. Jarausch and Michael Geyer, *Shattered Past: Reconstructing German Histories* (Princeton, NJ: Princeton University Press, 2003).

7   History, memory and civic education

Françoise Vergès

History's contribution to civic education and awareness is to alert to the existence of entangled histories, to bring light to the ways in which consent to political and economic systems is fabricated, the ways in which racist representations are created and circulated, and how networks of solidarity come to be. The group of scholars who created 'Historians Against Slavery' have articulated the relation between research and civic education and awareness. They want to 'bring historical context and scholarship to the modern-day antislavery movement in order to inform activism and develop collaborations to sustain and enhance such efforts'. This is also the goal of the Memorial of the Abolition of Slavery in Nantes inaugurated in March 2012, which connects the past history of the anti-slavery struggle with the present.[1]

In times of renewed xenophobia and all forms of discrimination and racism, historians have a duty to show society that the narrative of pure ethnos is a myth, that national history is also, always, global history, that colonial and post-colonial history are global history, that we live in a transnational and interconnected world. If we only look at Europe, we notice that for centuries it was in contact with cultures in Africa, the Americas and Asia. The long history of colonization transformed its arts, its laws, its philosophy, its social and cultural life and its politics. The end of colonial empires did not put an end to the circulations of people, ideas and cultural expressions. We might even talk of ongoing processes of creolization, whereby cultures are meeting and borrowing from each other.

In France, xenophobic impulses have found new ground in the resistance to make sense of the role and place of the colonial past in its post-colonial present. Under the pressure of groups asking for the acknowledgement of a history to which they identify because of family ties, progress has been made to recognize the entangled history and culture of French society with its former colonies. Yet French history remains framed within the borders of the Hexagon. In France, although the history of colonial slavery and post-slavery imperialism has made important progress in recent decades, allowing better understanding about past and present inequalities, racism and asymmetries of power, groups which feel connected to colonized societies still perceive an injustice insofar as republican narrative looks at their history. But in 1962, France reinvented itself within the

96 *Françoise Vergès*

borders of the Hexagon. As Todd Shepard and Kristin Ross have shown the 'invention of decolonization' redrew the borders of France and thus of the Fifth Republic which was born in 1958 out of a colonial war against the Algerians.[2] The Hexagon became the frame within which French history was made (and is still being made), foreclosing both the legacies of colonialism and the continuing French presence across the world in overseas territories inherited from the first (Guiana, Martinique, Guadeloupe, Reunion) and second (New Caledonia, Tahiti and other French territories in the Pacific, Mayotte in the Indian Ocean, St Pierre et Miquelon) colonial empire. Consequently, overseas territories have either disappeared from the French public debate, have come to exist as lands of 'hybridity' and 'Creoleness' or appeared in the news during times of riots or natural catastrophes. Lumped under the category '*outre-mer*', their differences are often ignored. Their regional environment, which has been, and continues to be, so important, is often ignored.

Historians can show that France was never homogeneous, that its colonial history is also the history of connected networks, that its current borders were invented in 1962 with the end of its war against Algerian movement for independence, that poverty is not the result of foreigners stealing jobs but of an economic system with a long history of dispossession. The space of the French Republic today covers many time zones, bringing together peoples who have different languages, religions, cultures and memories that are however not yet fully acknowledged in the republican narrative. Current republican narrative has adopted the model of the colonial exhibition, a centre, Hexagonal France surrounded by satellites around the world. Connected history shows nevertheless that the republican national narrative is a 'mutilating' narrative that excises entire chapters and societies.

Following the paths opened by anti-colonial thinkers and a wide range of recent historiography, I argue for a global, interconnected and transnational history. I look at the French case to explore ways in which history can contribute to civic awareness and education at a time of the renewed instrumentalization of history by advocates of a purified ethnos. History is not there to heal, to absolve or to distribute blame. It is about the unexpected, the unforeseen. It tells history 'from below', of the 'anonymous' and of the powerful. Interconnected macro-history shows that the division of history into well-defined periods masks the legacies and traces of the past in the present. It brings back complexity, grey zones, narratives of betrayal and complicity, indifference and cynicism, subversion and rebellion – in other words, a large range of thoughts and actions.

The path for a connected history had been opened by Fernand Braudel although his project remained heavily biased in the direction of European archives.[3] An interconnected approach challenges binary models (colonial state/ colony; south/north; centre/periphery) and suggests maps and representations of the world that connect Africa and Asia in the eleventh century, or Spain or England to western India in the early seventeenth century. It questions a periodization that reflects a European domination of the world that, however, emerged late (end of the eighteenth, beginning of the nineteenth century).

Finally, it reveals fraught encounters that 'usually did not take place between societies or cultural systems as such' ('Europe' meets 'Africa' or 'Asia') but 'between particular subcultures or segments of societies'.[4]

Before producing examples that illustrate the ways in which history can contribute to civic awareness and education, I would like to describe my first and very concrete encounter with a connected world. I am a Reunionnese; I am from a small island in the Indian Ocean, east of Madagascar. Uninhabited, it became a French colony in the seventeenth century, slaves were brought from Madagascar and East Africa, slavery was abolished in 1848, indentured workers were brought from India, China, Madagascar and Africa, migrants came from Gujarat and China, and colonial settlers from France. In 1946, it became a French department and in the 1980s a European region. From Reunion, it was clear that a compartmentalized approach from French and European colonialism (slavery, colonialism, decolonization and post-colonialism) impoverished the understanding of what had been and what was. Reunion history did not make sense if it was strictly studied in its relation with France. It had to be studied transversally in relation to emergences and developments in the Indian Ocean world and beyond, with flows of people, goods, plants, ideas, languages and beliefs.

Writing history from Reunion (not necessarily as a tangible place but as an archive on slavery, colonialism, accidents of history ...) meant looking at South–South, East–West, East–South exchanges and encounters, at processes of creolization, routes of solidarity across national borders and ethnic groups, circulation of ideas, tastes, images, objects, music, textiles, vernacular medical knowledge, ideas about servitude, freedom, faith and emancipation. Writing from Reunion led to a 'triple consciousness'; local (the island), regional (the Indian Ocean) and global (Europe and the world). It meant looking at local social formations, local tensions and forms of racism, observing how local reactionary and anti-colonial forces had come forth, how new social and cultural classes had emerged after the abolition of slavery (1848), the abolition of colonial status (1946), how new models of consumption had been adopted, how mutations in the region and in France had had an impact, to what extent the French model was hegemonic, and what had been the role of Reunionnese anti-colonial movements.

The colonial republic

In France, established historians such as Pierre Nora have attacked the turn to colonial memories arguing that they threaten their freedom and seek to impose on history a compensatory function for past damages and wrongs. Memory is fickle, subjective and prone to manipulation, they said. Their arguments have merit but it is a known fact that French historians have more than often produced their work in relative ignorance of the history of French colonies and overseas territories. And more than often, historians in French post-colonial territories have embraced republican ideology and adopted its chronology. It may be important to remind them that the second colonial French empire, the

98 *Françoise Vergès*

one that is associated with the French civilizing mission and the conquest of territories all over the world, was constructed under the Third Republic (1871–1940).

In its effort to build a French republican nation, the Third Republic sought to rework or erase memories of colonial atrocities and repression of the working class. It operated a rupture between the Ancien Régime or Bonapartism and the republic, associated republican colonialism with the abolition of slavery (the anti-slavery movement was never a vast social movement and it was never entirely constituted of republicans), scientific progress and bringing light and rights to colonized peoples. The rhetoric of the 'civilizing mission' (bringing French progress, science and education to peoples still caught in tradition and sorcery) was fully deployed against the 'mercantilism' of the British colonial empire. French republican colonialism was generous, secular and bringing progress and science to peoples subjugated by tyrants. Although unity among the colonized was not immediate or spontaneous and settlers did not all adhere to colonial racism, insurrections were always brutally crushed.

The connection between 'the Republic' and colonialism has, however, been refuted by a number of historians.[5] In his *Les empires coloniaux, XIXe-XXe siècle*, Pierre Singaravélou wrote that the notion of 'Colonial Republic' did not acknowledge the heterogeneity of the colonial empire and the plurality of its policies and practices; he added that the colonial empire was never supported by a large social base in the Hexagon.[6] Yet, as Bill Schwarz has remarked, 'To begin to narrate one's own life in the language of empire did not necessarily require obeisance to the full paraphernalia of high empire jingoism'.[7] The lack of a social base in the Hexagon did not hinder the existence in every colony of a French colonial social base founded on a racial divide that transformed French settlers into 'whites'. And heterogeneity was produced in local, regional and global context, not just by the diversity of colonial policies. Finally, heterogeneity went along with a common goal, supporting French economy and maintaining French world power. The plurality of practices and policies in the French colonial empire did not stop the republic from engaging in similar repressive policies regardless of local context or from treating the majority of the colonized with contempt. If periods of repression could be preceded or followed by politics of reform, but the politics of colonization were always in the hands of the Ministry of Marine and the Colonies.

Of course, the army, the government and business had their words to say; but though all these actors could have divergent interests and be at times at odds against each other, they all agreed on the moral superiority of the French civilizing mission and about the fact that colonies had been won to have their resources and populations exploited. Colonial cultural hegemony in France was about winning over hearts and minds to the existence of the colonial empire not by asking for direct support but by producing consent – and consent did not need to be loud. Thus, more important than the creation of a large social base was feeling entitled to sugar, coffee or tobacco regardless of where they came from and consent to the existence of empire as a proof of France's grandeur,

History, memory and civic education 99

even if few French travelled to the colonies or could name them. It was about the feeling of belonging to a great nation of white and free men. Too many French historians still ignore that 'the idea of a white man has less to do with empirical beings – men with pale skin – than with an entire fantasized discursive complex which underwrites its creation'.[8] The politics of consent, which rested on indifference, ignorance or interest, buried the voices of those who protested against French republican colonial politics. They were able to build a counter-force only in the mid-twentieth century.

Since the 1990s, however, memories of slavery and colonialism have been sites from where to challenge the narrative of the white republican bourgeois. An increasing number of festivals, exhibitions, colloquiums and debates have been exploring the role and place of slavery in the making of France, the fabrication of gender and 'whiteness' and the invention of a territory called 'France'. They come in between 1998 and 2012. I was personally engaged in two practices for which history proved very useful as a tool for civic awareness and education. I closely observed the ways in which memories served neither as a ground to write new narratives nor to support hegemonic claims in France and in post-colonial territories. Yet, in alternative revisions, French chronology was rarely challenged nor the binary link between the colonial state and the colony and in this revision of history, each colony was seldom inscribed in its cultural and political region.

One practice was my work around the memories of slavery and colonialism in France, notably as president of the French National Committee for the Memory and History of Slavery (2009–12, vice-president 2004–9) installed in application of the May 2001 Law recognizing slave trade and slavery 'crimes against humanity'. The other was as scientific director of a cultural project in Reunion Island, a museum on the history of its society. I applied a methodology of crossed memories and histories and looked at itineraries that challenged a mutilated cartography of history. For the memories of slavery, the objective was not simply to fill a lack, an absence, or to try to replace negative with positive images, but to question the logic behind an absence, to discern the invisible behind the visible, to show how social life had been permeated by the colonial past and post-colonial present. In Reunion, the objective was neither to recover the history of the island within the frame of French chronology, as historians of Reunion have done, nor to create a Reunion-centred history but rather to inscribe the Reunionnese society within its natural, geographical, cultural and political region, the Indian Ocean, in which Europe has been a late actor. Neither was it about attaching Reunion to one of the 'great civilizations' from which some of its inhabitants' ancestors came – India, France, China – as the ideology of multiculturalism has invited groups in Reunion to do with some success (in this list, Madagascar and Africa were often forgotten). It was about making visible the global flows of people, plants, ideas, goods, languages, gods and goddesses and the genealogy of a connected world. In both cases, it was about how the past meets the present in a dialectical relation to constitute a constellation of meanings.

100 *Françoise Vergès*

To illustrate crossing memories and history in multiple territories and the ways in which they can bring civic awareness to the fabrication of inequalities, racism and legitimacy of dispossession of native peoples, I present two examples. They tell of intertwined histories, trajectories imposed by power, histories of solidarities, lives reconstructed on foreign land with practices, beliefs and knowledge that have transformed local culture. They demonstrate that it is impossible to write the history of colonial slavery without looking at the history of consumption, social status, gender roles, or at larger French colonial politics, the circulation of officers and administrators throughout the colonial empire, or the competition among European powers. It is impossible to write about post-slavery colonialism without looking at the circulation between colonies of convicts, political exiles, at global capitalism, at the new flows of goods, plants, languages, ideas and practices. And finally, it is impossible to write about contemporary France while ignoring the traces of history colonization in its *longue durée*.

The study of the post-colonial present in France (Hexagon and overseas territories) reveals a 'prolific multicentredness' which questions historical causality.[9] Absolute discontinuity (total rupture between two periods) or complete continuity (nothing has changed) would not do. What is needed is to pull different threads together to bring multiple connectedness, differences and similarities. The diverse elements of connected history present a constellation of memories, a 'multidirectional memory', which again challenges the segmentation of history.[10] Reading these events together goes further than giving visibility to forgotten chapters of history; it shows the connection between the army, colonization, land and masculinity, how the colony was fabricated even out of the metropolitan revolutionary, how colonialism divided subalterns, and how the state used blind violence and brutality to impose its power.

Connected histories

Slavery and new forms of colonization

In France, colonial slavery was abolished first in the colony of Saint-Domingue in 1793 following the huge uprising of slaves in August 1791. (The uprising of Saint-Domingue led to victory for the slaves who defeated the Napoleonic armies in 1803, and on 1 January 1804 created the first Black Republic.) On 4 February 1794, slavery was abolished in all French colonies. It was re-established by Napoleon Bonaparte in May 1802. The second and final abolition of slavery in the French colonies occurred on 27 April 1848 under the Second Republic (24 February–10 December 1848). In the republican narrative, a clear separation was made between slavery and post-slavery colonization. The separation created a fictitious rupture insofar as it masked the difficult history of French abolitionism, persisting traces of the *Ancien Régime* and aristocratic culture in the Third Republic (between the Second and Third Republic, there was the Second Empire (1852–70), and the influence of Catholicism in the production of the 'civilizing mission'.

History, memory and civic education 101

If we look at the decree of 27 April 1848 abolishing slavery without looking at connected events in France and in the world, we miss a history of convergent and divergent elements within the global context of emerging new imperialisms. Textbooks tell the story of a colonization moving smoothly from slavery (associated with the *Ancien Régime*) to its abolition (accomplished by the republic) to post-slavery colonization. This is not just to point to the persistence of inequalities and racial hierarchy long after the abolition of slavery in the 'Old colonies' (as colonies which had experienced slavery became known), but to ask how the conditions of the abolition of slavery was considered *along with* concerns about the organization of labour, citizenship and rights in new French colonies.

The conquest of Algeria had started in 1830, *eighteen years* before the abolition of slavery. During these eighteen years, debates on the ways in which working and civic rights would be applied in the colonies (old and new) were the subject of intense debate and they were mixed with debates on civil liberties in France, the agitation of the working class and its repression (June 1848: 10,000 prisoners, 1,500 shot), the brutal crushing of Algerian resistance to colonial conquest, a new bourgeois order, new forms of consumption and the importance of reinforcing the colonial empire in competition with its old rival, England. In the 1840s, France was seeking to establish new colonies in the Pacific (New Caledonia, Tahiti and other islands), in the Indian Ocean (Madagascar, the Comoros islands) and in Asia (Indochina) and West Africa. It was clear that labour in the colonies could no longer be bonded labour. Beet sugar was threatening sugar cane and the colonial sugar lobby was closely following the shift, fighting to keep its privileges. Experimentation with indentured labour had already started in the plantations.

In 1848, the republican government both abolished slavery *and* transformed Algeria into three French departments. Algeria was from then on no longer a 'colony' but a part of France though its Muslim inhabitants were subjected to a specific status. On the other hand, contrary to the Algerians, the inhabitants of post-slavery societies retained colonial status though they had become citizens, had the right to vote and to be elected. They were 'colonized citizens'. The sugar lobby obtained not only compensation for the loss of slave owners' 'private property' (enslaved women and men) but also the right, under the government of Napoleon III and then the Third Republic, to bring from India and China thousands of indentured workers whose conditions of transportation, of living and working, were barely different from those of slaves.

Agreements between French and British imperialism facilitated the second organization on a global scale of a mobile, sexualized and racialized workforce. The first had been the slave trade. The organization of mobility meant a concerted effort from French and British to establish barracks at points of departure and arrival of indentured workers, to instal officers of registry and to ensure that ships would be ready to take their human cargo. The workforce was still sexualized because, as in the slave trade, the ratio was two-thirds men to one-third women. It was racialized because after anti-Black racism in the slave

102 *Françoise Vergès*

trade, new racialized categories appeared to tell the difference between Indian or Chinese 'coolies' and white settlers. Whiteness as a social and cultural marker was reinforced.

In September 1848, following suggestions in 1847 to replace the entire indigenous population in Algeria with settlers, the republican French Assembly voted a budget to support the settlement of 12,000 French, in the future colonial departments, who would receive upon their arrival a piece of land (stolen without compensation from Algerians), a home, cattle, seeds, and food for three years.[11] Army officers, writers and republican politicians were convinced that colonization went along with agriculture and required the twin policies of spoliation and settlement.

Land dispossession, repression of the working class and colonization

A similar interconnectedness brought together in 1871 the Paris Commune, the Algiers Commune, a vast and impressive Algerian insurrection, and New Caledonia. As a detailed history of these events would require a long, complex and careful description, I have chosen to point to the connection between land dispossession, the repression of the working class and colonization.

The 1843, the defeat of Abd el Kader who had led the resistance against the French conquest of Algeria had not put an end to local discontent. Revolts were followed by revolts. On 14 March 1871, a huge rebellion was launched in the east of Algeria. The heir of a long dynasty of local leaders, Muhammad al-Muqrani, raised around 25,000 troops against the French. Emissaries were sent throughout the country and spread the revolt to the eastern Sahara.

In France, the Second Empire, which was fighting Prussia, had been defeated and the new republic (established 4 September 1870) had signed a peace treaty on 26 February in which France lost the provinces of Alsace and Lorraine and agreed to pay 5 million francs to Germany. Republican Parisians took to the streets on 18 March and the Paris Commune was proclaimed on the 26 March. In May, the French leader, Adolphe Thiers, obtained from the German military authorities the agreement to bring back 60,000 soldiers to besiege the Commune. French troops launched their assault on 21 May. At the end of the *Semaine sanglante*, up to 20,000 Parisians were dead, and about 50,000 arrested. A further 4,500 were condemned to deportation to New Caledonia and 3,000 to Algeria. Many died in prison or on the transports.

French armies could now go to reinforce local troops in Algeria. Al-Muqrani was killed on 8 May. Villages and crops were burned, populations massacred, heads of leaders of the insurrection exposed publicly. The French army adopted the policy of General Bugeaud, who had declared in 1844: 'I will burn your villages and your houses; I will destroy your orchards, and you will yourselves be to blame.' Repression was 'an act of implacable revenge', wrote the historian Charles-Robert Ageron.[12] The uprising was finally suppressed in January 1872; one-fifth of the population had perished from hunger, disease and punitive expeditions. A fine of millions of francs was imposed on the population of Kabylie, which was used to pay the French debt to Prussia. Thousands of

Alsatian families were offered land among the 500,000 hectares confiscated without compensation. Overnight, thirty-three Algerian tribes became landless.

The fabrication of the colony went along with forced acquisition of land, spoliation, denial of rights and massacres of the native population. The army, colonization, land and masculinity were linked.

The Algerian insurgents were condemned to deportation to Guiana and New Caledonia. They awaited their departure with their fellow exiles, the Communards. They arrived in New Caledonia where all pre-colonial contracts had been annulled, especially around land ownership. The French colonial powers seized vast parts of land owned by indigenous communities, which they put into reservations (this was the only instance of a creation of reservations in the French colonial empire). Between 1862 and 1870, French land holdings increased from 27,000 to 78,000 hectares. By 1876, the Kanak population had considerably diminished and the French thought their extinction ineluctable. Yet, on 25 June 1878, the Kanak chief Ataï led an insurrection. Algerian exiles and Communards were offered to join the repression. Few accepted. The insurrection was crushed, Ataï taken prisoner and beheaded. His head was taken to France to be studied by scientists who would prove that his brain and the shape of his skull demonstrated 'Kanaks' inferiority'. A total of 5 per cent of the native population was massacred, entire tribes were displaced, and thousands of hectares confiscated for new colonies.

These disparate yet connected events bring together the history of labour, of colonized masculinity, of dispossession and colonial law, of agreements between European imperialisms despite their rivalry, of colonial lobbies and of new diasporic formations. They are not connected because of a coherent and well-planned colonial policy, but by a series of decisions and reactions that bring discrete elements into play.

These two examples show that colonial history is not only global history, but also regional history. A colony cannot be studied only within the frame of the relation to its colonial periphery, but must also pay attention to what is happening in its region (Caribbean, Americas, Indian Ocean, Pacific), to what are the global geopolitics, to the mutations in the global economic system in which its products are caught up, to the transformations of social, ethnic and cultural identities. Even though I have used the term 'Algerians', 'Kanaks', 'French', it is important to pay attention to differences within groups. They are not an indistinct 'mass' but are constituted of individuals even when they constitute themselves as a community. Finally, connected history questions French republican national narrative and its masked connection with the colonial past.

The slave in the Louvre: An invisible humanity

In 2011, for the Paris Triennial, I organized guided visits looking for the enslaved ghost in the Louvre. Created in 1793, the collections of the museum go up to the year 1848 (everything post-1848 being in the Musée d'Orsay). These two dates have particular resonance for the history of slavery in the French

104 *Françoise Vergès*

colonies. In 1793 (29 August) following the 1791 slaves' insurrection, slavery was abolished in the French colony of Saint-Domingue and in 1848 (27 April) slavery was finally abolished in the French colonies. (In May 1802, Bonaparte had rejected the 4 February 1794 abolition in all colonies and had reinstated slavery.) It was interesting to visit the Louvre, whose collection was framed between these two dates, to see how modern slavery had been represented, or not. I explicitly asked for no searching within the collections for representations of the enslaved. The guided visits concerned only the exhibited collections.

It was also important not to confuse representations of Blacks with representations of the enslaved. It is known that from the late 1400s to the early 1600s, Africans living in or visiting Europe during this time included artists, aristocrats, saints, slaves and diplomats. It was in the second part of the nineteenth century that abolitionist propaganda, especially British, popularized the representation of the suffering body of the enslaved and the cruelty of the slave trade and slavery. Art historians of the Louvre pointed out paintings of men smoking pipes, women wearing cotton dresses, still lives with cowries or tropical fruits and landscapes. The first part of the visit was about the history of a product (for example sugar, tobacco, cotton), pulling the thread from representation to history. Visitors heard first about the artists, then from what was represented – an aristocrat wearing cotton, a man smoking a pipe, the portrait of a young Black woman – slave trade and slavery were evoked through the story of tobacco, sugar, cotton, coffee, cowries … ; then a poet, an artist, a writer would freely comment on the painting. The relation between gender and consumption was discussed, sweet sugar with femininity, tobacco with masculinity, prostitution and revolution.

Rather than being about the lives of the enslaved (very few paintings represent them before the second half of the nineteenth century when British abolitionist propaganda made use of visualized representations of slaves' suffering), the guided visits were about the ways in which cultural and social life had been saturated by goods and products whose history brought back the world of colonial slavery. Colonial slavery had deeply and forever affected European taste and consumption, social and cultural life, transformed social gatherings, ways of presenting oneself, of celebrating births and weddings or representations of gender. It went along with a necessary erasure of the conditions of production, of the itineraries and living conditions of those who produced them. Coffee, sugar, cotton, precious woods or indigo were intimately connected with the slave trade and slavery but this connection had to be hidden. The creation of the consumer and its rights – easy access to goods at a reasonable price – required a distance from the producer, a naturalization of the economic system of slavery.

The programme 'The Slave in the Louvre' was about telling the French public that the centuries of slave trade and slavery were not about 'something over there' but about their own society as well, showing how their daily lives had been deeply affected by sugar, tobacco, coffee, cotton, all products of slavery; and talking about the birth of anti-Black racism, how colonial slavery had

History, memory and civic education   105

constructed a division between consumer and producer, and that even though the colonial empire had not visibly been part and parcel of the French social and cultural life, its existence has had impact on their society. 'Slavery is a ghost, both the past and a living presence; and the problem of historical representation is how to represent that ghost, something that is and yet is not', Haitian post-colonial thinker Michel-Ralph Trouillot has written.[13] The programme 'The Slaves in the Louvre: An Invisible Humanity' was about this ghost.

Hence, history was used to show that slave trade and slavery belonged to a global, economic, social and cultural system. It explained why Dutch paintings figured goods and products of slavery so prominently. Indeed, in the seventeenth century, ships sailed from Amsterdam to Africa, Indonesia, Brazil and the Americas and back, creating the basis of a worldwide trading network. Amsterdam became the port of entry into Europe for spices, tobacco and sugar. The 'Golden Age' of the Dutch city rested on slavery and 'free trade'. History could explain how and why the slave trade became the organization on a global scale of a mobile, precarious, racialized and sexualized workforce. It brought back the importance of the Treaty of Utrecht (1713) because for the first time, a transnational treaty spoke of an 'idea of Europe'. The work of two European thinkers (English and French), Abbé de Saint-Pierre and Charles d'Avenant, were important in its wording. In 1697, d'Avenant argued that '[i]n a trading nation, the bent of all the laws should tend to the encouragement of commerce, and all measures should be there taken, with a due regard to its interest and advancement'. The two pillars of free trade were the plantation in the Western colonies and free trade in the Eastern trading posts.

> The wealth England had once, did arise chiefly from two articles: 1st, Our plantation trade. 2ndly, Our East-India traffic. The plantation trade gives employment to many thousand artificers here at home, and takes off a great quantity of our inferior manufactures. The returns of all which are made in tobacco, cotton, ginger, sugars, indico, etc. by which we were not only supplied for our own consumption, but we had formerly wherewithal to send to France, Flanders, Hamburgh, the East Country and Holland, besides what we shipped for Spain and the Streights, etc.

Bonded labour and free trade were connected. In his *Project for Perpetual Peace in Europe* first published in 1712, Abbé de Saint-Pierre argued that a confederation resulting from a contract and a balance of power among European rival powers would allow the '[p]owers of Europe to form a sort of system among themselves, which unites them by a single religion, the same international law, morals, literature, commerce and a sort of equilibrium'.[14]

The treaty spoke of the necessity of establishing peace 'for the perpetual tranquillity of the whole Christian world', the need for 'an universal perpetual peace' and for 'securing the tranquillity of Europe by a balance of power'. It was a truly political programme with geopolitical consequences; it gave Europe the power to decide over international affairs in order to preserve a peace it had

106 *Françoise Vergès*

unilaterally decided to be universal. It asked European powers to forget the wrongs and damages that they had inflicted upon each other. Forgetting crimes at home served two goals: preserving European unity against common external enemies and turning a blind eye to crimes committed outside of Europe by a European power. Although Europe remained divided, its unity meant that European powers agreed that each could freely dispose of the spoils of its conquest. The fiction of the unity of Europe was important to maintain hegemony abroad. The new global order involved deporting captured and enslaved Africans, the pacification of First Nations, and working out internal European competition for the larger objective of preserving European global interests.

Finally, the treaty gave the *asiento* to England (the monopole of slave trade with the Spanish colonies) opening the way for the country to become the eighteenth-century global maritime power and the first slave trader. It gave a boost to the European slave trade, whereas between 1630 and 1640, between 20,000 and 30,000 Africans were taken per year as slaves to European colonies; between 1740 and 1840, the number increased to between 70,000 and 90,000 per year. During the European eighteenth century inaugurated by the Treaty of Utrecht, 60 per cent of the total African captives were deported. The connection between, on the one hand, the demand for goods, precious woods, precious stones, extraction of minerals, or the construction of palaces, fortresses ... and on the other, the necessity to enslave, is not, however, specific to colonial slavery. What colonial slavery did introduce was the idea that wealth rests on the capacity to move a workforce around and making it disposable.

Colonial slavery also contributed to the fabrication of 'whiteness' in Europe. The construction of 'Whites' vs 'Blacks' and of anti-Black racism does not belong only to the history of the colony or of the post-slavery empire. It is anchored in colonial slavery. In the eighteenth century, Europe had its own racialized minorities but the slave trade gave new meaning to racial hierarchy. In the case of France, the decrees taken to regulate the persons of African origin in France bring light to the history of whiteness. On 13 July 1315, the King of France had declared that 'the soil of France frees the slave that touches it' (*le sol de France affranchit l'esclave qui le touche*). France became a land of *free men* (not yet 'Whites'). In 1685, the *Code Noir* set a series of provisions to govern the lives of the enslaved in the French colonies. Poor French settlers brought as indentured workers became 'Whites' with the consolidation of slavery.

At the beginning of the seventeenth century, between 5,000 and 7,000 people of African origin were living in France, mostly in Paris, occupying different positions, as slaves, domestics, workers, craftsmen, tailors, seamstresses, musicians and so on. In 1694, the first limitations on the entry of slaves were issued. In October 1716, new provisions limited more severely the entry of slaves and for the first time, marriage between Blacks and Whites was forbidden. (In the colonies, it was forbidden by the *Code Noir*.) A slow shift began to make being Black and being enslaved synonymous. In August 1777, the *Police des Noirs* was created which forbade the entry of any Black, free or enslaved, into France. Colour became the fundamental marker.[15] Freed Blacks or *métis* had to carry a permit; arrested without them, they were imprisoned in barracks set up in every French port until they were expelled to a colony regardless of their preferred destination. On 5 April 1778, marriage between Blacks and Whites was rigorously forbidden. The French Revolution abolished these provisions but they were re-established by Napoleon in March 1802 along with slavery.

The guided visits 'The Slaves in the Louvre' made use of history to reflect on the impact of slavery *in* France, displacing the gaze from the colony to the periphery. The absence of the figure of the enslaved, or the ways in which he or she was represented, was not the focus of the visits.

History and civic education

Against the current abuse of history to support xenophobic and nativistic claims in Europe and the world, history is needed more than ever. Groups whose history has been marginalized or ignored are demanding recognition and inscription. The fact that their demands led to intense debate or controversy reveals that what is at stake goes beyond the discipline of history. The past acts as a fantastic reservoir of memories and experiences from which to draw on sources to consider the present and imagine the future. 'Ignorance is no excuse for inaction. Getting involved begins with education', historians against slavery have written. There is work to do.

Suggested further reading

Most key readings are clearly identified throughout the text and discussed. See in chronological order the works of:

K.N. Chaudhuri, *Asia Before Europe: Economy and Civilization of the Indian Ocean from the Rise of Islam to 1750* (Cambridge: Cambridge University Press, 1990).

John Thorton, *Africa and Africans in the Making of the Atlantic World, 1400–1800* (Cambridge: Cambridge University Press, 1998).

Kenneth Pomeranz, *The Great Divergence: China, Europe, and the Making of the Modern World Economy* (Princeton, NJ: Princeton University Press, 2000).

Sybille Fischer, *Modernity Disavowed: Haiti and the Cultures of Slavery in the Age of Revolution* (Durham, NC: Duke University Press, 2004).

Mélica Ouennoughi, *Les déportés maghrébins en Nouvelle-Calédonie et la culture du palmier dattier (1864 à nos jours)* (Paris: L'Harmattan, 2005).

Ehud R. Toledano, *As If Silent and Absent: Bonds of Enslavement in the Islamic Middle East* (New Haven, CT: Yale University Press, 2007).

Joachim Radkau, *Nature and Power: A Global History of the Environment* (Cambridge: Cambridge University Press, 2008).

Emmanuel Laurentin (ed.), *À quoi sert l'histoire aujourd'hui?* (Paris: Bayard, 2010).

Simon Gikandi, *Slavery and the Culture of Taste* (Princeton, NJ: Princeton University Press, 2011).

Emma Rothschild, *The Inner Life of Empires: An Eighteenth-century History* (Princeton, NJ: Princeton University Press, 2011).

108 *Françoise Vergès*

Enzo Traverso, *L'histoire comme champ de bataille. Interpréter les violences du XXe siècle (Paris: La Découverte, 2011).*

Pankaj Mishra, *From the Ruins of Empire: The Revolts Against the West and the Remaking of Asia* (London: Penguin Books, 2012).

Catherine Molineux, *Faces of Perfect Ebony: Encountering Atlantic Slavery in Imperial Britain* (Cambridge, MA: Harvard University Press, 2012).

Nico Slate, *Colored Cosmopolitanism: The Shared Struggle for Freedom in the United States and India* (Cambridge, MA: Harvard University Press, 2012).

Edward A. Alpers, *The Indian Ocean in World History* (Oxford: Oxford University Press, 2013).

Jonathan Curry-Machado (ed.), *Global Histories, Imperial Communities, Local Interactions* (Basingstoke: Palgrave Macmillan, 2013).

Françoise Vergès (ed.), *Exposer l'esclavage: Methodologies et pratiques* (Paris: L'Harmattan, 2013).

Christophe Granger (ed.), *À quoi pensent les historiens? Faire de l'histoire au XXIe siècle* (Paris: Autrement, 2013).

Greg Grandin, *The Empire of Necessity: Slavery, Freedom and Deception in the New World* (New York: Holt & Company, 2014).

Notes

1 http://www.historiansagainstslavery.org and http://www.memorial.nantes.fr, accessed 14 August 2014.
2 Todd Shepard, *The Invention of Decolonization* (Ithaca, NY: Cornell University Press, 2008); Kristin Ross, *Fast Cars, Clean Bodies: Decolonization and the Reordering of French Culture* (Cambridge, MA: MIT Press, 1996).
3 Fernand Braudel, *The Mediterranean and the Mediterranean World in the Age of Philip II*, vols I & II (Berkeley, CA: University of California Press, 1996).
4 Sanjay Subrahmanyam, *Courtly Encounters: Translating Courtliness and Violence in Early Modern Eurasia* (Cambridge, MA: Harvard University Press, 2012), p. xiv.
5 Nicolas Bancel, Pascal Blanchard and Françoise Vergès, *La République coloniale; Essai sur une utopie* (Paris: Albin Michel, 2003).
6 Pierre Singaravélou (ed.), *Les empires coloniaux XIXe-XXe siècle* (Paris: Seuil, 2013).
7 Bill Schwarz, *Memories of Empire, vol 1. The White Man's World* (Oxford: Oxford University Press, 2011), p. 15.
8 Schwarz, *Memories of Empire*, p. 20.
9 Frank Perlin, *Unbroken Landscape. Commodity, Category, Sign and Identity: Their Production as Myth and Knowledge from 1500* (Aldershot and Brookfield, VT: Variorum, 1994), p. 52.
10 Michael Rothberg, *Multidirectional Memory: Remembering the Holocaust in the Age of Decolonization* (Stanford, CA: Stanford University Press, 2009).
11 Mostefa Lacheraf, *L'Algérie, nation et société* (Paris: François Maspéro, 1965).
12 Charles-Robert Ageron, *Histoire de l'Algérie contemporaine, 1830–1966.* (Paris: Armand Colin, 1991).
13 Michael-Rolph Trouillot, *Silencing the Past: Power and the Production of History* (Boston: Beacon Press, 1997), p. 147.
14 From Abbé de Saint-Pierre, *Projet pour rendre la paix perpétuelle en Europe*. Full text: http://www.archivesdefrance.culture.gouv.fr/action-culturelle/celebrations-natio nales/recueil-2013/litterature-et-sciences-humaines/publication-du-projet-pour-rendre-la- paix-perpetuelle-en-europe, accessed 14 August 2014, my translation. See also Céline Spector, 'Montesquieu, critique du projet de paix perpétuelle?', in Jean Mondot and

Christian Taillard (eds), *Montesquieu et l'Europe* (Bordeaux: Académie Montesquieu, 2006), pp. 139–75 and 'Le projet de paix perpétuelle: De Saint-Pierre à Rousseau', in *Principes du droit de la guerre, Écrits sur la paix perpétuelle* (Paris: Jules Vrin, 2008), pp. 229–94.

15 Jean-François Niort, *Le Code Noir* (Paris: Dalloz, 2012).

8 'Different and better times'?

History, progress and inequality

Emily Robinson[1]

A great deal of recent academic work (my own included) has put forward the idea that we are living in an age of 'presentism', cut adrift from the great emancipatory and nationalist narratives of history. Instead, we look to the past not as a guide, but as an open-ended source of inspiration; a dressing-up box where we can find whatever form of historical identity we choose. 'Pastness' here has cultural cachet but no ability to bind or limit us. Rather than making us the end product of a linear narrative of development, this way of using the past allows us to be, in Peter Mandler's words, 'artists of our own becoming'.[2]

This is a compelling account of the uses of the past in an age of what has been called 'liquid modernity'.[3] It is fluid, unstructured, malleable. On the one hand, this has radical potential. In 1991 Keith Jenkins expressed the hope that recognizing history 'as what it is, a discursive practice that allows present-minded people(s) to go to the past, there to delve around and reorganise it appropriately to their needs' might create the space for 'fresh insights' to emerge about aspects of the past 'that have previously been overlooked or sidelined'. Jenkins believes this could 'actually make emancipatory, material differences to and within the present'.[4] On the other hand, as Tristram Hunt has argued more recently, it has left us without the necessary frameworks to critique historical and political structures. Hunt is particularly critical of the way in which traditional social history – with its 'social purpose, analytical relevance and contemporary relevance' has been replaced by an individual 'quest for identity and empathy' within a past that has become 'an attractive and lucrative media commodity'.[5]

The point I would like to make in this chapter is that contemporary uses of the past are not quite as free-floating as they appear. While the grand narratives of both left and right may have broken down, a more fundamental belief in Progress-with-a-capital-P persists and is embedded in many of the ways in which we encounter historical narratives in both daily life and as leisure activity. However, this progress is imagined as something that has already been achieved. It is the means by which we arrived at the present moment – with social discrimination, absolute poverty and the class system seemingly having dissolved along the way. But unlike grand narrative history, it does not point forward to an imagined future destiny. Indeed, as we will see, the idea that progress has gone 'too far' is also common. This militates against the radical emancipation looked for by Jenkins.

For instance, and as Hunt points out, an interest in the lived experiences of poverty and inequality is now a part of mainstream popular culture. The 'new heritage' sites invite us to explore the lives of working people, whether through industrial heritage exhibits or by foregrounding the 'below stairs' areas of country houses, while the experiences and hardships of 'ordinary people' also form the mainstay of 'living history' TV. All this invites us to confront and to condemn the inequality of previous ages, but, as Hunt recognizes, it has none of the political effect of the social history of the 1960s and 1970s, having replaced analyses of structure and agency with personal encounters with the past. Yet I would suggest that this focus on the individual (on how *I* would have coped in *their* shoes) is far from apolitical. And it is not just the personal aspect of these encounters that matters, it is also their 'pastness'. The fascination lies in the very difference between past and present. This works to convey a simple narrative with serious political consequences, namely that 'the past' was marked by structural inequality and the present, in contrast, is not.

The idea that a generic 'past' can serve as a repository of social ills is not new. Billie Melman's study of the *Uses of History* highlighted the extent to which nineteenth- and early twentieth-century ideas of history-as-progress ran alongside an 'uneasy', 'uncosy' sense of the past, defined more by Madame Tussaud's Chamber of Horrors than by edifying histories of constitutional freedoms.[6] Not only does this characterization of the past as a repository of 'horrors' persist – the success of the *Horrible Histories* franchise only being the most visible manifestation[7] – but I would suggest that this is, in important ways, inextricably connected to narratives of progress. The gruesome nature of the past dramatically counterpoints the civilization of the present. Whether we are marvelling at the rudimentary toilet facilities in a reconstructed farm worker's cottage, ridiculing the patrician arguments of anti-suffrage campaigners or condemning institutional child abuse as something that happened 'in the 1970s', we are also drawing a clear and congratulatory distinction between those periods and our own.

Some interesting recent work on the heritage industry has shown that although visitors are not the passive consumers that critics in the 1970s and 1980s feared, the distancing sense of pastness does have a depoliticizing effect. For instance, Bella Dicks's study of visitors to the Rhondda Heritage Park, based in a disused colliery, showed that many visitors are able to filter out messages about contemporary struggles. One couple, with family roots in the local mining industry, were clearly shocked by the extent to which 'the gentry were making money out of the poor old working class of the mines ... The big wigs, and Lord Bute, or whatever his name was. Built all these houses off the backs of the workers'. They therefore viewed protest against the inequities of the past as 'legitimate' and 'necessary' but clearly distinguished that from contemporary industrial action, which 'isn't in the same class'. Significantly, when asked whether the Park had revealed much about contemporary mining, one of the pair commented that

112   *Emily Robinson*

'Obviously, people aren't interested in that. I mean people want to know the heritage part of it and what happened 50, 100 years ago down the mines. I don't think I'd be interested really in the modern'.[8] Similarly, Laurajane Smith has found that visitors to country houses are well aware of the houses' connections with slavery and social inequity but that an overwhelming proportion feel 'comfortable' about this (that is the word they most frequently use), because it is now 'history'.[9]

There is clearly a self-congratulatory element to the belief that inequality is not relevant in the present, which many museums are keen to counteract. So the International Museum of Slavery in Liverpool has been very clear from the outset that the story of slavery does not end in nineteenth-century America but incorporates both contemporary slavery and the lasting legacy of the slave trade into its exhibits and events. Many of the commemorative events around the bicentenary of abolition in 2007 also sought to draw this connection. However, Smith found that visitors (particularly white Britons) were able to 'insulate' themselves from such messages, by drawing on narratives of temporal progress, the two most frequent tropes being 'It was a long time ago, you cannot turn back the hands of time' and 'the morals of the time were different then'. Over 50 per cent of the visitors she interviewed were 'unaware or uninterested' in the contemporary issues; another 20 per cent were 'aware but not engaged' and only 10 per cent were 'active in considering them'. Smith also found that the idea of apologizing for the slave trade 'often elicited agitated responses, this agitation frequently revealing the extent to which some respondents were confronted by the exhibitions'.[10]

The question of apologizing for the past raises a host of political and philosophical questions. The agitation felt by Smith's interviewees seemed to be associated with the sense that to apologize would be to concede that contemporary Britons are implicated in the injustices of the past. Not only might this carry tangible burdens of reparation, but it also seems to disregard the distance between past and present, to undermine the progress that has been made. David Cameron asserted in 2007 that he did not believe 'one generation can meaningfully apologise for something that a previous generation did'.[11] Of course, Smith's interviewees had chosen to visit exhibitions dedicated to the history of the slave trade and its abolition. They were neither ignorant of nor uninterested in *past* injustice, but preferred to separate this from their understanding of the contemporary world. Yet, apologies can also work to do exactly this. They provide a neat way of reinforcing our sense of ourselves as humane and enlightened; we are able to apologize because we are better than our predecessors. Tony Blair's not-quite-apology in November 2006 for the slave trade was a particularly explicit example of this, managing both to condemn the past and isolate it completely from an unproblematic present:

> It is hard to believe that what would now be a crime against humanity was legal at the time. Personally I believe the bicentenary offers us a chance not just to say how profoundly shameful the slave trade was – how we

History, progress and inequality 113

condemn its existence utterly and praise those who fought for its abolition, but also to express our deep sorrow that it ever happened, that it ever could have happened and to rejoice at the different and better times we live in today.[12]

A similar impetus seemed to underpin the posthumous pardons of both Alan Turing, chemically castrated for homosexuality in 1952–4, and the soldiers shot for desertion during the First World War. They were not pardoned for their crimes, but for having lived in an age when their actions were considered criminal. The Turing pardon was made particularly problematic because – as gay rights campaigners were quick to point out – it was only applied to a celebrated individual, to the exclusion of the 'ordinary' men who had received the same treatment. It seemed to be a way of rescuing Turing from his historical context in order to place him more straightforwardly in a story of national achievement. The pardon therefore relied upon not only contrasting what Justice Minister Chris Grayling described as the 'unjust and discriminatory' attitudes of the 1950s with their implicit inverse in 2014,[13] but also of presenting the latter as the embodiment of ahistorical, universal liberal values.

The more usual treatment of gay rights in Britain is, as Robert Mills observed of the 2006 'Queer is Here' exhibition at the Museum of London, a linear timeline beginning with the decriminalization of male homosexuality in 1967 and ending in the present day – in this case the launch of the second lesbian, gay, bisexual and transgender (LGBT) History Month in 2006;[14] now it would most likely run to the Marriage (Same-Sex Couples) Act 2013. Historians and theorists have tried to disrupt this narrative, pointing out that it misrepresents historical understandings of sexuality and promotes a culturally specific version of sexual mores, which circumscribes as much as it permits.[15] Indeed, it has been possible for Conservative politicians to explain their support for the 2013 Act in terms of conserving the institution of marriage and the family values it enshrines.

Yet we should not ignore the extent to which the idea of linear temporal progress has proved useful for campaigners – metaphors of 'roads' and 'milestones' being particularly common. The idea that equal marriage would be 'appropriate in Britain in 2010–11' was widespread.[16] As Nick Clegg put it, 'in this day and age I think most people think "come on, let's move with the times."'[17] The benefit of such arguments is that – however prescriptive – they are at least open-ended and leave the way open for new directions to come to seem 'inevitable' in the future. Of course, this was the fear of Conservative opponents of the Bill, who worried that the road was circular rather than linear and would inevitably take us 'back' to incest, polygamy and/or bestiality. Yet these critics themselves were placed within a temporal framework by which they were imagined as 'dinosaur[s]'.[18]

In the case of socio-economic inequality, the idea of progress has been more pernicious. Rather than presenting an ongoing journey marked by individual victories, the road seems already to have reached its end, or even, as we will see

114   *Emily Robinson*

below, journeyed beyond it. This is what enables condemnation of (or condescension towards) intolerant or inequitable attitudes in previous eras to sit alongside the acceptance of continuing, and even deepening, inequality in the political present. This dynamic is explicit in the narrative structure of the various 'living history' TV series, developed from the late 1990s by production company Wall to Wall. Their flagship 2001 BBC series, *Who Do You Think You Are?* (*WDYTYA?*) clearly has a levelling message: focusing on the lived experience of ordinary people, highlighting the prevalence of migration and racial mixing in Britain's past, and showing that even today's celebrities have humble roots. However, this last point means that it is inevitably predicated on the gap between past and present. The producers emphasize that most celebrities are first generation and so – for the purposes of a genealogy programme – are themselves 'ordinary people', with 'ordinary' family trees. They are descended from the same mixture of fame, infamy and obscurity as the rest of us. While this is clearly true, focusing on people who have transcended their backgrounds reinforces an idea of linear social progress. The tears, the realization, the sympathy all spring from the discovery of how tough things were 'back then' and the contrast with the celebrity's current situation. Poverty, discrimination, shame are therefore seen to be resolutely 'of the past'.

This problem is not exclusive to *WDYTYA?* In historical reality TV shows – again pioneered by Wall to Wall – the drama comes from the supposedly privileged and pampered citizens of modern Britain undergoing the hardships of the past. While these programmes may be asking us (and the participants) to identify personal and emotional continuities across time, the economic and social situation is conceived as entirely other. So outrage over historic inequalities does not translate into outrage in the present. The first of these programmes, *1900 House* (Channel 4, 1999) was predicated on the difficulty of giving up both the material comforts and the social equality of modern life in exchange for the privations and inequalities of the past. This was particularly apparent in the programme's treatment of gender and class. As Joyce, the mother, explained, 'Before I went to the 1900 House, I wasn't particularly a feminist. I wouldn't say I was that kind of a person.' It was due to the experience of discovering 'that so very recently, within the last 100 years, women's lives were so different to how they are today … it suddenly became more important'. Similarly, when the family employed a maid-of-all-work, this was presented as a squeamish subject for the family (and, by implication, their audience) who were unused to participating in such inequitable social arrangements. However, the maid, Elizabeth, was herself a third-generation cleaner. While she noted that '[f]or once in my life it did make me feel that I was under the Bowlers, that I was of a different class', there was no attempt to interrogate this statement or to compare the class-dynamics governing the life of a cleaner in 1999 with those faced by a maid-of-all-work in 1900. Any elements of continuity here were downplayed in favour of presenting the past as entirely alien to the present.

The implicit assumption is that *now* life is good. Absolute poverty, restrictive social relations, and classed and gendered inequality are all things of the past.

History, progress and inequality 115

To take an example from a rather more traditional form of TV history, Andrew Marr's series and books, *A History of Modern Britain* and *The Making of Modern Britain* make this point very well. One of the heroes of the first episode of the second series (confusingly the first chronologically) is Seebohm Rowntree. His realization that the poor were victims is taken as one of the stages en route to today's civilization. Marr invites us to condemn the Victorian and early Edwardian tendency to lay the blame on 'thriftless, drunken or immoral people'.[19] Our concepts of 'deserving' and 'undeserving' poor now place pre-welfare state Britons firmly in the 'deserving' camp, victims of time and history as much as of economics. And in sympathizing with them, we are implicitly drawing a favourable distinction between ourselves and the middle classes of their own time.

In the first book, dealing with more recent history, Marr had established that genuine hardship was abolished by the welfare state, and inequality caused by social class disappeared at some point in the late 1950s – when, as he confidently asserted, 'A Country of Cliques is Over'.[20] This story continued into the Blair years, when '[d]espite the growth of the super-rich, overall equality slightly increased'. Although Marr acknowledged 'Not everyone, of course, was invited to the party' and noted that the number of children living in relative poverty tripled between 1979 and 1997, this was presented as part of an overall story of progress: they are not 'physically worse off than the children of the late seventies, since the country generally became much richer'.[21] Victorian and Edwardian inequality provided the backdrop against which this story of social and economic progress made sense. While Marr invited us to be outraged over historic inequalities, he reassured us that there is no need to carry this forward into the present. The idea that we have progressed beyond the unjust social structures of the past leaves the individual in contemporary society apparently culpable for his or her own misfortune.

The current discourse on food banks is an excellent example of this. On the one hand is the idea that poverty and inequality are 'Dickensian', that they belong to the past and any return to them is deeply shocking. On the other, the disbelief that such conditions could be experienced in the present day leads to condemnations of the poor themselves in terms strikingly similar to that of the 'undeserving poor' in the nineteenth century. Yet it is precisely because we no longer live in those conditions that today's poor are seen to be undeserving. As one comment below an article in the *Hull Daily Mail* explained, 'nobody today needs to go without bread and milk unless they are vagrants outside of the safety net'.[22] The very narrative of progress seems to undermine support for contemporary attempts to address socio-economic inequality; not only because it allows us to be complacent about the present, but because it also makes available the argument that we have progressed 'too far', that too many concessions have been made and barriers removed.

A recent survey carried out by the Joseph Rowntree Foundation found that attitudes alarmingly like those attacked by their Edwardian founder not only persist but are becoming more entrenched. In particular they found highly judgemental attitudes towards the unemployed and an increasing tendency to label benefit recipients as 'scroungers'. This was in contrast with sympathy for the working poor, carers, the elderly and disabled – today's 'deserving poor'. When respondents were asked to consider the reasons why children are in poverty in Great Britain, the most frequent responses were all personal rather than structural – parents not wanting to work, alcoholism, broken relationships. Similarly the survey found that respondents tended to give highly individual and anecdotal responses to questions about life chances.[23]

To quote the report, there is 'a widespread belief about the availability of opportunity, resulting in highly individualised explanations of unequal outcomes'; these tend to emphasize hard work and effort. A total of 69 per cent agreed that '[o]pportunities are not equal in Britain today, but there is enough opportunity for virtually everyone to get on in life if they really want to. It comes down to the individual and how much you are motivated'.[24] These findings are echoed by the longitudinal British Social Attitudes (BSA) survey and show that despite the belief that the gap between rich and poor is too great and that government should reduce it, hostility to helping the poorest, including the unemployed, is not only high but has increased over time. Pride in the welfare state remains high (only 15 per cent of respondents to the BSA 2011 disagreed that it was 'one of Britain's proudest achievements'[25]), but is coupled with the belief that it is going too far, that welfare payments are too high and discourage recipients from finding work. Although 57 per cent of respondents agreed with this sentiment in 2013 – down from 62 per cent in 2011 – it is nevertheless still high in comparison with 24 per cent in 1993 and 35 per cent in 1983.[26]

There are two not quite contradictory beliefs at work here. First is the belief that we now live in a fairly equal society; we have progressed beyond the absolute poverty and brute inequality of the past and should be thankful for that – hence the pride in the welfare state. The idea that we have progressed beyond class is particularly pervasive. It is striking that nearly all of the respondents to the Rowntree survey placed themselves in the middle of the income scale, despite being drawn from a very wide range of socio-economic backgrounds. The roots of this belief lie in the post-war years when, as Lawrence Black and Hugh Pemberton have pointed out, the affluent society created the perception, if not the reality, of classlessness.[27] The lived experience of affluence, of declining deference, and of (limited) social mobility override the knowledge that deep structural inequalities not only remain but may again be increasing.

This faith in the levelling effect of historical progression perhaps underpins the resistance to government intervention to reduce inequality. However, the second belief at work is the rather less comfortable, not quite acknowledged sense that inequality has actually been a driver of historical progress. This is what underpins the fear that we are now going 'too far', and rewarding the wrong kinds of behaviour, that 'If welfare benefits weren't so generous people would learn to stand on their own two feet'.[28] Charles Moore in the *Telegraph* even attacked Andrew Marr's portrayal of Seebohm Rowntree,

History, progress and inequality **117**

asking 'Might Rowntree's idea that "the poor are victims" have helped produce the dependency culture which even people on the Left now recognise is a moral disaster?'[29]

It is significant that inequality at the top end of the income scale has generally been seen as far less of a problem than that at the bottom. In fact, it is often seen as a positive good in that it both drives economic development and provides an incentive for success.[30] This may be changing. The 2009 Rowntree study did find that attitudes to inequality at the top had hardened in response to the financial crisis, with their later focus groups being more inclined to support the idea of a maximum wage and a higher top rate of tax. But this was still minimal in comparison with judgemental attitudes towards the poorest.[31]

One particularly interesting example of the way in which these two beliefs play across one another was seen in a three-part Channel 4 series screened in August 2013, *Benefits Britain 1949*. Developing out of the *1900 House* format but with far more punitive intentions, this was one of a string of programmes developed by production company Twenty Twenty, with titles such as *That'll Teach 'Em* and *Never Did Me Any Harm*, which use historical comparison as a form of comeuppance for today's 'overprotected, apathetic' young people.[32] The past here functions both as a repository of 'horrors' and as a way of critiquing the softer values of the present. The premise of *Benefits Britain 1949* was that a return to the conditions of the 'original' welfare state would cut through debates about the 'crisis' of the welfare state and 'point a way out of this current mess'.[33] Much of the media commentary surrounding the series was black and white – for the *Daily Mail* the series was 'not just compelling television', but 'a revelation',[34] while *The Guardian* saw it as an excuse 'to bother and berate people on some flimsy historical premise until they burst out crying'.[35] However, the programme makers' attitude to the past was rather more grey.

Teaching the 'undeserving' a lesson was a clear theme of the series, as was the idea that many welfare recipients would be better served by a rather tougher form of compassion, underpinned by the capacity to provide full employment. But so also was the sense that the moralism, racism and parsimony of 1949 were best left behind. In the final summary of the first episode, one of the 'Welfare Enforcement Officers' asked, 'Although we're more compassionate today, do we want to maintain that, or do we want to get tougher on claimants?' Of course, this implicitly underscores the popular (mis)perception of the contemporary welfare system as unequivocally generous and compassionate to undeserving claimants. Yet her colleague countered, 'Today, cuts are being made to the welfare budget. Do we want to take this money from the most vulnerable? We've seen what happened to Melvyn [a pensioner] in 1949; would we want to see this happen again?' The general message seemed to be that while social progress is evident and should be celebrated, it had also gone 'too far' in coddling ungrateful and undeserving beneficiaries.

It is striking that all of these newer programmes that use ideas about the past explicitly to critique the values of the present, locate this past in the post-war years. This is when, as we saw with Andrew Marr's series, the worst

118   *Emily Robinson*

socio-economic inequities of history are seen to have been eradicated – at least in Britain. They therefore leave open the possibility of praising progress up to that point, while questioning its development since then. We come here to a different idea of inequality – visible from the late 1940s but growing in intensity from the 1970s. This is the idea that the welfare state system created new injustices by allowing some to take while others gave, that it discriminated against the hard working and rewarded the lazy. This is the means by which the idea that the welfare state had gone 'too far' gained popular currency and how ideas about social justice came to be replaced by those which spoke instead of just desserts.[36]

Despite these fears, a basic faith that meritocracy would drive social and economic progress survived. This is why the idea that millennials may be the first generation in living memory to experience declining living standards seems so shocking. Any stalling is seen to run not only against recent experience but against the very nature of historical time. This may sound surprising, given the preoccupation with national decline on both sides of the political spectrum in late twentieth- and twenty-first-century Britain. However, fears of relative decline have always run alongside faith in absolute improvement in both living standards and life chances – especially for those individuals who exhibit that magic combination of talent, hard work and personal ambition.

It is significant, then, that one of the most thoughtful and provocative pieces of TV history of the past few years did not anchor its narrative to a family or individual, instead it focused on particular places and the people that have passed through them. *The Secret History of Our Streets* (Century/Halcyon Heart Films, 2012) traced the stories of six London streets, from Charles Booth's 1886 poverty maps to the present day. Questions of class, race and inequality were foregrounded, as the producers probed the consequences of both political decisions and socio-economic trends: of municipal welfare schemes and demolition policies; of the abolition of rent controls and introduction of the right to buy; of immigration and the rise of finance capital. The layering of viewpoints highlighted the extent to which one person's social mobility is another's social exclusion. The series presented housing as

> the product of a social relationship between classes and fractions within classes, in terms of the needs of factory owners and the needs of their workers; the profits of builders, rents of landlords, and the standard of living of tenants; the ideology of owner-occupation; the struggle between classes within which housing is one issue, as it takes place in street and council chamber.[37]

The quotation is taken from Jerry White's contribution to Raphael Samuel's 1981 edited collection of articles on *People's History and Socialist Theory* and was part of his vision of what a socialist local history should be. This was a reaction against the tendency he saw for people's history collectives to focus on personal experience, to the exclusion of social and political analysis. He noted that one of the 'dangers' of this approach 'is not so much the romanticisation of the past, but the romanticisation of the *present*' (emphasis in the original); memories of inequality in the past are used to legitimate inequality experienced in the present, creating the perception that poverty no longer exists.[38] White's observation was controversial at the time, criticizing as it did the grassroots people's history movement. In the intervening decades a more intentionally apolitical form of people's history has come to prominence within mainstream heritage culture. Its romanticization of the inequalities of the past and legitimation of those experienced in the present has become so pervasive we barely even notice it.

Conclusion

Linear trajectories from unequal past to more equal present provide a compelling means of structuring stories of both civil rights and socio-economic inequalities. Despite historians' attempts to unsettle such narratives they remain robust because they chime with both common sense and lived experience – whether the journey from the decriminalization of male homosexuality to same-sex marriage in fewer than fifty years, or the effects of affluence, the decline of deference, and rise of a demotic popular culture on perceptions of social class.

We have, then, a rather whiggish story of the gradual advancement of both civil liberties and personal freedoms, coupled with a tale of social mobility, which operates on a national scale but is felt more viscerally at a deeply personal level, both individual and familial. The former allows us to be grateful that we do not have to live under the social strictures of the past; the latter enables us to celebrate exactly how far we (as individuals) have come. Rather than looking to genealogy as a way of demonstrating noble origins and legitimating our inherited social standing, it is now more frequently employed to underscore the distance we have travelled. This, in turn, confers a new form of social legitimacy, rooted in the authenticity of working-class experience, but also in the achievement of transcending it.

Sara Ahmed has written about 'the politics of bad feeling' and how it can feel good to feel bad on behalf of others.[39] In feeling bad for past victims of inequality we are able to feel good for feeling bad, while also keeping the object of that bad feeling isolated from the political present. If those victims are our own ancestors we can add further levels of feeling, by basking in a little reflected compassion and imagining their pride at our own, more privileged, situation. Feeling bad for our contemporaries requires rather more effort. It means acknowledging that social and political factors, of the kind explored in *The Secret History of our Streets*, have underpinned most of our stories of personal becoming. And it means recognizing that structural inequalities not only persist but that they can be challenged. At root, this is about recovering the sense that our current situation is not the outcome of an inevitable historical process, and the faith that the future can be different from the present. That is what 'history from below' was always supposed to be about.

120 *Emily Robinson*

Suggested further reading

In addition to the works cited, the idea of cultural presentism can be seen in, for instance, Fredric Jameson's *Postmodernism: Or, the Cultural Logic of Late Capitalism* (Durham, NC: Duke University Press, 1991); Pierre Nora (ed.) *Realms of Memory: Rethinking the French Past, vol. I, Conflicts and Divisions* (New York: Columbia University Press, 1996); and – more recently – Douglas Rushkoff, *Present Shock: When Everything Happens Now* (New York: Current, 2013). My own work in this area is *History, Heritage and Tradition in Contemporary British Politics: Past Politics and Present Histories* (Manchester: Manchester University Press, 2012), and on the attractions of 'pastness', 'Touching the Void: Affective History and the Impossible', *Rethinking History* 14(2) (2011): 503–20.

On the uses of the past in popular culture, the classic texts are Raphael Samuel, *Theatres of Memory*, vol. 1 *Past and Present in Contemporary Culture* (London: Verso, 1994); Patrick Wright, *On Living in an Old Country: The National Past in Contemporary Britain* (London: Verso, 1985) and Robert Hewison, *The Heritage Industry: Britain in a Climate of Decline* (London: Methuen 1987). More recent work includes Jerome de Groot, *Consuming History: Historians and Heritage in Contemporary Popular Culture* (London: Routledge, 2008), and Tony Bennett's *The Birth of the Museum: History, Theory, Politics* (London: Routledge, 1995) and *Pasts Beyond Memory: Evolution, Museums, Colonialism* (London: Routledge, 2004). More specifically on television history see Ann Gray and Erin Bell, *History on Television* (London: Routledge, 2013); Ruth McElroy and Rebecca Williams, 'The Appeal of the Past in Historical Reality Television: Coal House at War and its Audiences', *Media History* 17(1) (2011): 79–96; and Jerome de Groot, '"Perpetually Dividing and Suturing the Past and Present": *Mad Men* and the illusions of history', *Rethinking History* 15(2) (2011): 269–87.

Matt Houlbrook's work is helpful in problematizing the linear narrative of the achievement of gay rights. In addition to the chapter cited in the text, see his blog post 'Pardoning Alan Turing might be good politics, but it's certainly bad history', http://tricksterprince.wordpress.com, accessed 8 August 2013. For a more theoretical take on these questions see Jasbir K Puar, *Terrorist Assemblages: Homonationalism in Queer Times* (Duke University Press, 2007), and on the idea that inequality resides 'in the past', see Angela McRobbie, *The Aftermath of Feminism: Gender, Culture and Social Change* (London: SAGE, 2009). Finally, on British declinism see Jim Tomlinson, *The Politics of Decline: Understanding Post-war Britain* (Harlow: Longman, 2000) and Richard English and Michael Kenny (eds), *Rethinking British Decline* (Basingstoke: Macmillan, 2000).

Notes

1 I am grateful to Pedro Ramos Pinto, who invited me to contribute to this volume and organized the workshop on 'Rethinking Inequality in Historical Perspective' at the University of Manchester in May 2012, at which the first version of this paper was given. I benefited from the insights of those at the workshop, and students in my

History, progress and inequality 121

Special Topic class on Ideas of Progress and Decline in Modern British Politics. I am grateful to Cathy Elliott, Pedro Ramos Pinto, Bertrand Taithe and Jon Croker, who commented on drafts of this piece.

2 Peter Mandler, *History and National Life* (London: Profile Books, 2002).

3 Zygmunt Baumann, *Liquid Modernity* (London: Polity Press, 2000).

4 Keith Jenkins, *Rethinking History* (London and New York: Routledge, 1991), p. 68.

5 Tristram Hunt, 'Reality, Identity and Empathy: The Changing Face of Social History Television', *Journal of Social History* 39(3) (2006): 843–58 (843).

6 Billie Melman, *The Culture of History: English Uses of the Past, 1800–1953* (Oxford: Oxford University Press, 2006).

7 Books by Terry Deary, beginning with *The Terrible Tudors* (London: Hippo, 1993). Later books published variously by Hippo, Scholastic Children's Books and Andre? Deutsch Children's. Also CBBC TV series (2009–13) and stage show, http://horrible-histories.co.uk/, accessed 22 October 2014.

8 Bella Dicks, *Heritage, Place and Community* (Cardiff: University of Wales Press, 2000), pp. 233–234.

9 Laurajane Smith, *The Uses of Heritage* (London: Routledge, 2006).

10 Laurajane Smith, 'Affect and Registers of Engagement: Navigating Emotional Responses to Dissonant Heritages', in Smith et al. (eds), *Representing Enslavement and Abolition in Museums: Ambiguous Engagements* (New York: Routledge, 2011), pp. 260–303 (268–270).

11 David Cameron, quoted in Hugh Muir, 'Livingstone weeps as he apologises for slavery', *The Guardian*, 24 August 2007, http://www.guardian.co.uk/politics/2007/aug/24/london.humanrights, accessed 2 November 2009.

12 'PM's article for the *New Nation* newspaper (27 Nov 06)' from http://webarchive.nationalarchives.gov.uk/20080910134927/http://number10.gov.uk/page10487, accessed 11 August 2014.

13 Ministry of Justice, press release, 24 December 2013, http://www.gov.uk/government/news/royal-pardon-for-ww2-code-breaker-dr-alan-turing, accessed 31 December 2014.

14 Robert Mills, 'Queer is Here? Lesbian, Gay, Bisexual and Transgender Histories and Public Culture', *History Workshop Journal* 62(1) (2006): 253–63.

15 See, for instance, Matt Houlbrook, 'Daring to Speak Whose Name? Queer Cultural Politics: 1920-67', in Marcus Collins (ed.) *The Permissive Society and its Enemies* (London: Rivers Oram, 2008).

16 Simon Hughes, quoted in Adam Wager, 'Has the time come for gay marriage in the UK?', *Guardian*, 21 July 2010, http://www.theguardian.com/law/2010/jul/21/gay-marriage, accessed 31 December 2014.

17 Nick Clegg speaking to *The Agenda* (ITV). Quoted in *The Guardian*, 6 March 2012, http://www.theguardian.com/world/2012/mar/06/archbishop-westminster-same-sex-marriages, accessed 22 October 2014.

18 Nick Clegg, speech to Liberal Democrat Conference 2013, http://www.libdems.org.uk/nick_clegg_speech_to_the_liberal_democrat_autumn_conference, accessed 31 December 2014.

19 Andrew Marr, *The Making of Modern Britain: From Queen Victoria to VE Day* (Basingstoke: Macmillan, 2009), p. 18.

20 Andrew Marr, *A History of Modern Britain* (Basingstoke: Macmillan, 2007), p. 224.

21 *Ibid*, pp. 574-578.

22 'Level of food poverty among Hull families "is like Dickensian times"', *Hull Daily Mail*, 12 May 2012, http://www.hulldailymail.co.uk/Level-food-poverty-Hull-families-like-Dickensian/story-16062223-detail/story.html#ixzz3GrziWdg6. Comment by hcfchcfc09, 7.57am, 12 May 2012, accessed 17 May 2012.

23 Louise Bamfield and Tim Horton, *Understanding Attitudes to Tackling Economic Inequality* (York: Joseph Rowntree Foundation, 2009), p. 26.

122   *Emily Robinson*

24 *Ibid*, pp. 6; 23.
25 Alison Park et al, (eds), *British Social Attitudes 29* (London: NatCen, 2012), p. 12.
26 Alison Park et al, (eds), *British Social Attitudes 31* (London: NatCen, 2014), p. 6-7.
27 Lawrence Black and Hugh Pemberton, 'Introduction', in Black and Pemberton (eds), *An Affluent Society? Britain's Post-war 'Golden Age' Revisited* (Aldershot: Ashgate, 2004).
28 *British Social Attitudes 29* (2012). 55% agreed; 20% disagreed.
29 Charles Moore, 'Andrew Marr's The Making of Modern Britain is a patronising and ignorant piece of history', *Daily Telegraph*, 3 November 2009, http://www.telegraph.co.uk/comment/columnists/charlesmoore/6491340/Andrew-Marrs-The-Making-of-Modern-Britain-is-a-patronising-and-ignorant-piece-of-history.html, accessed 22 October 2014.
30 Peter Dorey, *British Conservatism: The Politics and Philosophy of Inequality* (London: IB Tauris, 2010).
31 Bamfield and Horton, *Tackling Economic Inequality*, p. 24, Table 7.
32 http://www.twentytwenty.tv/program/Never-Did-Me-Any-Harm_445.aspx, accessed 31 December 2014.
33 *Benefits Britain 1949* (Channel 4/Twenty Twenty, 2013). Introductory voiceover.
34 Melissa Kite, 'The extraordinary experiment that PROVES the welfare state has lost its way', *Daily Mail*, 12 August 2013, http://www.dailymail.co.uk/news/article-2389525/Channel-4-series-documents-extraordinary-experiment-PROVES-welfare-state-lost-way.html#ixzz3GrwSmmsm, accessed 22 October 2014.
35 Tom Meltzer, 'Benefits Britain 1949: TV review', *The Guardian*, 13 August 2013, http://www.theguardian.com/tv-and-radio/2013/aug/13/benefits-britain-1949-horizon-tv-review, accessed 22 October 2014.
36 I am grateful to participants at the workshop on 'Rethinking Inequality in Historical Perspective' for this suggestion – particularly Patrick Joyce and Ben Jackson.
37 Jerry White, 'Beyond Autobiography', in Raphael Samuel (ed.), *People's History and Socialist Theory* (London: Routledge and Kegan Paul, 1981), pp. 33–42.
38 I am grateful to Fiona Cosson for pointing me towards this piece.
39 Sara Ahmed, 'The Politics of Bad Feeling', *Australian Critical Race and Whiteness Studies Association Journal* I (2000): 72–85.

9 Campaigning histories

Peter Yeandle

Since the global economic meltdown of the late 2000s, the world has witnessed numerous incidences of social unrest, ranging from strikes and occupations to riots and revolutions. The suppression of popular uprisings in Brazil, Turkey and Thailand has demonstrated the extent of violence the state is prepared to use to put down dissent. Discontent – especially the awareness of financial inequality at a time of near universal economic hardship – has resulted in high-profile mass demonstrations in Bangladesh, Saudi Arabia and Uzbekistan, to name but a few. The 'West' (howsoever defined) has not been immune from large-scale and sometimes violent displays of civic discontent, however. Hundreds of thousands of protesters surrounded financial districts in Madrid, London, Frankfurt, Hong Kong, Tokyo, Toronto and New York in the years following 2008. Occupy camps became global phenomena in the autumn and winter of 2011: from long-term encampments in Brussels, London, New York, Sydney and Vancouver to flash camps all around the world (Wikipedia documents occupations as far afield as Armenia, Mongolia, Chile, Indonesia and New Zealand. *The Guardian* went so far as to publish an interactive 'Occupy Map of the World').[1] The Spanish *indignados* and Greek *aganaktismenoi* are examples of political movements which have developed outside of the party political tradition, articulating demands for social justice in opposition to austerity economics and the perceived corruption of conventional politics. The physical mobilization of thousands of environmental activists in Australia – the so-called Bentley Blockade – has succeeded in stalling the use of high-risk gas-extraction technology. Similar mass acts, seeking eco-justice, have been witnessed in Canada, Ecuador and Romania. It would not be difficult to extend this list: mass acts of unrest have become a fixture of global politics.

On the one hand, there appears something new about these instances of social unrest. Perhaps this sense of newness is owed to the widespread reach of social media; Facebook and Twitter have not so much served as call to arms, but have provided the relative freedom of broadcast and a method for the instantaneous distribution of information. Perhaps, then, these movements seem modern because there is something unprecedented in the way we learn about them; something original in both their conduct and their development. On the other hand, however, to an historian of political activism, some of these

124 *Peter Yeandle*

demonstrations seem acutely historical in nature: not so much new (as in *novel* or *original*), but new in the sense that they engage typical protest traditions but make use of the toolkit of modern media.

Each modern action has its echoes in the past. Two poignant images serve to illustrate this: the 'Standing Man' of Taksim Square (Turkey, June 2013) and the infamous 'kiss scene' at Tahrir Square (Egypt, January 2011), in which an old lady was photographed kissing a policeman in full riot clothing. These images have been given life by social media, converted into powerful and visually arresting memes in which the *moment* of dissent has not only been captured but recycled and replayed hundreds and thousands of times. But despite the novelty of the technology, the symbolism is not new. The imagery of the vulnerable confronting the militarized state with kindness – of gentleness in the face of state violence (of speaking 'truth to power' in Quaker adage) – immediately recalls the Pulitzer Prize winning photograph by Bernie Boston of a protester inserting a flower into the barrel of a gun during an anti-Vietnam war demonstration in 1967. The silence and passive resistance of the Standing Man recalls the non-violence of Gandhi as well as the passivity of the Prague Spring of 1968. One does not have to spend much time reading newspaper reports to see how social unrest is often linked back to historical moments. The London riots of August 2011 were reported as similar to the Rodney King riots in Los Angeles, 1992, which in turn recalled the Detroit Riots of 1967: in each case, the spark was the perception of police injustice igniting racial tension. Student demonstrations in the UK, Chile, Spain and elsewhere were compared to the student revolutions of the 1960s. Past bread riots are used to explain modern hunger marches; rallies against political corruption are narrated, according to the level of violence, in the context of velvet or violent revolution. The past is present in modern dissent. But, as I thought further on these quite obvious links – on the regurgitation of familiar narrative connections in the media – I wondered about the extent to which movements understood themselves as historical phenomena. Do campaign groups make conscious use of history as part of their protest? And if so, how so? What techniques, tropes and props are used? And how might we as historians think about these incidences as acts of public engagement with history?

I cannot survey global unrest in a chapter as short as this. Given that I work on late-Victorian and early twentieth-century British history, my intent here is to explore the use of history in modern British protest movements and draw connections between past and present. I analyse two very different types of protest: the 'traditional' trades union march, and the Occupy camp.

The former celebrates its history, identifying itself as part of a strong historical tradition and draws from that collective story in order to formulate group identity and articulate its grievances. Banners and placards are carried, the visual and textual symbolism of which invoke long traditions of dissent and recall histories of protest in which gains were achieved by acts of industrial unrest: the eight-hour day, holiday entitlement, maternity pay and equal pay, to name but a few.

The latter – Occupy – presents itself as something new: unlike the trades union march from A to B and culminating in a rally in public space, Occupy understood itself as radical since its form was located not in a demonstration of strength through mobility, but stasis. In common with past occupations, it took control of public space, occupying time as well as location; it introduced a language of consensus into debate, and was absolutely clear it had no party political allegiances. It learnt from the prevalence of social media during the Arab Spring. Protests were broadcast in real time via live-streaming websites (such as Bambooser) and discussed in synchronic time via Facebook and Twitter. There seems a blending of the physical with digital protest, in which acts of dissent are both larger than their physical presence but also far wider reaching.

Both types of demonstration indicate not only different uses of public space, but contrasting invocations of history. In particular, both understand themselves as performative movements and it is on this notion of performed activism that I will conclude, since it presents particular issues for the historian seeking to explore public engagement with history.

The trades union movement

The March for the Alternative was a Trades Union Congress (TUC) organized demonstration in central London on 26 March 2011. It was the largest protest in the UK since the anti-Iraq war march of 2003; and the largest union-organized demonstration since the Second World War. Various estimates of numbers have been made, ranging from a quarter to half a million demonstrators. The official march was colourful, musical and carnivalesque (video is easily found on YouTube). Although the actions of breakaway groups provided alarmist copy for newspapers and television news – masked anarchists attacking West End hotels and occupying upmarket shops (201 warrants for arrests for trespass, most of which were subsequently cancelled) – I want to focus on the majority: on the banners, the music, the procession; and how the past was invoked in these various forms.

The carnivalesque atmosphere of the march was owed in part to the range of sounds: accompanying a cacophony of chants led by megaphone, one could hear music ranging from traditional brass bands to a bhangra brass band, a steel band, plastic trumpets, vuvuzelas (first heard during the 2010 Football World Cup but since then a staple of the outdoor event), whistles, rattles and guitars. This was a protest that captured the modern: portable sound systems, mass-produced kitsch instruments, all recorded by hand-held video and mobile phone camera, and populated by protesters of all ethnic, religious and economic backgrounds. But amid the noise, most media reporting focused on brass bands playing traditional union tunes. Brass band tunes included the *Internationale* (obviously – it is *the* most recognizable left-wing anthem played at demonstrations since the nineteenth century); *Solidarity Forever*; and the *Blackleg Miner* (a traditional song most evocatively – in my recent memory – performed by the band Steeleye Span during the miners' strikes in Britain in the 1980s).

126 *Peter Yeandle*

Given their rich historical relationship with workers' movements (especially collieries), the brass bands themselves served as a narrative connection between past and present. When the march arrived at Regents Park for the rally, demonstrators processed past a socialist choir singing *Red Flag* and *The Union Makes us Strong* (written in 1913), among other songs. The songs of the procession invoked the 1960s' tradition of protest music (for instance Woody Guthrie, Bob Dylan), connecting the present to a musical heritage, not in the least because they were often – when sung – sung collectively. Some of the sounds of the march were captured by the London Sound Survey and can be heard online.[2] George McKay uses some telling phrases to describe protest music. Music, McKay writes, provides the 'aural architecture' of the demonstration; protests are choreographed by tradition, as much 'ritualised dance' as march, serving as a reminder of past protests as well as providing a collective focus for the here and now. On the one hand, then, modern sounds – and multicultural performers – reflected the vibrancy of London as a progressive city.[3] On the other, the blending of modern and traditional connotes a privileging of the historical; the march can be understood not only as the physical union of protesters from across the country, but also as a coming-together of past and present.

A similar juxtaposition of traditional and modern can be seen in the colours of the march; in particular in the designs of trades unions banners and home-made and mass-produced placards. Some of the banners invoked clear historical tropes, recalling the Peterloo Massacre (1819), Copenhagen Fields demonstration (1834) and other incidents in which workers stood up to oppression and were often injured in the process. Some contain quotations from leftist luminaries such as Karl Marx, Thomas Paine and William Morris. Others, however, reflect more modern themes. One banner for the National Union of Teachers, for instance, depicts a playground in which children of all religious and ethnic backgrounds are seen playing together: the slogan is 'Together we can build a happy and prosperous future'. Similar images are evident in banners for those working in health and the postal service. Recently made banners using slogan and visual imagery blend past and present in order to suggest an agenda for the future. I will return to this notion of a usable past in a moment – first, I think it is important to say a little about the historical significance of banners themselves.

The curious absence of research into the history of trades union banners is being corrected by the analyses by Nick Mansfield,[4] John Gorman[5] and Annie Ravenhill-Johnson. Ravenhill-Johnson and Paula James make the important observation that the banner has received more analytical attention from art historians than from social and political historians; an incongruity they argue requires repair since the production and use of banners is a key part of British social and political history.[6] One of their findings relating to nineteenth-century banners is just as relevant to those of the twenty-first century: that is, that banners invoked specific historical images as a means both to depict local and collective identities but also to shape debate about the future. Some banners used images from biblical and Greco-Roman history, depicting the honesty and integrity of men at work and using visual codes by appealing to deified abstract figures such as Truth, Justice and Virtue.

When London dockworkers went on strike in 1889 for instance their strike banner displayed the figure of Hercules strangling the snake of capitalism (Hercules had been recast during the French Revolution as a proletarian hero). The banner made for the Hull branch of the Associated Shipwrights Society (1885) showed a commanding ship in the background (occupational pride), but also positioned imperial icons – Britannia, with customary shield, and regal Lion – at the front. The purpose of the banner was to remind those viewing it of the contribution of British labourers to the acquisition, maintenance and profits of empire. Most banners, however, depicted multiple layers of collective identity (and still do): occupational, regional, national and sometimes international. Photographs of historical banners can be seen via the People's History Museum website,[7] but it is worth visiting in person – not only to gain a sense of their size, but the intricacy and craftsmanship required to produce such stunning pieces of art (and the intensive labour-of-love which has been put into maintaining and restoring them).

If you were to visit the People's History Museum in Manchester, you would also note that not all banners were intended for exhibit during protest processions. Some were made to be displayed at fairs and civic celebrations. You would also note that not all banners were made for trades unions. A significant number were made for clubs and leisure societies, others for guilds and cooperatives. This is worth bearing in mind since the majority of nineteenth-century banners which remain are trades union oriented – probably because the superior organizational and storage capabilities of the unions meant their banners would be more likely to be retained. A quick visit to the Trades Union Congress website 'The Union Makes us Strong: TUC History online' (note the title's evocation of the folk song mentioned earlier) evidences the sheer volume of archival material; so, too, does a visit to the Tolpuddle Martyrs Museum and their online platform[8] (similarly, Durham Miners Museum and countless others).

I mention this historical variance of banners for two reasons: the first is that it reminds us that not all banners were intended as props for protest; the second is that those banners which were used in demonstrations belonged not only to official unions and their branches. Indeed, at the March for the Alternative, central London was awash not only with trades union banners from across the country but independent ones. Some groups' visual display demonstrated their anger at environmental issues, others – for instance – targeted businesses newsworthy for their unscrupulous tax arrangements.

There is a clear sense, however, that banners perform cultural work in their use of history – and this is most noticeable in trades union visual material. The new Islington TUC banner, first paraded in 2008, bears the slogan 'Reclaim our Past; Organise our Future'. It includes a quotation from Paine ('My Country is the World and My Religion is to do Good'), contains reference to the six Tolpuddle Martyrs transported in 1834 and the subsequent 100,000-strong solidarity march

128   *Peter Yeandle*

from Copenhagen Fields in North London. In a black text box, the Pentonville Five are mentioned: these were five unionists arrested in 1972 for refusing a court injunction to desist from forming picket lines; their arrest led to a London-wide multi-union strike. The image is a collage, bringing together past and present into a coherent whole: Paine is joined in the picture by Vic Turner (one of the Pentonville Five) and contemporary workers, including a nurse in modern uniform. The multiculturalism of modern London is made clear in the mixture of workers from different ethnic backgrounds. The Red Flag is flying and the Angel Inn – a local landmark and the public house where Paine was believed to have written *The Rights of Man* in 1792 – is prominent.[9]

The banner deliberately seeks to merge past and present, to depict a narrative of workers' struggle. The martyrs were transported for forming a union; the Pentonville Five arrested for defending union rights. The future on offer is collaborative and prosperous. Such themes are redolent in other recently manufactured banners. A banner, commissioned by the National Union of Rail, Maritime and Transport (RMT) Workers Union in 2011 for the Three Bridges branch, features a picture of a local viaduct built in 1842 and the slogan 'the past we inherit, the future we build'. The South Wales and West of England RMT, in order to mark the centenary of the 1906 Trades Dispute Act, commissioned in 2005 a new banner: the spectacular resulting image contrasts a modern high-speed train (an Intercity 125, at the time the fastest diesel-fuelled engine in the world) and the 'Castle' class steam engine of Great Western Railway which would have been carrying customers and cargo a century before. Again, the connections between past and present are made explicit; so too is the appeal to local history through the visual depiction of iconic buildings, local manufacturing products, and local historical figures of note or indeed the workforce of a local area.

Banners thus recall moments of civic pride yet also connect to an ongoing national story. They serve as sites for aesthetic unity. Recent banners follow templates established in the nineteenth century: they provide commentaries on histories of struggle, define local and collective identity – solidarity – and project the spectator's gaze to the future. They serve several functions in their use of history. They recall historical moments of success (eight-hour day, equal pay, etc.) and causes for civic pride such as feats of manufacturing and engineering. In doing so, they document the importance of working-class protest as a core component of national history. They also serve as visual reminders of moments of working-class trauma (Taff Vale Disaster of 1904, Peterloo Massacre of 1819, the Levant Mining Disaster in Cornwall in 1919 are a few examples). They document injustices, demonstrating past struggles and implying the struggle goes on (the Pentonville Five, local to Islington, could be replaced up and down the country by others: in Shrewsbury, for instance, a union banner recalls the controversial arrest of twenty-four union activists, also in 1972). Banners, therefore, connect past and present in their iconography and imagery. Collated at a national march, local and regional come together in a collective display of shared heritage. History, complemented by the sound and technology of the present, becomes a usable and potent tool in modern protest.

Occupy

Of the hundreds of banners and placards produced during the time Occupy was camped in the forecourt of St Paul's Cathedral, the most iconic – and the most used in the mainstream media – was the one that read 'Capitalism isn't Working'. The banner made no appeal to union history, but it was an ironic commentary and reworking of a well-known historical symbol. In 1979, the Conservative Party launched their election campaign with the 'Labour isn't Working' poster; an image depicting a seemingly unending snake-like queue of unemployed people waiting to sign up for their social-security benefit. The Occupy banner reproduced the image, replacing the word Labour with Capitalism. The strapline in the original poster read 'Britain's better off with the Conservatives'; Occupy's stated 'Another World is Possible'. There is a clear negotiation of the past here; an adaptation of an historical image to address a current grievance. Occupy took some of its intellectual origins in the Adbusters campaign, which included 'subvertising': the idea was to undermine corporate power by using modern methods of visual communication to challenge big business. To this extent, the 'Capitalism isn't Working' banner both encapsulates Occupy's playfulness, but is also symptomatic of the movement's reworking of history in order to project a collective, fairer, future.

The Occupy encampment both hailed itself as radical because of its newness but also positioned its activists as inheritors of human rights campaign histories: including the Abolitionist, the American Civil Rights and the suffragettes movements. 'We are the new suffragettes. #Occupy' claimed one placard, itself demonstrating a juxtaposition of the hastily assembled and modern where pen on plywood met Twitter hashtag. Other banners invoked Martin Luther King, student revolutions of the 1960s, and (a version of) Gandhi's dictum that 'A nation's greatness is measured by the way it treats its weakest members'. Another, with a clever play on words, appropriated the Peasants' Revolt in a placard proclaiming 'welcome to the pLeasant revolt'. In a video documenting several arrests on 12 May 2012, an Occupy campaigner – when asked to comment on the value of peaceful, direct action – commented:

> ... the best people in history put themselves on the line. Speaking out against injustice is a profoundly political act. And I take heart in what other people have done. Martin Luther King, the suffragettes, Abolitionists, and all great people in history. To protest against an unjust law, to paraphrase Martin Luther King, to break a law which conscience tells you is unjust is in reality to express the highest respect for the law. I strongly believe that is what we're doing.[10]

There is a clear sense here that a narrative of successful protest has been identified: Occupy identifies itself with those who in the past, through mass mobilization and non-violent direct action, deviated from the normalized trades union protest model and achieved significant breakthroughs. To the list cited in the quotation above, other inspirations included workers' occupations of their factories, Mario Savio's famous 'bodies under the gears' speech (Berkeley, 1964)[11] and cross-political and internationally coordinated campaigns such as those in the 1980s against apartheid in South Africa.

Occupy's use of history, as with the trades union movement, included music. From bonfire sing-alongs to staged performances on the steps of St Paul's Cathedral, protest music was invoked to generate a sense of historical legitimacy. Artists who contributed ranged from Billy Bragg and Tom Morello (of the band Rage Against the Machine) in London, to Loudon Wainwright III, Patti Smith, David Rovics and Rufus Wainwright in America. Morello won an MTV award for his live performance. Activists in London launched a record label, Occupation Records, and an album, *Folk the Banks*, which featured songs by such bastions of protest music as Leon Rosselson, Peggy Seeger, the Oysterband and Chumbawamba. Music served its purpose to unite the present with the past. It is noticeable that, whereas social movements in the 1960s and 1970s generated a distinctive soundtrack of dissent, more recent campaigns lack a clear and characteristic musical identity. On the one hand, this may be because contemporary activists are able to draw from a rich historical tradition. It may also be because, in the age of the iPod, music is nowadays less of a collective experience. Nonetheless, the rise in popularity in Britain of hip-hop protest musicians and punk poets – artists such as Akala, Lowkey, Henry Raby and Alexander Anaxagorou as well as the revival of those who made their name in the 1980s (Attila the Stockbroker and John Cooper Clarke) – suggests the ongoing importance of creativity and the art of sound as a complement to protest activity. What Occupy and the trades union demonstrations have in common is the use made not only of past protest songs but of the performers themselves.

Other examples of the invocation of history include the explicitly religious. Whereas some union banners in the nineteenth century invoked biblical symbolism, few do so nowadays. Not unsurprisingly, given the location of the camp – the age-old question 'What Would Jesus Do?' – was asked both in media narratives and documented in banners. The answer in Occupy's rhetoric, of course (and seemingly endorsed by the high-profile resignation of Giles Fraser, one of the Canons of St Paul's), was that Jesus was a revolutionary anti-capitalist and would have joined the campers rather than endorse the corrupt ties between finance and politics symbolized by the Cathedral's thrall to the City of London Corporation. A protester dressed as Jesus carrying a placard reading 'I threw the money lenders out of the temple for a reason' was filmed by all four major British television news channels and found himself on the front page of several newspapers. Home-made placards, pinned to safety fencing and tent canvas, and on display in the Tent City University, drew from the biblical quotations: 'He that oppresses the poor to increase his riches shall surely come to want' (Proverbs, 21:16); 'I was hungered and ye fed me not; naked and ye clothed me not' (Matthew, 25:42); 'My House is a House of Prayer, but ye have made it a Den of Thieves' (Matthew, 21:13).

The use of direct biblical quotation positions the Occupy placard in a different protest genre from that of the trades union banner. The history of the relationship between the labour movement and the church has been rocky; indeed, for (most) strict adherents to Marxist doctrine, religion is a tool used by the state for subduing and controlling the workers (this despite a rich collaborative history between Christian Socialists and other activists at the turn of twentieth-century Britain). Yet, despite Occupy's hostility to the Cathedral, it was not religion per se that was in dispute. Rather, it was the relationship between the Cathedral authorities and the City of London Corporation; a relationship that was seen to epitomize the corruption of both church and state. Occupy's demands were reminiscent of late-Victorian campaigners: evident in the placards is the plea for the Cathedral to rethink its ethical priorities; to become more 'Christian' in the sense of the gospel of Jesus. Hence, Occupy made use of history in a way that sought to make moral arguments by comparing past and present as a means to expose the inequities of the here and now. It was a question that jabbed at the church, to the extent that the then Archbishop of Canterbury agreed that Jesus would have joined activists. Occupy was right, he argued, since they articulated the public's 'deep exasperation with the financial establishment'[12] and, according to the incoming Bank of England officer for fiscal responsibility, 'it is the analytical, every bit as much as the moral, ground that Occupy has taken'.[13]

This is one noticeable area in which the visual ephemera of the Occupy movement diverged from that of the traditional Left. Emphasis on morality and fairness – here deployed through religious language – was not to be achieved by forcing changes in workplace conditions and legislative change (as demanded in union banners) but by collective empowerment through communal action. It is no surprise, then, that Occupy rejected the democratic centralism favoured by left-wing political parties and instead drew from a different historical approach: that of consensus decision making (CDM). Various forms of CDM have been used over the last 500 years or so, by Quakers and indigenous Americans, but more specifically by American and European anarchist movements and postwar feminist and environmental activist campaign groups. It is no surprise that a significant proportion of the visual artefacts collected from the camp by the Museum of London were made up of 'how-to' guides with instructions and explanations of CDM.

I mention this for two reasons. First, Occupy's rejection of the 'traditional' decision-making process highlights its commitment to participatory democracy. That required both open access and transparency, as well as documentation (live streaming, use of social media to distribute minutes), and the conduct of discussion in public space. At the end of October 2011, more than one hundred people (more at weekends) would gather daily on the steps of St Paul's and take part in a general assembly. These were conspicuous displays of open democracy. Second, then, the operation of CDM very much encapsulated Occupy's approach to political engagement as performative. It is to a brief exploration of the performative element of modern protests that I now turn.

132 *Peter Yeandle*

Protest and the performativity of the past

There is thus clear use made of the past in these public performances of historical traditions. As historians, what can be said about the significance of these invocations of protest heritage? My main observation is that both trades unions and Occupy conceptualize their public displays as performances. The carnivalesque of the March for the Alternative is indicative of a deliberate display of collective identity: of solidarity, of the power of a unified working class. In Bakhtin's definition of the carnivalesque, simply put, the modern carnival is an event in which the usual codes of social order can be challenged – the world turned upside down – but normalcy is returned once the event is completed.[14] Sounds and images of the March for the Alternative demand change but, in doing so, conform to the model of a traditional trades union demonstration. The march has a start point and end point, the planned route culminating in a rally, the presence of banners and brass bands themselves indicative of a narrative connection between past and present.

The march is obvious. Protesters form in a procession, walk in the same direction, marked out from an audience not only by their participation in the ritual, but by hundreds of stewards in high-vis safety tabards. There is a separation of protester and audience, which, in performative terms, implies the march is a spectacle – a pageant, an 'us and them' event in which the audience are required to agree with the message in order to join the procession. Occupy, however, is much more difficult to quantify (witness the media confusion at the time: *What is it? What do they want? Who is their leader?*) By occupying space and embracing stasis, traditional boundaries of performer (the protester) and the spectator are deliberately blurred. Occupy was an example of a porous movement, a type of social movement which shared commonalities with *zapatistas* and *indignados* – the audience could join in, by physical or digital participation, but the audience did not need to bodily involve themselves in protest in order to be part of dissent. The most widely known of Occupy's slogans – 'we are the 99%' – deliberately framed a movement in which those belonging to all political interest groups, or none, could join.

It is little surprise that in November 2011, the *Telegraph* reported that 'Occupy' was 'the most commonly used English word on the internet and in print' for 2011.[15] Such techniques, making use of social media, also explain the surge in the last few years of the online petition and that curious embodiment of modern protest: the armchair activist, colloquially known as the clicktivist. The opportunity to protest is available to an increasing number of people, itself both an indication of the newness of the method but also a return to eighteenth- and nineteenth-century traditions of the mass petition (for example, the People's Charter, signed by millions and presented by the Chartist Movement to Parliament in 1838).

It is possible to witness the ingredients in social movements that Charles Tilly describes as 'contentious politics'.[16] For Tilly, movements can unite across nominal divisions in seeking to claim something – justice, retribution, enfranchisement, etc. – through making communal 'claims' and 'coordinating efforts on behalf of

Campaigning histories 133

shared interests or programs'. For Tilly, campaigners make their claim to a third party: who it is that forms that third party differs, in this analysis, for trades unions and Occupy. This is evident in their respective uses of history. Performance theorist Peggy Phelan writes that protest performances are defined by their disappearance; in their state of *being* they grasp political power in a moment of time, to be recorded and documented, but to be confined to the past tense.[17] The trades union march exists as a modulated repetition of previous marches, learning and drawing from tradition, but addressing power through familiar modes.

Occupy sought to incorporate multiple aspects of traditional dissent – socialist, anarchist, environmentalist and religious – and, crucially, made conspicuous use of multiple means of representation: it aimed to become a permanent fixture, it was a new movement, it was a digital phenomenon, there were no criteria for being part of the movement nor was there a clearly delineated boundary for inclusion or exclusion. In Tilly's sense of 'contentious', Occupy and unions make similar claims but through different methods – and it is the method that explains mixed reception. In both Phelan's conceptualization of performance and the Bakhtinian notion of carnivalesque, Occupy shook the system, momentarily, precisely because it defied traditional modes of dissent and refused – like the trades union march – to go home at the end of the day and, in doing so, threatened commerce and the usual order of things.

The trades union march has a long history. It will, no doubt, have a rich future. It is chronologically embedded in the narrative of the Left. The size of membership of marches fluctuates, often according to economic context: in the 1920s they were sizeable enough to provoke serious concern about their revolutionary potential. In the 1990s they dwindled. The return of the march, since the late 2000s, has drawn from trades union history; not repetition so much as adapted re-enactment developing from carefully selected histories of victory and defeat. The use of history on the trades union march and rally serves two functions: solidarity through remembrance, and solidarity through collective activity. The audience for the protest is the protesters, separated out from the spectator: their power of persuasion and the ingredients of their 'claim' (in Tilly's sense of the word) is their conspicuous display of present-day unity strengthened by shared appropriation of a single historical narrative.

The Occupy movement, on the other hand, captured the national imagination for a few months but, despite the persistence of Occupy groups around the world, has been fetishized as part of the past. The activist quoted earlier was also aware that, in identifying and selecting Martin Luther King and suffragettes as part of an historical tradition, Occupy – too – would be subject to a rewriting by the present: remembered as a campaign group located in a moment of time and written about in the past tense. The representation of the past, then, is subjected to the sins of selectivity and omission; not just by the mainstream press and the textbooks, but self-consciously by the movements themselves.

As an historian of activism, I am led by these observations to three concluding thoughts. First, there is clear evidence of a high degree of historical literacy.

134 *Peter Yeandle*

Social movements are aware of their traditions. Their narratives might be selective, but if history is understood as an indicator of communal culture and the work of collective memory, then these histories connote a specific identity relationship with the past. Moreover, these narratives provide the discursive power to shape collective understanding of the present and future. These are usable histories, presented in public settings, making use of a range of visual and musical media in order to disseminate information.

My second conclusion relates to the documentation of protest so that it can be researched by future historians. In a fascinating essay on the challenges of archiving the Occupy movement, Jim Gledhill – as curator – summarized the difficulty of his task: how is it possible, he asked, to preserve 'the historical memory of the active present?'[18] The problem with both the digital and the performative turn is that there is not one single archive available, but an ongoing, evolving, and multifaceted series of protest moments and social relationships. Each of these generates multiple layers of material culture and provenance: is a lollipop placard, boldly stating 'No Cuts', as valuable for archival retention as transcripts of interviews with participants or sound recordings? Does it matter that, because of social media, modern movements document themselves? Perhaps the biggest challenge confronting historians of protest is less the task of fathoming the historical dimensions of contemporary social unrest, but – instead – the impact of modern technologies on the documentation of dissent.

My final thought – if we are analysing these movements as performative – is the ways in which these performances of shared history construct their public as part of a self-conscious process of democratization: not democratization in the sense of documenting the struggle to win voting rights alone, but democratization in Raphael Samuel's sense of equal access to archives, repositories and the writing of history itself. The research and writing of 'History', in Samuel's opinion, 'mobilises popular enthusiasm and engages popular passions'.[19] If 'History' – as discipline, research process, and publication technique – has been defined by its domination by the academies, then these public conspicuous displays of shared heritage suggest a public retention of self-identified traditions and alternative methods for their dissemination. Movements are aware that very few people *know* the kind of history they wish to tell – the histories told in their performances are therefore both straightforward, but also the attempt to maintain tradition and influence how people think about the present and the future. As historians, we should not underestimate the importance of these renditions of history, nor should we take them lightly. As witnessed with the kiss scene in Tahrir Square and the Standing Man of Taksim Square, modern moments – through localized performances of dissent – have the power to become historically significant.

Suggested further reading

A recent conference of historians, with specialisms in various geographical and chronological topics, sought to historicize recent protest movements. Katrina

Navickas records their findings in 'Protest History or the History of Protest?', *History Workshop Journal* 73(1) (2012): 302–27. One theme that emerges is the question of the historian's bias. Are those of us sympathetic to past (and sometimes present) dissent likely to tell our stories in certain ways? Are we likely to draw connections, in a Whiggish manner, between past and present because we are conditioned to think in terms of historical connections? Navickas's essay explores such methodological issues and addresses others. For further information on the development of the trades unions and their histories, see Keith Laybourn, *A History of British Trade Unionism, c.1770–1990* (Stroud: Sutton, 1992). On the relationship between early labour, socialism and religion, Stephen Yeo's essay 'A New Life? The Religion of Socialism in Britain, 1883–96', *History Workshop Journal* 4(1) (1977): 5–56 remains a definitive text. On leftist narratives of history, and history as 'popular', see the various essays by Raphael Samuel in his *Theatres of Memory: Past and Present in Contemporary Culture* (London: Verso, 1994 – but reprinted with a fascinating preface by Bill Schwarz in 2012). Samuel's short essay 'What is Social History?,' written for the popular magazine *History Today* 35(3) (1985) is an excellent introduction to his ideas on popular histories and the democratization of the past.

I have written a short blog for the *Journal of Victorian Culture* online on the topic of church occupations in the later nineteenth century, which playfully suggests some historical echoes of the Occupy movement: 'What Would Jesus Do? The Occupation of St Paul's Cathedral, February 1887' (8 November 2012), http://myblogs.informa.com/jvc/2012/11/08/what-would-jesus-do-the-%E2%80%9Coccupation%E2%80%9D-of-st-paul%E2%80%99s-cathedral-february-1887/, accessed 14 July 2014.

On trades union banners, Nick Mansfield's reflection on his curatorial work at the People's History Museum rewards reading: 'The Contribution of the National Banner Survey to Debates on Nineteenth-century Popular Politics', *Visual Resources* 24(2) (2008): 133–43 and 'Radical Banners as Sites of Memory', in Paul Pickering and Alex Tyrrell (eds), *Contested Sites: Commemorative, Memorial and Popular Politics in Nineteenth-century Britain* (Aldershot: Ashgate, 2004), pp. 81–100. Annie Ravenhill-Johnson, with Paula James, *The Art and Ideology of the Trade Union Emblem, 1850–1925* (London: Anthem Press, 2013) is the best introduction to the production and emblems of banners. Katy Layton-Jones offers some intriguing suggestions on how historians can deconstruct the semantic value of banners and placards: see 'Visual Quotations: Referencing Visual Sources as Historical Evidence' and 'Editorial: Visual Collections and Historical Research', both in *Visual Resource* 24(2) (July 2008): 105–7 and 189–99. John Gorman's *Banner Bright: An Illustrated History of the British Trade Union Movement* (Buckhurst Hill: Scorpion, 1986) is an engaging exploration of banners as a visual guide to labour history.

Histories of music in general are told in Stuart Maconie's *The People's Songs: The Story of Modern Britain in Fifty Records* (London: Random House, 2013). Chapter 17 'Part of the Union' offers an introductory overview of left-wing popular music. For more detailed analyses of music performed at protests,

136 *Peter Yeandle*

see George McKay, '"A Soundtrack to the Insurrection": Street Music, March-
ing Bands and Popular Protest', *Parallax* 13(1) (2007): 20–31; Ron Eyerman and
Andrew Jamison, *Music and Social Movements: Mobilising Traditions in the
Twentieth Century* (Cambridge: Cambridge University Press, 1998); and Jennifer
Whitney, 'Infernal Noise: The Soundtrack to Insurrection', in Notes from
Nowhere Collective (eds), *We Are Everywhere: The Irresistible Rise of Global
Anticapitalism* (London: Verso, 2003).

On brass bands in particular, see both the fascinating essays in Trevor Herbert
(ed.), *The British Brass Band: A Musical and Social History* (Oxford: Oxford
University Press, 2000) and Roy Newsome's *Brass Roots: A Hundred Years of
Brass Bands and Their Music* (Aldershot: Scolar Press, 1998). Information and
track listing for the *Folk the Banks* record can be found here: http://occupation
records.bandcamp.com/album/folk-the-banks.

The Occupy movement has attracted considerable interest from political
scientists, but, as Cathy Ross – the current curator of the Museum of London –
points out, most historians have focused on the question of archival retention:
Ross, 'Occupy Collecting', *History Workshop Journal* 75(1) (2013): 237–46.
Her former colleague, Jim Gledhill, offers his thoughts in Gledhill, 'Collecting
Occupy London', *Social Movement Studies*, 11(3–4) (2012): 342–8. Some
ephemera collected at the Occupy camp has been photographed and uploaded
to the Museum of London's online collections. There is much in storage yet
to be documented. http://collections.museumoflondon.org.uk/online/object.aspx?
objectID=object-796175&start=0&rows=1.

Various repositories and museums have provided high-resolution photographs of the trades union banners in the collection. The People's History
Museum can be visited at www.phm.org.uk/; the Tolpuddle Martyrs Museum
at www.tolpuddlemartyrs.org.uk/. The trades union archives are available here:
www.unionhistory.info/. By the time of this book's publication, the Victoria and
Albert Museum will have opened its 'A World to Win: Posters of Protest and
Revolution' exhibition: www.vam.ac.uk/whatson/event/3171/a-world-to-win-
posters-of-protest-and-revolution-4588/. Some of the recordings made by the
Sounds of London project have been made available online at www.soundsurvey.
org.uk/index.php/survey/soundacts_po1/poli tical1/1310/. *The Guardian*'s
'Occupy Map of the World' is here: www.theguardian.com/news/datablog/
interactive/2012/sep/17/occupy-map-of-the-world.

On the use of performance studies to analyse protest, see Peggy Phelan,
Unmarked: The Politics of Performance (London: Routledge, 2013) and Charles
Tilly, *Contentious Performances* (Cambridge: Cambridge University Press,
2008). James Epstein's *In Practice: Studies in the Language and Culture of
Popular Politics in Modern Britain* (Stanford, CO: Stanford University Press,
2003) focuses on the nineteenth century but makes some very important interventions into the relationship between visual, written and spoken culture as sites
for radical politics. See also Baz Kershaw, 'Fighting in the Streets: Dramaturgies
of Popular Protest', *New Theatre Quarterly* 13(51) (1997): 255–76. A recent
collection of essays, *Performing Religion in Public*, edited by Joshua Edelman,

Claire Chambers and Simon du Toit (Basingstoke: Palgrave, 2013) explores the various opportunities afforded by performance theory to interrogate histories of public dissent. The focus may be on religion in general, but the introduction provides an intriguing insight into the relationship between performance and protest.

Notes

1 *The Guardian*'s 'Occupy Map of the World' is here: http://www.theguardian.com/news/datablog/interactive/2012/sep/17/occupy-map-of-the-world, accessed 6 November 2014.
2 London Sound Survey, http://www.soundsurvey.org.uk/, accessed 6 November 2011.
3 George McKay, '"A Soundtrack to the Insurrection": Street Music, Marching Bands and Popular Protest', *Parallax* 13(1) (2007): 20–31.
4 Nick Mansfield, 'The Contribution of the National Banner Survey to Debates on Nineteenth-century Popular Politics', *Visual Resources* 24(2) (2008): 133–43; Mansfield, 'Radical Banners as Sites of Memory', in Paul Pickering and Alex Tyrrell (eds), *Contested Sites: Commemorative, Memorial and Popular Politics in Nineteenth-century Britain* (Aldershot: Ashgate, 2004), pp. 81–100.
5 John Gorman, *Banner Bright: An Illustrated History of the British Trade Union Movement* (Buckhurst Hill: Scorpion, 1986).
6 Annie Ravenhill-Johnson, *The Art and Ideology of the Trade Union Emblem, 1850–1925*, ed. Paula James (London: Anthem Press, 2013).
7 The People's History Museum can be visited at http://www.phm.org.uk/, accessed 6 November 2014.
8 The Tolpuddle Martyrs Museum can be visited at http://www.tolpuddlemartyrs.org.uk/, accessed 6 November 2011; the trades union archives are available here: http://www.unionhistory.info/, accessed 6 November 2011.
9 Thomas Paine, *Rights of Man, Common Sense, and Other Political Writings* (Oxford: Oxford University Press, 1995).
10 The video, made and produced by You and I films in 2012, was used in the court cases against activists. It was taken offline in 2014. It could be found at: http://occupylondon.org.uk/case-dismissed-for-occupy-londons-m12-five, accessed 8 January 2015.
11 Robert Cohen, *Freedom's Orator: Mario Savio and the Radical Legacy of the 1960s* (Oxford: Oxford University Press, 2009), pp. 326–8.
12 *The Guardian*, 3 November 2011.
13 Speech widely reported but can be found in full here: Andrew Haldane, 'A Leaf being Turned'. Speech given by Andrew G. Haldane, Executive Director, Financial Stability and member of the Financial Policy Committee. At the Occupy Economics, 'Socially Useful Banking' event, Friend's House, Euston, London, 29 October 2012, p. 2, http://www.bankofengland.co.uk/publications/Documents/speeches/2012/speech616.pdf, accessed 6 November 2014.
14 Mikhail Bakhtin, *Rabelais and his World,* trans. Helene Iswolsky (Bloomington, IN: Indiana University Press, 1984).
15 Murray Wardrop, '"Occupy" is the most commonly used word in English language media, claims study', *Daily Telegraph*, 10 November 2011, http://www.telegraph.co.uk/news/newstopics/howaboutthat/8881273/Occupy-is-most-commonly-used-word-in-English-language-media-claims-study.html, accessed 6 November 2014.
16 Charles Tilly, *Contentious Performances* (Cambridge: Cambridge University Press, 2008).
17 Peggy Phelan, *Unmarked: The Politics of Performance* (London: Routledge, 2013).

138　*Peter Yeandle*

18 Jim Gledhill, 'Collecting Occupy London', *Social Movement Studies* 11(3–4) (2012): 342–8.

19 Raphael Samuel, *Theatres of Memory: Past and Present in Contemporary Culture* (London: Verso, 1994, reprint 2012); Samuel, 'What is Social History?', in Juliet Gardiner (ed.) *What is History Today?* (Basingstoke: Macmillan, 1988), pp. 42–8; Samuel, 'What is Social History?', *History Today* 35(3) (1985).

10 History, science and environment policy

Paul Warde

In 1959 C.P. Snow delivered his famous description of the 'two cultures' that he perceived in academic life, each hunkered down in their trenches and myopically pursuing their own agendas; not so much locked in a recursive struggle for intellectual pre-eminence, as barely aware of each other's existence. On one side was 'science', exact, experimental, factual, unsentimental, pursued by people who 'naturally had the future in their bones' (or alternatively, 'shallowly optimistic, unaware of man's condition'). On the other, were what Snow called 'literary intellectuals', but that we might now call the 'Arts and Humanities', fuzzy, discursive, interpretative and inconclusive, fomenting endless debate about values and meaning (or, alternatively, 'totally lacking in foresight, peculiarly unconcerned with their brother men ... traditional culture ... wishing the future did not exist').

Of course, these views were and are stereotypes, and it is notable that while we still may easily evoke a divide between science and the arts, the differences that Snow proposed would not sit so comfortably today; the putative divide is perhaps more persistent than the precise qualities of that division. The labels above are poor descriptions of what many scientists or humanities scholars actually spend their time doing and the work they deliver. Any one of the words in the list above could easily be transferred 'across the barricades' to describe some work that was being done on 'the other side'. Yet such caricatures contain sufficient truth to be recognizable to public and practitioner alike, and even to be adopted by people working in each broad field as a (possibly virtuous) description of what they do (notwithstanding an intemperate counterblast by the literary critic F.R. Leavis, who described Snow as 'intellectually as undistinguished as it is possible to be'). This is reflected still in the protected funding given to 'STEMM' (science, technology, engineering, maths and medicine) subjects within the United Kingdom, and in the defensive posture of humanities scholars, driven to justify not simply the level of financial support required for their subjects, but the value of being given any support at all.

Historians find themselves in a peculiar double bind in their relationship with the natural sciences and policymaking. Science is the purveyor of real, concrete information about the world, while historians still, after all these years, cannot agree about the causes of this or that revolution ... At the same time, the apparently more open and easily comprehensible nature of the humanities – anyone with

140   *Paul Warde*

a computer, a library, or maybe a pint in the pub can 'do' them – means that policymakers and publics are less likely to feel the need to defer to specialist knowledge. Yet taking the long view, the emergence of this great divide between science and the humanities (or 'arts') is really very recent, going back no further than the middle of the nineteenth century.

The consequences and conundrums of this divide are illustrated perfectly in the emergence of one area of policy that is almost entirely novel since World War Two: the environment. Not that what we now call 'environmental' concerns were new. But thinking of them as a group of *problems in common,* that required central government action, and giving rise to a broader political movement, only clearly emerged on the public stage in the 1960s. The British Ministry of the Environment was created in 1970, the same year that the Environmental Protection Agency was founded in the United States, now the second largest federal employer after the military. Concern for the environment as we know it thus appeared in an age where the cleft between humanities and the natural sciences was well established, and environmental problems, with their measures of chemical toxicity, species depletion and soil erosion, seemed to belong pre-eminently in the scientific realm. Later, this catalogue of problems would be joined by anthropogenic climate change, hypothesized in the late nineteenth century and then from the 1950s increasingly measured in the development of climate models and atmospheric chemistry.

And yet … the overwhelming consensus of the scientific community seems unable to put debates about the cause and extent of climate change (to take just one environmental problem) to bed. It is not just a case that people find *solutions* difficult to agree about. The person in the pub with their pint, or sitting at home reading blogs on their computer, is happy to call into question the merits of large-scale scientific investigation, and might get a public hearing for doing so. 'Science' turns out not to be able to resolve, in the public mind, apparently scientific problems, even though all sorts of people with opposing views continually make appeals to science to legitimize their claims (of course, one might note that *within* sciences this is the norm for scientific practice). One common response to this problem is what is called by some the 'deficit model' of science. The apparent inability of science to win political arguments is simply caused by a lack of scientific knowledge among the public.

As too many of the public do not appreciate what scientists tell them, then maybe humanities scholars, with their fabled communication skills (aside from when they are writing impenetrable academic texts) should be drafted in for the purposes of 'communication'. In this model history might operate as one of the spokespeople for the real work of scientific research. The two cultures model remains blissfully intact: natural scientists create 'real' knowledge, while historians tell stories, generate meaning, inspire and motivate. This is a model that underestimates the contributions to knowledge in the traditional domain of science that history can make, just as it underestimates the expressive and communicative capacities of scientists. Clearly, at least, something in the present model of knowledge cultures is not working.

Irrespective of perceptions of two cultures, or the division of school curricula and university departments, history has been engaging with science for a long time, most prominently in writing the history of science. This is a vast field in itself that helps us understand that science is in fact a diverse and changeable field of activity. It is not the purpose of this short chapter to delve into that huge literature, but it suffices to point out for now that historians have been at the forefront of a crucial activity: examining *what scientists actually do* as opposed to *what they say they should do*, which can be a major help for understanding how scientific knowledge and practice relate to policy, and how it responds to demands for information from policymakers. Policymakers' demands can be urgent but also seek and create pressure for assessments of risk when issues may have been little studied and no scholarly consensus exists, such as in the danger posed by levels of pesticides in the food chain, mercury toxicity in water, the relationship between cancer and radioactivity, or the causes of extreme weather phenomena such as drought or floods.

Historians have also long recognized the intimate connections between developments in human society and its environment. Such theorizing goes all the way back to Herodotus in ancient Greece, and for much of the nineteenth century it was still widely accepted that social and racial characteristics were closely related to climate, producing a fear of climate change. Such environmental determinism became less respectable in the twentieth century. However, other strands of historical writing, most notably from the *Annales* school in France and in particular its founder Lucien Febvre, insisted on anthropogenic change to the environment as a normal state of affairs. The landscape and the distribution of species within it, although not yet the climate, were understood as the *effects* of human choices, as well as being a stage that shaped the possibilities for human action. In that sense, the environment was already a cultural artefact, and no scientist should seriously assess an environment as if it was free from human 'interference'. The baselines by which one could judge what was 'normal' in nature were already profoundly shaped by millennia of human action. However, in the post-war framing of the environment this lesson was largely ignored, and there was a strong tendency to treat the very recent past as some sort of norm which industrial society was in the process of destroying.

The historical conditioning of science and environmental policy

We will return to the question of how natural scientists and historians can profitably work together. A more oblique, but significant view is of how scientists and policymakers have interacted historically. Being aware of this process can aid reflection on the likely course of such relationships today. Numerous studies have now shown that there has been no direct line from scientific observation to policy response; not because the messy and compromised world of politics simply refuses to take notice of the scientific facts (although sometimes this is true), but because science itself does not provide any clear answer to political problems, even those problems that scientists play a strong role in

142 *Paul Warde*

defining. Indeed, history can show how things work the other way round: the political definition of what a 'scientific' problem should be can bring science into play in a way discomforting to scientists, demanding 'answers' or advice for which there is no clear precedent or evidence (requiring assessments of dangerous levels of toxins or radioactivity are cases in point). Thus what counts as environmental policy is itself the product of a history that has included some things and excluded others, setting us on particular paths and valorizing certain kinds of expertise. Revisiting this history can help us understand its successes and failures. In the more traditional mode of 'learning from history', we can also look at analogues that might give more insight into current problems: How have societies dealt with similar problems in the past, or what effect have similar policies had in the past? This is not to argue that the past can simply be translated into the future, any more than we should expect a policy to have the same effect in two different countries.

Perhaps more straightforwardly, history also provides information, the gold-standard in an age demanding evidence-based policy. History is a vast repository of knowledge about environments and how they have changed over the long term. Once you have taken the step of looking at long-term environmental change, you quickly discover that environments are dynamic and the 'baseline' chosen for when the environment was in a 'good' state is essentially a choice about the desirability of a certain previous historical state. Of course, some environments can remain stable for hundreds or even thousands of years – depending on the scale at which we examine them – but others change much more rapidly, whether under human influence or not. To be aware of this dynamism, that the environment is not fixed, is not to say that 'anything goes' for the future, that one environment is no better than any other. Rather, it helps make explicit what values are being applied when a judgement is made about the desirability of a landscape or environment. In fact in some ways, as we will see, this kind of thinking was more explicit before the environmental turn in policy – hardly half a century old – when nature reserves and national parks were protected for their 'beauty'.

At this point we can begin to recognize that far from being a self-evident object demarcated and comprehended by scientists, the environment is a complex, fragmented beast that is difficult to grasp and that is managed through a range of different institutions, all with their own experts, goals and ways of doing business. These all change over time. Today, the environment in Britain is dealt with by the Department for Environment, Food and Rural Affairs (DEFRA), set up in 2001. At this point the environment ceased to be intimately linked in the official mind with transport and the regions, as it had been since 1997 under the Department of the Environment, Transport and the Regions. Henceforth it was married to what had previously been the Ministry of Agriculture, Fisheries and Food, founded in 1955 (but with predecessors running back to the Board of Agriculture founded in 1889). A Ministry for the Environment was originally created in Britain in 1970. Climate change, the premier 'environmental issue' of our time, was allocated its own separate department in

2008. The list could be extended back in time and internationally. There are also many agencies that interact with these government departments, such as the Environment Agency, established in 1996, whose mandate is 'to protect or enhance the environment, taken as a whole'.[1] In practice, this primarily means the management of waterways and coastal sites, regulation of waste disposal and monitoring of air pollution; generally issues to do with safeguarding property (flood prevention), ensuring access and preventing contamination.

When it comes to the protection of species in nature reserves, or Sites of Special Scientific Interest (SSSI), or the power to nominate and manage cherished landscapes in national parks or 'Areas of Outstanding Natural Beauty' we find a different constellation of institutions. The larger areas have their own statutory bodies that work with local councils to ensure access and influence planning. Some areas enjoy regulatory protection determined by the European Union, and conservation work is led in England by Natural England, a rebranding in 2006 of English Nature, merged with the Countryside Agency. These were the inheritors of early changes in 1991 which had seen the amalgamation of the Countryside Commission and Nature Conservancy Council, which in turn had their roots in the founding in 1949 of Nature Conservancy as part of the National Parks Act.[2]

What this indicates is that, politically, the domain actively marked out as 'environmental' may shift with time and place, and indeed is not always given the same name. While we could argue that environmental policy has been around since medieval times, given that legislation has existed on issues such as fire prevention, street lighting, air and water pollution, management of fields, fishery protection, wood supply, and so on, what makes modern environmental policy distinct is the idea that all these things should be governed by the same institution, and belong to the same policy area.

Thinking about and legislating around nature, in the sense of modern conservation, took off in the nineteenth century as two movements: towards the protection of species where extinction was feared (and especially where the birds were in decline because of allegedly frivolous demand, such as for feathers in women's hats); or where nature provided 'green lungs' for recreational and health reasons. From the 1860s we also see the gradual emergence of a global movement for protecting spaces as parks, often focused on ideals of grandeur and wilderness, and as 'national parks' linked to nationalist and nation-building sentiment. Notably, England and Wales got round to establishing them by law in 1949, in the tumult of post-war enthusiasm that saw novel ventures from the establishment of comprehensive planning and the National Health Service to the foundation of the UN agencies and the International Union for the Conservation of Nature.

None of these ventures were thought of as environmental policy. The 'Environment' – a word popularized in English during the nineteenth century by Thomas Carlyle, but above all the polymathic thinker Herbert Spencer – was a thing that affected you, rather than *vice versa*, although plenty of earlier writers since antiquity had noticed our capacity to affect soils, forests, water flows and

144 *Paul Warde*

so on. But the environment had not acquired a name as something that had an interconnected life of its own that could be endangered by us. This changed after the Second World War, with mounting evidence of worldwide impact, and fears over population growth and scarcity of raw materials in an increasingly globalized logistics system – especially to the military.

Intellectually, this 'environmental turn' paved the way for developments by the end of the 1960s – the setting up of Environmental Protection Agencies, the National Environmental Research Council, and by 1970, the new Conservative government's Ministry of the Environment. The explicit call for 'environmental policy' was made by American planner Lynton Caldwell in 1963, as a way of linking together things previously dealt with in isolation: in his words, 'In our characteristic concentration on intensive, specialized analysis of our public problems we may omit so many data from our normal field of vision that the integrating profile does not appear … [I] ask whether "environment" as a generic concept may enable us to see more clearly an integrating profile of our society'.[3] Around the same time, Rachel Carson's famous *Silent Spring* popularized research that demonstrated the dangers of pesticides and introduced ecological thinking to a new audience.

'The environment' was thus in essence a plea that we were not doing enough 'joined-up' thinking about the world that we lived in. But in truth, that demand for integration was not fulfilled in the way that might have been hoped. Environmental policy tended to fall into two distinct areas – in fact, following Caldwell, it developed new forms of intensive, specialized analysis. First was protection from hazards – new regulatory and monitoring systems for dealing with chemicals, flooding, and so forth. Second was preservation – using the nature conservancy, applying planning restrictions, protecting species and areas, but with limited budgets that have restricted the scale of action, especially as protection often entailed compensation of landowners. Indeed, the second mission tended to be split between very small areas monitored by scientists, and larger landscape-scale protected areas with the emphasis on amenity, recreation and character. In large part this work was negative, rather than positive. It forbade rather than inspired.

In Britain the result has been a fragmented system that has struggled to live up to the ambition of the idea of 'the environment'. Policy has been fairly successful in mandating and employing scientific experts dealing with very specific problems. But the wider problem of integration, and deciding what we collectively want from our environment, remains. This desire for integration to some degree explains the rapid recent uptake of the idea of the 'ecosystem services', borrowed from environmental economics, as a way of making 'what nature does for us' comparable with what we get out of economic activity, and even to create monetary values for these services. Nature is valued for the 'service' it provides, whether the capacity to grow plants or provide clean water, in the same way that a car provides the service of mobility or a bank the service of storing money. In fact analogues have been created many times before, in the 'cost–benefit analysis' that appeared in the late 1940s as a way of deciding whether governments should invest in infrastructure projects. Numerous local studies attempted to put a money value on what nature does for us. While such attempts then and now can be enlightening and interesting, they told us little new about the functioning of the environment, or indeed why we value it. One can value scenery by the tourist revenue it brings, or how far we are prepared to travel to see it. But does this mean that scenery becomes less valuable if, say, air transport becomes cheaper so we can fly elsewhere, or incomes decline so we spend less on holidays? Do we value something less because we can see it out of our back window rather than if we have to drive there?

Cost–benefit analyses quickly found that opponents in debates simply produced similarly styled analyses that put different values on things, mostly by including different sets of criteria in the valuations. Instead of allowing one to see more clearly what was valuable, the numbers were used to shore up already existing positions (although on the part of civil servants in the UK it is a requirement that they produce them). We see the same today with debates over the High Speed 2 (HS2) rail link. If the terms of the analysis are not relatively simple, we find methodological debates acting as screens for what are in fact political debates. Scientists, sometimes with the aid of economists, are being asked to come up with some metric by which the 'goods' and 'bads' of a particular way of managing the environment – as a whole! – could be measured and reconciled, such that the politicians' work is done for them. The reality is different, as only a small amount of historical reflection would reveal. Indeed, the reality is often recurrent rounds of conflicting evidence from different scientists, frustrated politicians (who blame policy failure on bad advice, as with the floods in southern England in the winter of 2013–14), and accusations of 'bias' or cynicism among a wider public. Structurally, the system wrestles with the very same dilemmas highlighted by Caldwell in 1963:

> The public decision-maker ... has been compelled to seek some calculus of objectivity that would pass as defensible rationality and simultaneously afford room to manoeuvre among the fixed or conflicting political forces – the pressures of public life.[4]

This is not to say that the search for better evidence is fruitless, whether by the natural sciences, social sciences or humanities. It is rather to highlight the fact that science can no more generate indisputable answers to complex problems than history can deliver definitive verdicts on the causes and justice of past behaviour. So often, attempts to provide a 'magic bullet' answer to policy problems by appeal to the apparent indisputability of science is not really a means to integrate better values and forms of knowledge into the policy process, but a way to subsume those values and forms into one specialized form of analysis – that *appears* 'objective', but may conceal more than it reveals. This is a classic problem with many economic valuations, as was highlighted by Ross Garnaut to the Australian Multi-party Climate Change Committee in 2011, in talking about the 'discount rate' – effectively the rate of interest we use to value the

146 *Paul Warde*

money of the future in today's terms, to assess whether an investment is worthwhile or not.

> If we used the share market's discount rate to value the lives of [the future] ... and if we knew that doing something now would give lots of benefits now but would cause the extinction of our species in half a century, the calculations would tell us to do it.

In reply, Julia Gillard declared that the entire committee – even in fractious Australian politics – were 'against the extinction of the human species'.[5]

Scientific knowledge and cultural choice in environmental policy

One thing is clear: the mere existence of environmental policy was not enough to protect the environment. Indeed, a spurious correlation could even argue that destruction has accelerated alongside the measures to prevent it. But what other policy lessons lie in the past? In one sense, all of history can be a source of analogues. The question is: Which ones are useful? I want to pick up on just one question, in relation to the current demand for 'evidence-based' policy. That is: Does more knowledge help make better policy? There can be little doubt that some knowledge is essential for policy of any kind. But has policy been a reaction to better knowledge, thus improved knowledge would drive us towards better policy? Here, the answer is more equivocal; at least, accumulating more of the *same kind* of knowledge does not necessarily impact favourably on policy.

This can be exemplified in two cases: first, air pollution, and second, global warming from carbon dioxide emissions. By the late nineteenth century it was already clear that air pollution was a major – perhaps the major – cause of death in Britain. Or, in the words of the Chief Sanitary Inspector of Glasgow, Peter Foyle, after a fog of November 1909:

> Let us use no euphemisms, no glossing words, to cover our own misdemeanours in the vain attempt to blame Dame Nature. The citizens themselves, along with some manufactures, are alone to blame; and the dire effect, death – this excessive death – is due to one thing and one thing alone, and that is smoke![6]

Factories were widely blamed as the greatest culprits, so gradually regulation emerged of factors such as chimney height to disperse smoke. But as Foyle argued, domestic hearths were actually the main source of the problem in cities. Voluntary efforts to change behaviour, such as introducing better technology, or alternative energy sources such as gas and electricity, had relatively little effect. Factors encouraging resistance to change included a persistent popular belief in the healthy ventilating effects of coal fires; the fact that they remained much cheaper than alternatives; and a dominant rental sector, where neither

History, science and environment policy 147

landlord nor householder had much incentive to invest in the long-term value of the house for a problem that was perceived as social rather than personal.

Hence no really effective action came until after the great London smog of 1953, and then the Clean Air Act had to wait until 1956. Change was facilitated by a rapid cheapening of alternative fuels after the Second World War; but most immediately, by the stick of a ban on smoky fuels coupled with the carrot of large subsidies for new heating equipment. It was not a question of either/or with the carrot and stick, but both being deployed simultaneously. The political will to do so was created by a large number of people dying in a very short space of time from a highly visible phenomenon (that obfuscated the view of everything else) in the capital city. But no new knowledge was required, because the problem had been absolutely clear in medical circles for decades.

In the case of climate, it was already hypothesized at the end of the nineteenth century that burning a lot of fossil fuel was likely to heat the world up because of CO_2 emissions; the most famous writer on the theme was the Swede, Svante Arrhenius. However, this was not much of a preoccupation of climate scientists at the time, who focused on other things: developing an understanding of regional weather; the obviously important focus on variations in incoming solar radiation; and more localized phenomena such as polar warming in the 1920s and 1930s, or as it was called at the time, 'climate embetterment'. Early and fairly accurate production of measures of global warming linked to coal combustion produced by the engineer G.S. Callender were largely dismissed by mainstream science as being outside of the serious preoccupations of the time, and done by someone without recognized meteorological training. Only after the Second World War and with the advent of modelling of the global climate system (funded to a large extent by the cold war military) did the potential for warming from CO_2 emissions become the subject of more attention. By the late 1950s it was widely accepted in climate science as a potential issue, and a decade later the 'Keeling Curve' measuring increasing atmospheric CO_2 concentrations in Hawaii was suggesting these models were correct. Frank Fraser Darling's Reith lectures from 1969 already warned of dangers from the 'greenhouse effect' from burning fossil fuel, which would melt polar ice caps and cause massive coastal flooding.[7] It took another eight years, until April 1977, before the first warning about 'the greenhouse effect' from fossil fuels appeared in *The Economist*.[8]

Yet policy impact was delayed another decade; and still moves only slowly, despite huge refinement of data and greatly more sophisticated modelling across the 1970s, 1980s and 1990s. None of this changed the basic story, although we have realized that climate change could happen more rapidly than previously suspected. Again, no new 'knowledge' was essential to change wider attitudes on climate change. Instead, what *was* needed were political interventions to get policymakers to perceive global warming as an issue worthy of their attention.[9] Yet ineradicable uncertainties in our capacity to predict the climate system, and assign plausible costs to the consequences, remain a continuing source of contention, and justification for inaction. Despite appeals to 'evidence', in practice

148   *Paul Warde*

such logic is certainly not applied to crime or education policy, or military interventions. This is clearly something to do with the very framing of environmental policy from an early date: that it should be determined by science (and any environmental policies that venture beyond this are based merely on emotion).

What these histories show us is that while the scientific underpinnings of environmental understanding are clearly essential, what changes policy is, unsurprisingly, the policymakers, and the political world they inhabit. These histories also suggest that policies reliant on an appeal to what should be rational in theory – (that surely people can see they will be better off in the long term if they change their boiler or reduce their chance of dying) – have rarely, in themselves, had very much effect on the ground. In the realm of historical environmental policy, carrots have not tended to work well without sticks, because it is not enough to give people a 'choice' that may even be skewed in favour of a beneficial result to them and the environment: they also have to be forced to make that choice. The alternative to 'the stick' is to build from the ground up, as now happens with the UK's land management policies where environmentally friendly farming is generally encouraged on a case-by-case basis, locking farmers into agreements after voluntary negotiation. It is successful to a degree, but it is immensely time consuming and inevitably marginal. Of course, this particular observation may not be applicable in all cases.

What applies to policymaking and the science–policy interface also applies to wider public understandings and values about the environment. It doesn't take much thought to recognize that our preference for how a landscape should look is a preference for the landscape of a particular historical period (and one that can be reconstructed to demonstrate how this is the case). The idealized English landscape of hedgerows and copses and a mix of arable and pastureland – think Constable – is essentially that of the 'old enclosed' countryside of parts of southern England; throw in a few heaths and moorlands to keep the Romantics – Coleridge or Wordsworth – happy.

The current distribution of open and uncultivated country has partly been preserved because it was what had been created by sheep farming and grouse shooting when campaigns for access and rambling emerged in the nineteenth century, a movement as much about health and equity against big landowners, as about nature.[10] These landscapes have hence been preserved in the form they happened to have then. More recently, with the proposed sale of the Crown's forest estates in 2010 in England, it was proposed that certain woodlands would be designated as 'heritage' forests and sold off to appropriately minded non-governmental organizations (NGO). These were essentially the relicts of areas designated by royal fiat as hunting forests in medieval times, and managed accordingly. Ironically, it was the drive to retain these for the nation that led to the privatization plan being scuppered, rather than the fate of 'commercial forests' which had actually been created with public money for public benefit, to provide a secure supply of timber to the nation in the wake of the world wars. Understanding why we value something – and why it is as it is – are

History, science and environment policy 149

fundamentally historical questions. It is hard to conserve a landscape without understanding how it got there, or to measure the impact of changes without any knowledge of how it once was. Here history must come to the fore.

It is also good to be aware of how we class and protect things. We show great concern today – as in many parts of the world – for 'native species'. But 14,000 years ago northern Britain was deep under ice, and the south a windswept tundra. There wasn't much in the way of native species. Today, we classify plant species as native; as introduced, but nativized (archaeophytes) or non-native (neophytes). The boundary date is 1500. Suffice to say that this date is completely arbitrary, or at least, if you want to exclude plants and animals that come from really far away – the Americas – you could perhaps make it 1492. Eight out of ten of our most endangered archaeophyte species were introduced alongside people, in connection with agriculture, but thousands of years ago.[11] If a species arrived a mere 514 years ago, it has no such 'nativized' rights. Such judgements may be justified, but they are hardly 'scientific'. Nor do they distinguish a human and non-human natural world. Such distinctions are not just true of lists of protected species, or our valuing of obviously 'historic' landscapes. Dig a little into those who advocate 're-wilding' and you will soon find that their notion of 'when wild was' can differ, wildly – some essentially wanting to restore medieval times, some the Mesolithic, some actually before the last Ice Age. All this may be reasonable and justified – but it is not restoring some 'untrammelled nature'.

Invasive species and diseases are now one of the most pressing environmental – and security – issues of our day. But the idea of invasion that was coined by ecologist Charles Elton in the 1950s is, of course, pejorative, and its application reflects judgements about the desirability of environmental change, not whether plants or animals really should 'belong' (as some minor reflection on some of our most familiar fauna would reveal: rabbits, turtle doves, grey squirrels). Gardens are full of introduced species that we rather like, while we put a lot of energy (rightly) into eradicating others. Himalayan balsam (*Impatiens glandulifera*) is an example of an introduction about which opinions have changed. Beloved of Victorian landscapers, it is now loose in the countryside, and certainly can extend its territory rapidly. Now, land managers frequently seek to eradicate it. But does this make it bad? It does not, in fact, drive any native competitor to extinction. Should we also remove all that invasive Victorian architecture added or alongside medieval buildings, for example (sometimes actually with the intention of making them look more medieval)? The point here is that the way we treat both buildings and landscapes are cultural choices, and we might be more conscious of this fact. This works both ways. We can, as I have just done, question the arbitrariness of how we decide whether a species in the natural world is good or bad, or at least understand it as a cultural judgement. But equally, given that we bind ourselves tightly with building regulations and planning rules in regard to buildings, we show relatively little regulatory concern for what constitutes an acceptable standard of landscape.

150　*Paul Warde*

There is, of course, no reason for us to restore, perfectly or 'authentically', the buildings or landscapes of any particular period – unless we want to. And in any case every landscape throughout history has itself been the result of long historical accretions of all the ages before, just as an old house does not just contain furniture from the year it was built. But this kind of historical perspective and juxtaposition can make us far more aware of what we are actually doing and the basis on which we are spending resources.

Shared concerns and collective approaches

History is thus a reminder that environmental problems – and hence many problems of environmental policy – are *political*. Science advice is not the only kind of relevant advice; we should involve other kinds of thinking in the framing of the problem. But the approach of history (or humanities) to science is not to be destructive, or undermine confidence in scientific evaluations – far from it. Any assessment of the state of past environments from the documentary sources typically employed by historians is going to be very partial, and becomes far more convincing when allied with sources of information drawn on by scientists (sometimes through archaeology), such as pollen analysis, ice-core data, dendrochronology (tree-ring studies), or an understanding of the biological and ecological functioning. The same goes for data collected by scientists, that can often be linked much more accurately to past landscapes through the use of maps, official records or court disputes, or indeed by interpretations of current traces in the landscape by those who understand their origins.

Such interaction and cooperation is long-standing, especially in the study of landscape. This has sometimes been driven by individuals straying over supposed boundaries, such as the renowned ecologist Oliver Rackham who has left a deep imprint on our understanding of the English countryside. In the twenty-first century, such work is increasingly done by interdisciplinary teams that might bring together historians with soil scientists, palynologists and others: an approach pioneered in the UK especially at the University of Stirling. In historical climatology, teams of historians and climate scientists have built up vast databases from documentary records, especially chronicling extreme weather events, but also the more mundane collection of weather diaries, data from ships' logbooks, or use harvest records to reconstruct past climate and weather patterns over the centuries. The History of Marine Animal Populations has been a massive and global project to reconstruct historical fish and whale populations (and hence baselines for current management policies) using historical records ranging from the direct returns of fishing fleets to the changing patterns of consumption and price in restaurant menus.

None of these interdisciplinary efforts involve any usurpation of scientific methods, but rather close collaboration among those who use different kinds of quantifiable and qualitative data. The dividing line does not necessarily fall between science and the humanities; indeed, such approaches have been familiar for decades among historical demography and the 'new economic history' which emerged in the late 1950s and 1960s, and was already cited by C.P. Snow in his Rede Lectures of 1959.

Equally, some historians have found conceptual commonality, perhaps unsurprisingly most markedly in the environmental field. It is perhaps a curiosity that evolutionary approaches to change, although inherently historical and path dependent, have had little direct endorsement from historians. The running in applying evolutionary thinking to human societies has usually been made by non-historians, and indeed it is some of these associations, pioneered in the nineteenth century by Herbert Spencer – now remembered somewhat inaccurately as a 'social Darwinist' – that may have discouraged later engagement. Now, in the fields denoted as 'deep history' or 'big history' historians seek both to engage with science and evolutionary approaches, and see human history as part of much longer sequences of patterning, contingency and development.

In the case of David Christian, history reaches all the way back to the beginning of the universe, setting 'historical time' into ancient processes of adaptation and complexity, a recurrent story of 'fragile ordered patterns'; John L. Brooke has applied theories of 'punctuated' evolution from earth systems theorists like Stephen Jay Gould to the long span of human history, both with a view over millions of years, and as explanation for events that happen over decades or even years. The medieval historian Daniel Lord Smail has engaged with comparative studies of other primate societies and the deep history of human social and technological development over tens of thousands of years, identifying patterns of continuity and moments of rupture. Others have evoked the idea of 'co-evolution' to examine how particular human societies exist in co-dependency with species that have evolved or become prevalent in that social and environmental context, whether domesticated beasts, parasites, grasses or the varieties of cotton amenable to mechanized picking that supplied the mills of the Industrial Revolution.

Such approaches indicate that the 'two cultures' may not be so far apart after all, or at least that work in the sciences and humanities may have much in common, whether conceptually, in the use of particular methods, or the problems posed; even if generally the style of output and argument in different disciplines generally remains distinct, sometimes awkwardly so. This is a significant observation at a moment when geologists are debating whether to designate the last two centuries as the beginning of 'the Anthropocene', a new era supplanting the Holocene epoch of the last ten thousand years, as humans have become the main driving force for change in the global system. If such a designation is accepted, it suggests a present, and all the more a future, where no scientific work on ecology, oceanography, climate and even geology can avoid taking human actions and impact into account. Equally, all human actions will be understood to have environmental consequences. The divides between research in the environmental sciences and social sciences and humanities are likely to become far less clear-cut. Indeed, one could argue that the particular historical moment that gave rise to the concept of 'the environment' and the associated

152 *Paul Warde*

expertise of the scientists who manage it may give way to a new distribution of knowledge creation and policy advice.

Suggested further reading

C.P. Snow's classic lectures are published, with additional reflections, as C.P. Snow, *The Two Cultures: And a Second Look* (Cambridge: Cambridge University Press, 1965); a recent reflection in the same vein is Jerome Kagan, *The Three Cultures: Natural Sciences, Social Sciences, and the Humanities in the 21st Century* (Cambridge: Cambridge University Press, 2009). For discussions of engagement between environmental historians, 'practitioners' and policy see Peter Coates, David Moon and Paul Warde (eds), *Local Places, Global Processes* (Oxford: Windgather, 2015). For some examples of recent historical works that seek to mix conceptual approaches from the sciences and humanities, see John L. Brooke, *Climate Change and the Course of Global History: A Rough History* (Cambridge: Cambridge University Press, 2014); David Christian, *Maps of Time: An Introduction to Big History* (Berkeley, CA: University of California Press, 2004); Andrew Shryock and Daniel Lord Smail, *Deep History: The Architecture of Past and Present* (Berkeley, CA: University of California Press, 2011); and Edmund P. Russell, *Evolutionary History: Uniting History and Biology to Understand Life on Earth* (Cambridge: Cambridge University Press, 2011).

Notes

1 See http://www.environment-agency.gov.uk/ and http://www.defra.gov.uk/environment/, accessed 14 August 2014.
2 John Sheail, *Nature in Trust: A History of Nature Conservation in Britain* (Glasgow: Blackie, 1976); W.M. Adams, *Future Nature: A Vision for Conservation* (London: Earthscan, 2003, 2nd edn); Margaret A. Anderson, 'Areas of Outstanding Natural Beauty and the 1949 National Parks Act', *Town Planning Review* 61 (1990): 311–39.
3 Lynton K. Caldwell, 'Environment: A New Focus for Public Policy', *Public Administration Review* 23 (1963): 132–9. See also Caldwell, *Environment: A Challenge for Modern Society* (Garden City, NY: Natural History Press, 1970).
4 Caldwell, 'Environment'.
5 Ross Garnaut, *The Garnaut Review 2011: Australia in the Global Response to Climate Change* (Cambridge: Cambridge University Press, 2011), p. ix.
6 Stephen Mosley, *The Chimney of the World: A History of Smoke Pollution in Victorian and Edwardian Manchester* (Cambridge: White Horse, 2001), p. 100.
7 Frank Fraser Darling, *Wilderness and Plenty: The Reith Lectures 1969* (London: Oxford University Press, 1970).
8 'Weather: Magnificent Ignorance?', *The Economist* (9 April 1977), p. 14.
9 A very useful introductory discussion can be found in Mike Hulme, *Why We Disagree about Climate Change* (Cambridge: Cambridge University Press, 2009).
10 T.C. Smout, *Nature Contested: Environmental History in Scotland and Northern England since 1600* (Edinburgh: Edinburgh University Press, 2000).
11 T.C. Smout, 'Nature, Cultural Choice and History', in Peter Coates, David Moon and Paul Warde (eds), *Local Places, Global Processes* (Oxford: Oxford University Press 2015).

11 History and practitioners

The use of history by humanitarians and potential benefits of history to the humanitarian sector

John Borton and Eleanor Davey

For decades humanitarian practitioners have subjected their work to sustained reflection and critique. Over the last fifteen years or so, the humanitarian sector has developed a range of initiatives to systematize its learning from its operations during and in the aftermath of conflict and natural disasters. Yet due to the myopia of much of the sector, these efforts have not benefited from the historical awareness that is so important to strategic thinking and effective practice. This chapter explores the relationship that the humanitarian sector has with history – what 'the past' becomes when it is channelled into narrative – focusing on the use of history and historical materials for and by practitioners.

Humanitarian assistance is defined as assistance and actions intended to save lives, alleviate suffering and maintain and protect human dignity during and in the aftermath of emergencies resulting from natural disasters, armed conflicts and extreme forms of economic and social crisis. Despite accounting for just 7 per cent of the total overseas development assistance provided by members of the Organisation for Economic Co-operation and Development (OECD),[1] humanitarian assistance constitutes a significant sector in its own right, employing an estimated 274,000 workers worldwide and expending around US$16 billion annually.[2] While the organizations and agencies associated with these figures such as the United Nations (UN), the Red Cross and Red Crescent movement, and national and international non-governmental organizations (NGOs) by no means exhaust the list of those who respond during emergencies, the formal and informal links between these actors make them a distinct and prominent sector within emergency response.

The sector's collective efforts to learn from response operations have led to a significant increase in the use of formal evaluation processes for accountability and learning purposes. Through their focus on such criteria as relevance, effectiveness, coverage, efficiency and impact, these evaluations provide preliminary retrospective analyses of the response to the humanitarian needs created by the disaster or conflict. While many limit their scope to the programmes of a single organization, the more comprehensive evaluations, such as the Joint Evaluation of Emergency Assistance to Rwanda conducted after the 1994 conflict and genocide or the Joint Evaluation of the international response to the Indian Ocean Tsunami, cover whole operations in an effort to draw system-level conclusions.[3]

154   *John Borton and Eleanor Davey*

When coupled with the development of mechanisms for sharing such evaluation reports (like the Active Learning Network for Accountability and Performance (ALNAP)'s Evaluative Reports Database and the more recent Humanitarian Genome Project), it has become much easier for humanitarian practitioners to search for potential lessons from humanitarian operations conducted ten or fifteen years previously.

However, this desire to learn from immediate past experience has not meant the embrace of a deeper historical perspective. Preoccupied by the present, the sector and those working in it are often poorly aware of the sector's past and display a marked lack of appreciation for the value of historical knowledge and methods.[4] Initiatives aimed at fostering improved practice often reference only recent experience while ignoring decades of prior practice which are not only contextually pertinent but have an important role to play in strategic analysis and critical thinking. This situation must continue to be challenged in the name of more effective and appropriate humanitarian action.

The uses of history for humanitarian action

It is very rare for a manager of a humanitarian response programme, let alone his or her staff, to put effort into identifying literature on previous responses to earlier disasters in the same area, regardless of whether they took place one hundred, fifty or only twenty years previously. Even back in the manager's head office, where staff arguably have more time and space to identify and make use of the relevant historical expertise, few agencies will seek out historical literature or develop connections with individual researchers. Some agencies might identify staff who worked in earlier comparable operations and deploy them as resource persons to a particular operation,[5] but this approach limits the historical period that might be accessed to thirty years or so. Consequently, lessons that earlier operations might have for current operations are often overlooked. The result is humanitarian decision making and action that is based on incomplete and inadequate evidence and may not be appropriate for the context.

The benefits of a greater use of history by, and for, the humanitarian sector can broadly be categorized as either contextual or strategic, though both are mutually influencing and reinforcing. The history of a place and the people living there should be integral to the contextual analysis and needs assessments undertaken by agencies, yet often such fundamental contextual issues are not considered. A review of a dozen inter-agency, inter-sectoral needs assessments found that '[i]nformation on conditions prior to the emergency is often available but seldom sought or integrated into analysis. Such background is essential for understanding the context of the current situation'.[6] Its omission, as that of past operations, represents the loss of a vital tool to ensure the effectiveness and appropriateness of humanitarian action and of understanding how current operations may be perceived.

On a strategic level, history underpins innovation by providing a knowledge base for understanding, discussion and debate and by supporting informed

The use of history by humanitarians   155

analysis and decision making that is more open and risk-willing. Studies have suggested that organizations with a clear understanding of their history are better able to negotiate change and engage with new challenges.[7] Historical methods also shape the understanding of complexity which should be at the heart of all strategic planning and organizational prioritizing. They provide an analytical tool that, in evaluating outcomes and emphasizing contingency, has much to offer programmes undertaken in complex settings such as conflicts and natural disasters.[8] An attention to history helps to draw attention to received truths, challenging comfortable accounts and shedding light on assumptions, distortions and omissions.

Thinking at a global level can also benefit from knowledge of historical studies. Perceptions of the humanitarian landscape are changing rapidly as a wide range of national and local actors participate in the sector, each with their own past informing and shaping their particular perspective. Adopting an historical approach to this trend indicates the need for more nuanced understanding and for recognizing how this may influence the way actors, incorrectly labelled as 'new', are approached. For the humanitarian sector to understand and respond effectively in a difficult operating environment, it is vital that its historical myopia be addressed.

Factors contributing to the demand for and supply of humanitarian history

The sector's neglect of history is often, and not without cause, attributed to the situations of emergency in which humanitarian work is done. According to this view, there is little time for reflection and even less for the consideration of history. For instance, in the days immediately following the January 2010 earthquake in Haiti or when Cyclone Haiyan struck the Philippines in November 2013, agencies will have focused all their efforts on ensuring that their teams gained access to the affected areas as rapidly as possible; or, if they were already present in the affected areas, on reinforcing and supporting their teams with minimum delay. Lessons-learned reports from previous evaluations of responses to earthquakes and cyclones prepared by ALNAP will, most probably, have been shared with these teams. For the teams on the ground, priority will have been given to the myriad of tasks that they have to undertake: carrying out needs assessments; coordinating with other agencies; planning their programme interventions; establishing logistics systems; recruiting staff; and preparing funding proposals. Not only are lives at stake but the ability to rapidly establish programmes is expected by agencies' staff, supporters and funders. Though agencies coordinate to a degree on the ground, there is often strong competition between them when raising funds, and the pressure to be seen to be responding quickly can be intense. To be perceived as having been 'slow to respond' could be damaging for an agency's ability to raise funds in the future and the staff involved could expect criticism from their peers.

156   John Borton and Eleanor Davey

This situation corresponds to a demand-side factor that helps to explain a certain lack of motivation for accessing relevant historical materials. It is also arguably distinctive of the humanitarian sector with its emergency focus. However, while the prioritization of action in pressured contexts and sudden-onset disasters is understandable, it is more difficult to account for the lack of consideration of history in subsequent, less time-pressured phases of high-profile operations such as Haiti and the Philippines, as well as operations in contexts that are less time-pressured throughout. Crucially, these contexts are actually more typical of those in which humanitarian agencies operate: 'the reality is that most humanitarian assistance goes to countries that are chronically poor, that experience recurring disasters, and that have been receiving humanitarian assistance for many years.'[9]

From this point of view, the line between the humanitarian and development sectors is not as clear as the terminology might suggest. In theory, humanitarian assistance differs from other forms of foreign assistance and development aid in that it is intended to be short-term in nature and provide for activities in the immediate aftermath of a disaster, and is often understood as governed by the principles of humanity, neutrality, impartiality and independence.[10] However, in many situations of prolonged vulnerability it is difficult to distinguish between 'humanitarian' and other types of assistance, and the term has also come to cover disaster prevention and preparedness activities including early warning systems, contingency planning and the holding of contingency stocks. The policy environment is similar for both humanitarian and development work and individual personnel move between them, whether working at field or headquarters level, in government, public service, or in NGOs. As a result there is significant overlap between the development and humanitarian sectors in terms of their relationship to history; and the criticism that international development assistance policy tends to neglect or actively devalue history has been made by a number of commentators and scholars.[11] David Lewis, for example, described the 'perpetual present' of the development policy world:

> a state characterized by an abundance of frequently changing language and 'buzzwords', by frequent discussions of new approaches that promise better chances of success than those currently in use, and by a strong – and in many ways understandable – sense of wanting to look forward rather than back.[12]

In such contexts the lack of motivation by agencies and their staff for accessing historical resources appears to be due to a range of factors. In both high-profile, time-pressured operations and in less time-pressured, more chronic, operations, most humanitarian personnel have the attitude that they have little time and space to consider history and, even if they did, that history would probably not have much relevance to their current work and their agency's programmes. The limited funding base that is typical of humanitarian operations in areas of continuing, 'chronic' need, coupled with the short planning

The use of history by humanitarians   157

cycles of humanitarian programming, keep staff under pressure to perform, yet perpetuate uncertainty as to whether their posts and perhaps even the programme will still exist even just a year ahead. Related to this, high levels of staff turnover are common among international humanitarian personnel, with many serving no more than one year in a particular operation. Inevitably such staff are focused on understanding the current context and programmes so as to perform well, rather than delving into what may have occurred decades earlier.

However, the acknowledgement that demand-side factors can work against the consultation of historical material should not be mistaken for a justification. Agencies and analysts are not, of course, unaware of the disadvantages that the neglect of past experience brings. That the humanitarian sector should make a more sustained and sophisticated use of history is supported in principle at least by leaders within the sector. For instance Valerie Amos, UN Under-Secretary-General for Humanitarian Affairs and Emergency Relief Coordinator, has declared that 'to shape our future, we must understand our past'.[13] The field-level relevance of history has also been recognized. As an evaluation by the UK's Disaster Emergency Committee (DEC) noted,

> DEC agencies appear to suffer from some loss of institutional memory concerning their longer-term engagement in Ethiopia. Some of the organisations concerned have been working in Ethiopia for forty years, but government officials sometimes appeared more familiar with this history than agency staff.[14]

Yet, as the evaluation continued, 'That history is surely a strength' and agencies lost a valuable resource in neglecting it.

A number of supply-side factors, however, limit the accessibility of the history of relief operations to humanitarian workers and their agencies even where there is demand. Humanitarian action spans a wide range of specialist disciplines: the 'life-saving' sectors are identified with health, water and sanitation, food and nutrition, shelter, and protection work, complemented by other programmes including education, agriculture, mental/psychosocial health, and livelihoods or income generation. As a consequence, the specialist literature is widely dispersed; in parallel, historical studies of conflicts and other crises are carried in a wide range of disciplinary and area-specialist journals. The combined result is that potentially relevant historical literature is spread across an extraordinarily large number of sources. For instance, work to identify 500 key monographs and journal articles on humanitarian history found that the 238 journal articles that had been included in the selection spanned no fewer than 133 journals. Only eleven journals accounted for more than two selected articles.[15]

The highly dispersed nature of the relevant historical literature is accentuated by the fact that humanitarian agencies tend to spend very little on research resources and knowledge management systems. Even large, comparatively well-resourced international NGOs subscribe to only a handful of journals, if any, and preference is inevitably given to those journals deemed to be of greatest

158   John Borton and Eleanor Davey

professional relevance. Unlike university-based scholars who are able to access full text articles of thousands of journals through the Athens or Shibboleth systems, so far as the present authors are aware, no humanitarian agency pays for, or has access to, such accumulated academic knowledge. While recent Open Access developments are to be welcomed, the process is slow and its impact is yet to be felt.

The material available, moreover, has not always been well suited to the goal of improving humanitarian practice. There are relatively few comprehensive histories or overviews of humanitarian action, and a significant body of work has been institutionally driven by the commissioning agencies in terms of its framing, methodology and critical perspective.[16] Certain schools of historiography are also of less utility for practice, notably those written in a 'denunciatory' style and, at the opposite end of the spectrum, hagiographic studies that serve mainly to build identity myths. Programming, and practitioners in operational roles, stand to benefit from the use of history as much as other parts of the humanitarian sector, yet have often been overlooked as both subject and audience of history. The operational history of humanitarian action – histories, for instance, of emergency shelter, nutrition, camp management, water and sanitation, protection work or livelihoods in crisis – largely remains to be written.

Using humanitarian history in practice

In the absence of comprehensive operational histories of the different sectors, many agency handbooks and field manuals focus almost exclusively on recent contexts or present expertise as technically rather than historically grounded. Nonetheless, there are some exceptions. This section considers four cases.

The first is provided by the Shelter Project Series produced by UN-Habitat, the United Nations High Commissioner for Refugees (UNHCR), and the International Federation of the Red Cross and Red Crescent (IFRC). Since 2008, summaries of both historical and contemporary cases, designed as learning tools, have been provided in an effort to draw lessons for the improvement of future responses. The second report explained this objective with reference to the difficulties of building institutional memory *collectively* – fostering a shared, deployable memory across a sector of practice, instead of housed within and confined to one organization alone. The evaluations and reports that best capture past experience, they note, are often consigned to 'sit on the shelves of agency headquarters, are buried inside field manager's laptops or become anecdotal "snapshots" passed on by the people involved. If not properly documented, memories fade away, year after year, disaster after disaster'.[17]

Fifty years earlier, similar thinking had motivated the production of a comparable, though multi-sectoral, learning tool for relief workers prepared during the Second World War – *International Relief in Action 1914–1943*.[18] The book contains fifty-seven records from different relief and refugee programmes, grouped into disciplines, each compiled from one or more texts, including field

The use of history by humanitarians 159

reports, commissioned studies, newspaper articles and academic literature, and annotated with discussion questions. These project records are supported by histories of the organizations featured and an extensive bibliography. A joint project of the American Friends Service Committee (AFSC), the Brethren Service Committee (BSC) and the Mennonite Central Committee (MCC) – three organizations with long-standing experience of aid work – the book explicitly linked past practice to future response. The author, pioneer German social worker Hertha Kraus, expressed their shared belief that

> These scenes may help to clarify the attitudes and the types of skills, the knowledge, and the information, which will be widely needed in the task before us. There can hardly be any question that contemporary knowledge and the best of professional practice in public and community service must be mobilized.[19]

Kraus's work draws attention to how we might historicize professionalism in the humanitarian sector, as well as its operations – as humanitarian action has evolved, so too have ideas of what it means to be 'professional' within relief work and how the aspiration of professionalism might be achieved. Michael Barnett has argued that relief in the 1940s was characterized by the adoption of a number of learning, planning and coordination measures, aiming to consolidate and improve upon the performance of humanitarian action during the First World War.[20] Arguably, then, and as represented in Kraus's book, humanitarian professionalism at the time of the Second World War was associated with the proactive redeployment of operational experience. The inclusion of historical cases in the Shelter Project Series appears as a comparable effort to build on past practice within current and future operations. This can be contrasted with recent professionalization debates that have adopted the less chronologically oriented lens of standardization and accreditation. While standards of practice are important, the importance of contextual and strategic planning should demand the inclusion of more sustained and sophisticated use of past experience as part of today's image of a professional and self-reflexive sector.

A recent initiative along these lines which also, crucially, seeks to maintain the accessibility of this material as it becomes 'historical', is the series of Speaking Out Case Studies developed by Médecins Sans Frontières (MSF) and led by researcher Laurence Binet. Begun in the late 1990s following the request of the MSF International Council for case studies for internal educational use, the organization began to make the series publicly available online during 2013. Each case study takes the form of a dossier compiling extracts from internal MSF documents such as field reports and minutes of meetings; other contemporary material including press releases and research (by MSF and others) and media reports; and the personal testimony of key figures captured through subsequent interviews. The approach explicitly rejected the idea of developing guidelines: '*Témoignage* cannot be reduced to a mechanical application of rules

160 *John Borton and Eleanor Davey*

and procedures as it involves an understanding of the dilemmas inherent in every instance of humanitarian action.'[21]

The sources are curated with a minimum of editorial intervention. This approach gives voice to multiple viewpoints and interpretations both synchronically and diachronically: the different positions adopted by operational centres and individuals and the evolution of understandings over time. While the precise extent to which this 'curatorial' approach entails a more objective stance is open to discussion, the Speaking Out Case Studies highlight the potential for using history as part of a broader culture of reflection and debate. The decision to make them public is a brave attempt to open up what goes on within agencies to facilitate reflection and learning. It is also an exercise in transparency: selected internal documents are placed online in full for the first time to accompany the studies that cite them. The Speaking Out project sets a good example for agencies wanting to be considered as being reflective and professional in their approach to learning. Not only should other agencies be following the lead set by MSF, ideally such case studies would also be prepared for whole operations using operation-wide analysis so as to complement the perspective of individual agencies.

An example of a resource platform that could support operation-wide analysis is the Sudan Open Archive that was originally established in 2004 to preserve and make accessible the records of Operation Lifeline Sudan (OLS). At that time, in light of steps towards the end of civil war in Sudan, there was very real concern that the records would be lost; images of OLS records stacked in jumbled disorder in old shipping containers are evidence of the neglect of 'the long view' that is so prevalent in the humanitarian sector. Since its establishment, the archive has been expanded to include historical sources, personal papers and other grey literature.

The aim of the Sudan Open Archive, to help improve practice and policy through consolidating knowledge, has driven its format. As Dan Large, its Project Director, explained, the ambition was

> to create a practical, usable resource for aid practitioners [in Sudan], who could use it to better understand what they were doing, how they were doing it, and what had been done before. That's why the emphasis was really on something that was accessible, easy to use, and could really allow for immediate access to this deeper history of aid interventions in Sudan but also other forms of Sudanese history as well.[22]

The example of the Sudan Open Archive highlights the importance of preserving today's documentary record. A commitment to improving humanitarian responses should also mean a commitment to transparently recording activities and decisions, sharing this and other information, and returning to it later in time. While this kind of sustained engagement for the most part remains aspirational for the humanitarian sector, there is no reason to think that the above examples of the use of history, and others that adopt different approaches, cannot be consolidated.

The use of history by the military

The humanitarian sector's relationship with its own history stands in marked contrast to the military – a sector alongside which it often has to operate and with which it is sometimes compared.[23] Both operate in high-stress environments and are strongly affected by technological change; for both the frontline field worker and the infantry soldier, historical study can seem far removed from daily reality. Of course the comparison can only go so far: not only are their fundamental objectives profoundly in opposition, but most militaries enjoy far higher resourcing levels and have very clear hierarchical structures intended to facilitate command and control – all very different from the modest resource levels of 'low-profile' emergencies, the wide range of agency types and nationalities involved in most humanitarian operations, their often disorderly attitudes to hierarchy, and the voluntary basis of most humanitarian coordination arrangements. Nevertheless, in its potential strategic role, the allocation of resources, and in efforts to apply 'lessons', the military's approach to history could serve as both a precedent and an instructive caution for the humanitarian sector.

One area where the military appears to lead the humanitarian sector is in attributing an important role to historical study in the development of strategy. Whether understood as a military question or on a more general level that includes peace-time diplomacy, strategy has been broadly defined as 'the art of winning by purposely matching ends, ways, and means'.[24] Carl von Clausewitz, the Prussian theoretician of conflict, gave history an important place in *On War*, first published in 1832. Discussed notably in book two of *On War*, history is portrayed as the necessary subject of detailed study and the starting point of any theoretical analysis.[25] Other elements of preparation and training, such as battlefield experience or technological proficiency, continue to be regarded as 'ultimately sterile unless grounded in a careful and thorough examination of the past'.[26]

Different national militaries have thus recognized the value of history, not only for posterity but also for training purposes, and have invested accordingly in recording and capturing that history. In Britain, for example, regimental histories detailing the composition, deployments and combat engagements of each regiment date back in some cases to the English Civil War (1642–51).[27] 'Official histories' complement regimental histories by providing accounts and analyses of conflicts in which many regiments were involved. The UK's Official History Programme was established in 1908 to learn lessons from perceived failings during the Second Boer War (1899–1902). It was under its auspices that the massive official histories of the First and Second World Wars were prepared. 'The History of the Great War Based on Official Documents', for instance, comprised twenty-nine volumes published between 1923 and 1949. Until 1941 the Official History Programme focused solely on military and naval histories but, in recognition of the significant role then being played by 'the Home Front' in the Second World War, its remit was expanded to include civil history. This expansion of what is considered relevant, to include not only military operations but broader questions of society and culture, is one of the ways that 'war studies' have influenced more traditional military history and serves as another reminder of the importance of context to humanitarian history.

Although attitudes towards the use of history have oscillated over time and according to different national military and political cultures, the belief in capturing past experience has led to a significant deployment of resources. In the United States prior to the Second World War, the concept of official history had been limited to an archival function, and the preparation of 'narrative' history was discouraged. But this changed in 1943 when a new Historical Office was created and historical detachments began to be despatched to the different theatres where they collected and preserved primary historical documents. Early on, it was recognized that there were gaps and discrepancies in the operations records maintained by combat units, and so the work of the historical teams was expanded to include ensuring proper record keeping and obtaining additional on-the-spot information through interviews with participants.[28] Militaries invest heavily in professional military education at national service academies such as Sandhurst, the École de Guerre and West Point where the courses make substantial use of history.

Yet the use of military history is often discussed in the same breath as its abuse. It should come as no surprise that the objectivity and accuracy of the histories produced by army regiments and some of the official histories have been challenged. Perhaps the best-known British example has been the long debate over the account of the Battle of the Somme prepared by Brigadier General Sir James Edmonds who was not only the official historian but also the overall leader of the official history of the First World War.[29] The lessons drawn are equally open to disagreement. In the words of the leading military historian Michael Howard, 'Like the statesman' – and we might add the humanitarian –

> the soldier has to steer between the danger of repeating the errors of the past because he is ignorant that they have been made, and the danger of being bound by theories deduced from past history although changes in conditions have rendered these theories obsolete.[30]

The failure of French strategy in 1940 (of having strong but static fortified defensive lines), based on an erroneous reading of the lessons of 1914–18, is probably the most famous.[31] To guard against such flawed readings, Howard advocated that officers should study military history in *width*, in *depth* and in *context*.

Others have already called for a 'humanitarian equivalent of military science' to address the fact that humanitarian agencies 'do not possess, and are unwilling to invest in the capabilities to process information, correct errors and devise alternative strategies and tactics'.[32] Reflection on the military's own experience suggests that history should be essential to this endeavour, but that the process is far from simple and requires effort and critical skills.

Building a more historical culture in the humanitarian sector

Apart from a few instances of good practice and useful initiatives, the humanitarian sector has yet to appreciate the potential value of history and to seriously engage with it. The humanitarian sector does have a healthy strain of self-criticism and has accumulated a body of analysis of its own work but, because of its short-sightedness, does not always gain full or long-term benefits from this analysis. This offers opportunities and a point of departure for more historically grounded examination of recurring challenges faced by practitioners.

Improving the accessibility of material (fostering supply) and enhancing interest in and demonstrating the benefits of a familiarity with past perspectives (increasing demand) are important first steps in developing an historically informed humanitarian sector. There are a number of intersecting avenues through which this influence may be felt. Existing initiatives to retain and make available the historical records of operations, particularly those records built up in the field, should be expanded and properly resourced. In order to make these as complete as possible, multiple methods should be embraced including oral history and digital archiving. The increasing interactions between academic research and the sector, whether through institutional links, collaborative initiatives, or in the personal trajectories of individuals with experience of both, are a positive sign for the prospect of history in the humanitarian sector. These have the potential to contribute to and multiply instances where those within the sector use history for their own work. As these links multiply, and especially in the current context of an increased investment in education and training programmes in the sector,[33] it will be important to integrate humanitarian history into operationally oriented programmes as well as academic curricula.

Belief in the importance of a dialogue between history, policy and practice has motivated the work of the Overseas Development Institute (ODI) to promote the use of an historical perspective in humanitarian action. This work has been led by ODI's Humanitarian Policy Group (HPG) in a project entitled *A Global History of Modern Humanitarian Action*.[34] The project has three objectives designed to contribute to its goal of promoting the use of history in humanitarian response: first, to advocate for a more inclusive humanitarian history that includes diverse and changing perspectives on the nature, meaning and practice of humanitarian action; second, to offer historical analysis to inform current discussions and debates on improving humanitarian policy and practice; third, to help the sector more fully engage with the history of humanitarian action, including past contributions and experiences outside the Western narrative. The project thus seeks to highlight where history might make a difference and to provide a platform for others to develop its insights further.

To challenge the issues around supply and demand outlined above, however, will require changes in work cultures and reflective practices. It will be difficult to achieve without a basic infrastructure to make the history of humanitarian action more accessible to aid workers, the media, scholars and the interested public and to facilitate more scholarly exchange and collaboration with humanitarian agencies. As an outgrowth of HPG's programme on humanitarian history, a joint project has been established with the Humanitarian and Conflict Response Institute (HCRI) at the University of Manchester to develop a website that will provide this basic infrastructure.[35]

Once the infrastructure has been established and as demand grows, it might then be feasible to take a lead from the approach of the US military and consider humanitarian historians being deployed in the field to encourage and support agencies in maintaining their records, to gather key documentation and fill in gaps through oral history interviews. This might be done directly by some of the larger agencies interested in improving the historical record of their own operations, though ideally such efforts would be based within agencies such as the UN Office for the Coordination of Humanitarian Affairs (OCHA) with its operation-wide coordination remit. Alternatively, research centres and networks specializing in humanitarian history might seek to field such teams themselves with the objective of preparing and interrogating 'official histories' on behalf of and with support from a wider grouping of humanitarian agencies.

Over time, a more sustained engagement with historical perspectives has the potential to contribute to a shift in the decision-making culture within the humanitarian sector. The sector will benefit from an expansion of its knowledge base, the fostering of historical understanding, discussion and debate, and above all the integration of much-needed contextual and strategic perspectives into policy analysis and operational decisions. Such steps should aid the sector in reflecting critically on its own position, understanding others, and shaping a more rounded analysis of its future – ultimately informing more appropriate and effective action in support of people in need. To build a culture in which history is respected and valued alongside the focus on the present and immediate future will take time, but it is a process that has begun and which can only be positive if it manages to take root.

Suggested further reading

The historiography of humanitarian action cited included Michael Barnett, *Empire of Humanity: A History of Humanitarianism* (Ithaca, NY: Cornell University Press, 2011), which provides a valuable introduction to and overview of humanitarian history. It also mentioned André Durand, *From Sarajevo to Hiroshima: History of the International Committee of the Red Cross* (Geneva: Henry Dunant Institute, 1984); Pierre Boissier, *From Solferino to Tsushima: History of the International Committee of the Red Cross* (Geneva: Henry Dunant Institute, 1985); François Bugnion and Françoise Perret, *De Budapest à Saigon, histoire du comité international de la Croix-Rouge, 1956–1965* (Geneva: Editions Georg, 2010); Silvia Salvatici, '"Help the People to Help Themselves": UNRRA Relief Workers and European Displaced Persons', *Journal of Refugee Studies* 25 (3) (2012): 428–51. Two older classic texts on humanitarian assistance are Randolph Kent, *Anatomy of Disaster Relief: The International Network in Action* (London: Pinter Publishers, 1987) and Peter Macalister-Smith, *International*

The use of history by humanitarians 165

Humanitarian Assistance: Disaster Relief Actions in International Law and Organization (Dordrecht and Lancaster: Nijhoff, 1985). More recently, a number of journal special issues have contributed to this literature, including in *Journal of Nutrition* (2002); *Journal of Contemporary History* (2008); *French Historical Studies* (2011); *Ethnologie française* (2011); *Journal of Imperial and Commonwealth History* (2012); *Past & Present* (2013); *Journal of Modern European History* (2014).

For reflections on the use of history in the humanitarian sector, we drew upon Eleanor Davey, *Humanitarian History in a Complex World*, HPG Policy Brief (London: ODI, 2014); Julia Steets and Claudia Meier, *Coordination to Save Lives: History and Emerging Challenges* (New York: OCHA, 2012); Sean Keogh and Yvonne Ruijters, *Dangerous Liaisons? A Historical Review of UNHCR's Engagement with Non-State Armed Actors* (Geneva: UNHCR, 2012).

In relation to the use of history in humanitarian practice, we discussed *Shelter Projects 2009* (Geneva and Nairobi: IFRC/UN-Habitat, 2010); Hertha Kraus, *International Relief in Action, 1914–1943* (Scottsdale, AZ: Herald Press, 1944); MSF Speaking Out Case Studies, online at www.speakingout.msf.org, accessed 3 November 2014; the Sudan Open Archive, online at www.sudanarchive.net/, accessed 3 November 2014.

In discussing how operational evaluations represented a step towards gathering historical materials, we highlighted John Telford and John Cosgrave, *Joint Evaluation of the International Response to the Indian Ocean Tsunami: Synthesis Report* (London: Tsunami Evaluation Coalition, 2006) and John Eriksson et al., *The International Response to Conflict and Genocide: Lessons from the Rwanda Experience: Synthesis Report* (Copenhagen: Danish Ministry of Foreign Affairs, 1996). For more detail on humanitarian aid and its effects, see the latter project's third study, led by John Borton; readers interested in this area may also wish to consult Adrian P. Wood, Raymond Apthorpe and John Borton (eds), *Evaluating International Humanitarian Action: Reflections from Practitioners* (London: Zed Books, 2001).

Resources cited on humanitarian assistance today included Active Learning Network for Accountability and Performance in Humanitarian Action (ALNAP), *State of the Humanitarian System* (London: ODI, 2012); *Global Humanitarian Assistance Report 2013* (London, Nairobi and Kampala: Development Initiatives, 2013); *Disasters Emergency Committee – East Africa Crisis Appeal: Ethiopia Real-time Evaluation Report* (Oxford: Valid International, 2012); Didier Fassin and Mariella Pandolfi (eds), *Contemporary States of Emergency: The Politics of Military and Humanitarian Interventions* (Cambridge, MA: Zone Books, 2010).

Discussion of various facets or examples of Southern humanitarianism can be seen in Jonathan Benthall and Jérôme Bellion-Jourdan, *The Charitable Crescent: Politics of Aid in the Muslim World* (London: IB Tauris, 2003); Miwa Hirono and Jacinta O'Hagan (eds), *Cultures of Humanitarianism: Perspectives from the Asia-Pacific*, Keynotes, vol. 11. (Canberra: Australian National University, 2012); Julia Pacitto and Elena Fiddian-Qasmiyeh, *Writing the 'Other' into*

166 *John Borton and Eleanor Davey*

Humanitarian Discourse: Framing Theory and Practice in South-South Humanitarian Responses to Forced Displacement (Oxford: Refugee Studies Centre, 2013); see also the publications of HPG's project *A Global History of Modern Humanitarian Action*, available online at www.odi.org.uk, accessed 3 November 2014.

On organizational knowledge in the humanitarian sector and beyond, see John Borton, 'Learning and Knowledge Management: The Literature and Experience of "Comparable" Sectors', in ALNAP, *Annual Review of Humanitarian Action* (London: ALNAP, 2002); Thomas G. Weiss and Peter J. Hoffman, 'The Fog of Humanitarianism: Collective Action Problems and Learning-challenged Organizations', *Journal of Intervention and Statebuilding* 1(1) (2007): 47–65; Charles Booth and Michael Rowlinson, 'Management and Organizational History: Prospects,' *Management & Organizational History* 1(1) (2006): 5–30.

For comparative discussion of the uses of history in relation to the development sector, we drew upon C.A. Bayly et al., *History, Historians and Development Policy: A Necessary Dialogue* (Manchester: Manchester University Press, 2011); David Lewis, 'International Development and the "Perpetual Present": Anthropological Approaches to the Re-historicization of Policy', *European Journal of Development Research* 21 (2009): 32–46; Michael Woolcock, Simon Szreter and Vijayendra Rao, *How and Why Does History Matter for Development Policy?* (Washington, DC: World Bank, 2010).

In relation to the military, we used Edward J. Drea, 'Change becomes Continuity: The Start of the US Army's "Green Book" Series', in Jeffrey Grey (ed.), *The Last Word? Essays on Official History in the United States and British Commonwealth* (Westport, CT: Praeger, 2003), pp. 83–104; Michael Howard, 'The Use and Abuse of Military History', *Royal United Services Institution Journal* 107(625) (1962): 4–10; Williamson Murray and Richard Hart Sinnreich (eds), *The Past as Prologue: The Importance of History to the Military Profession* (Cambridge: Cambridge University Press, 2006).

Notes

1 OECD Aid Statistics 03/04/2013, http://www.oecd.org/dac/stats/aidtopoorcountries slipsfurtherasgovernmentstightenbudgets.htm, accessed 3 November 2014.
2 Active Learning Network for Accountability and Performance in Humanitarian Action (ALNAP), *State of the Humanitarian System* (London: ODI, 2012), 26–8.
3 John Eriksson et al., *The International Response to Conflict and Genocide: Lessons from the Rwanda Experience: Synthesis Report* (Copenhagen: Danish Ministry of Foreign Affairs, 1996); John Telford and John Cosgrave, *Joint Evaluation of the International Response to the Indian Ocean Tsunami: Synthesis Report* (London: Tsunami Evaluation Coalition, 2006).
4 For the purposes of this chapter we take 'historical' analysis to refer to contexts and events that took place more than ten years ago.
5 Alistair Dutton, former Humanitarian Director, Caritas Internationalis, in an interview with John Borton, 19 February 2014.
6 Richard Garfield et al., *Common Needs Assessments and Humanitarian Action*, HPN Network Paper 69 (London: ODI, 2011), p. 6.

7 See for example Charles Booth and Michael Rowlinson, 'Management and Organizational History: Prospects', *Management & Organizational History* 1(1) (2006): 5–30.

8 Eleanor Davey, *Humanitarian History in a Complex World*, HPG Policy Brief (London: ODI, 2014).

9 *Global Humanitarian Assistance Report 2013* (London and Nairobi; Kampala: Development Initiatives, 2013), p. 98.

10 The historical articulation of these principles is associated with the Red Cross, especially in the work of Jean Pictet, but they have also been affirmed by the UN, notably in Resolution 46/182 of 19 December 1991.

11 C.A. Bayly et al., *History, Historians and Development Policy: A Necessary Dialogue* (Manchester: Manchester University Press, 2011); David Lewis, 'International Development and the "Perpetual Present": Anthropological Approaches to the Re-historicization of Policy', *European Journal of Development Research* 21 (2009): 32–46; Michael Woolcock, Simon Szreter and Vijayendra Rao, *How and Why Does History Matter for Development Policy?* (Washington, DC: World Bank, 2010).

12 Lewis, 'International Development and the "Perpetual Present"', p. 33.

13 Valerie Amos, 'Preface', in Julia Steets and Claudia Meier (eds), *Coordination to Save Lives: History and Emerging Challenges* (New York: OCHA, 2012). See also Sean Keogh and Yvonne Ruijters, *Dangerous Liaisons? A Historical Review of UNHCR's Engagement with Non-state Armed Actors* (Geneva: UNHCR, 2012).

14 *Disasters Emergency Committee – East Africa Crisis Appeal: Ethiopia Real-time Evaluation Report* (Oxford: Valid International, 2012), p. 32. This example was identified using the Humanitarian Genome Project.

15 The 11 journals were: *Disasters*; *International Review of the Red Cross*; *Journal of Contemporary History*; *Journal of Refugee Studies*; *American Historical Review*; *International Affairs*; *Refugee Survey Quarterly*; *American Ethnologist*; *Journal of Global History*; *Journal of Nutrition*; *The Lancet*. The list of 500 sources was published in May 2013 on the pilot site http://www.humanitarianhistory.org, accessed 3 November 2014.

16 A humanitarian organization with a strong historical engagement is the International Committee of the Red Cross (ICRC), which has an extensive archive and has produced a number of studies of its own history drawing upon these collections. See for example André Durand, *From Sarajevo to Hiroshima: History of the International Committee of the Red Cross* (Geneva: Henry Dunant Institute, 1984); Pierre Boissier, *From Solferino to Tsushima: History of the International Committee of the Red Cross* (Geneva: Henry Dunant Institute, 1985); François Bugnion and Françoise Perret, *De Budapest à Saigon, histoire du comité international de la Croix-Rouge, 1956–1965* (Geneva: Editions Georg, 2010).

17 Esteban Leon and Graham Saunders, 'Foreword', in *Shelter Projects 2009* (Geneva; Nairobi: IFRC/UN HABITAT, 2010), p. iii.

18 Hertha Kraus, *International Relief in Action, 1914–1943* (Scottsdale, AZ: Herald Press, 1944). The authors are very grateful to Peter Gatrell for bringing this work to our attention.

19 Krauss, *International Relief*, p. 1. On Kraus's work, see Beate Bussiek, 'Hertha Kraus: Quaker Spirit and Competence. Impulses for Professional Social Work in Germany and the United States', in Sabine Hering and Berteke Waaldijk (eds), *History of Social Work in Europe (1900–1960): Female Pioneers and their Influence on the Development of International Social Organizations* (Opladen: Leske + Budrich, 2003), pp. 53–64.

20 Michael Barnett, *Empire of Humanity: A History of Humanitarianism* (Ithaca, NY: Cornell University Press, 2011), 107–12. See also *A Reading List for Relief Workers* (London: Royal Institute for International Affairs, 1944).

21 Speaking Out Case Studies Editorial Committee, 'Foreword', in Laurence Binet (ed.), *Somalia 1991–1993: Civil War, Famine Alert and UN 'Military Humanitarian' Intervention 1991–1993* (Geneva: Médecins Sans Frontières (MSF), 2013), p. 3. This

168 John Borton and Eleanor Davey

and other studies are available at http://www.speakingout.msf.org, accessed 14 August 2014. *Témoignage* is the policy of witnessing and speaking out about inhumanity and injustice, a central tenet of the MSF movement.

22 Rift Valley Institute, 'The Story of the Sudan Open Archive', interview with Dan Large, 2013, http://riftvalley.net/project/sudan-open-archive#.Uw3ipPl_uSo, accessed 26 February 2014.

23 For example Thomas G. Weiss, *Military-civilian Interactions: Intervening in Humanitarian Crises* (Lanham, MD: Rowman & Littlefield, 1999); Borton, 'Learning and Knowledge Management: The Literature and Experience of "Comparable" Sectors', in ALNAP, *Annual Review of Humanitarian Action* (London: ALNAP, 2002); Didier Fassin and Mariella Pandolfi (eds), *Contemporary States of Emergency: The Politics of Military and Humanitarian Interventions* (Cambridge, MA: Zone Books, 2010).

24 John Andreas Olsen and Colin S. Gray, 'Introduction', in Olsen and Gray (eds), *The Practice of Strategy: From Alexander the Great to the Present* (Oxford Scholarship Online, 2012), http://www.oxfordscholarship.com/view/10.1093/acprof:oso/978019960 8638.001.0001/acprof-9780199608638-chapter-1, accessed 14 August 2014.

25 Thomas Waldman, *War, Clausewitz and the Trinity* (Farnham: Ashgate, 2013), pp. 37–9.

26 Williamson Murray and Richard Hart Sinnreich, 'Introduction', in Murray and Sinnreich (eds), *The Past as Prologue: The Importance of History to the Military Profession* (Cambridge: Cambridge University Press, 2006), p. 8.

27 Arthur. S. White, *A Bibliography of Regimental Histories of the British Army* (Dallington: Naval and Military Press, 1992).

28 Edward J. Drea, 'Change Becomes Continuity: The Start of the US Army's "Green Book" Series', in Jeffrey Grey (ed.), *The Last Word? Essays on Official History in the United States and British Commonwealth* (Westport, CT: Praeger, 2003), pp. 83–104. The role of oral history was significantly expanded in the late 1980s and the first guide for conducting oral history was issued in 1992. Stephen Lofgren, *U.S. Army Guide to Oral History* (Washington, DC: Center of Military History of the United States Army, 2006).

29 David French, '"Official but Not History?": Sir James Edmonds and the Official History of the Great War', *Journal of the Royal United Services Institute for Defence Studies* 131(1) (March 1986): 58–63; Andrew Green, *Writing the Great War: Sir James Edmonds and the Official Histories 1915–1948* (London: Frank Cass, 2003).

30 Michael Howard, 'The Use and Abuse of Military History', *Royal United Services Institution Journal* 107(625) (1962): 7. Resonant with this caution, Silvia Salvatici points out that relief workers' planning ambition during the Second World War did not necessarily mean clear or appropriate professional formation, in Salvatici, "Help the People to Help Themselves": UNRRA Relief Workers and European Displaced Persons', *Journal of Refugee Studies* 25(3) (2012): 3–8.

31 Julian Jackson, *The Fall of France: The Nazi Invasion of 1940* (Oxford: Oxford University Press, 2004).

32 Thomas G. Weiss and Peter J. Hoffman, 'The Fog of Humanitarianism: Collective Action Problems and Learning-challenged Organizations', *Journal of Intervention and Statebuilding* 1(1) (2007): 58.

33 See Peter Walker and Catherine Russ, *Professionalising the Humanitarian Sector: A Scoping Study* (London: Enhanced Learning and Research for Humanitarian Assistance, 2010).

34 See Humanitarian Policy Group (HPG), *A Global History of Modern Humanitarian Action Research Framework*, 2013, http://www.odi.org.uk/hpg, accessed 14 August 2014.

35 A pilot version of the site is available at http://www.humanitarianhistory.org, accessed 14 August 2014.

12 The impact of the state

Peter Mandler[1]

British universities are self-governing corporations, but like most universities in the developed world in the second half of the twentieth century they became increasingly dependent on state aid; by the mid-1970s, nearly all of their income came from various agencies of the state. While universities have grown rapidly since the early 1990s, the state's contribution per student has fallen, and more recently cutbacks in public expenditure have reduced the state's contribution in absolute terms. Today the British state invests less in higher education as a proportion of GDP than almost any other OECD country.[2] At the same time, paradoxically, the strings attached to state aid have multiplied and become more onerous. This chapter considers the history of those strings as they bear on research in the humanities. It argues that while the 'arm's length' arrangements developed over the first two-thirds of the twentieth century were underpinned by an emergent philosophy, based on the culture of governance, the specified needs of academic freedom, and the further specified needs of the humanities, the reduction of the 'arm's length' has not been accompanied by any similarly reasoned case. The impact of the state has been driven by *ad hoc* decisions motivated by the need for cost savings twinned with greater accountability. This impact has thus accumulated many dimensions, not all of them compatible, and by no means limited to the requirement that humanities research should have wider 'impact' on economy and society.

I

Since the early years of the twentieth century, state aid to academic research has been mostly channelled through what later became known as the 'dual-funding system'. The most important source of funding came in the form of a basic grant to support teaching and research, beginning in 1889, and from 1919 allocated to individual institutions by the University Grants Committee (UGC), a largely academic body. By 1946 the UGC accounted for a majority of British universities' income and by 1974 its share had peaked at 78 per cent.[3] For most of this period universities were considered primarily teaching institutions, but research played a role of increasing importance, both in the state's view of the universities and in the universities' view of their own mission. UGC funds for

170   *Peter Mandler*

research were distributed on the 'block-grant principle', which sought funding from government based on its own assessment of the universities' plans and needs, and then determined allocations to individual institutions based on the universities' statements of their own plans and needs, but left it entirely to the institutions to allocate internally to departments, individuals and projects. As the UGC put it in 1964,

> In relation to recurrent income, the general principle has been accepted that the State, though contributing over 70 per cent of the universities' income, does not intervene formally or by direction. The allocations of recurrent grant are, in the main, block allocations without strings. The principle of this seems clearly essential ... If money were allocated among departments and developments by an outside body the decisions would be taken without full knowledge of the individual university's circumstances and needs, and possibly on non-academic grounds.[4]

Though this principle may today sound impossibly high-minded, even naive, it was then consistent with the general practice of the British state in the twentieth century, as it extended its reach and its funds into realms previously considered the province of personal freedom and individual choice, especially where the expression of opinion was concerned: that is, the 'arm's length' principle, whereby funds were allocated by the state but disbursed by a non-state or para-state body, deemed to be less immediately motivated by short-term political considerations, usually under Treasury oversight. This practice had emerged in the nineteenth century to fund the national galleries and museums, but it extended more generally in the twentieth century, to the BBC, to the Arts Council and to the universities.

The second arm of the dual-funding system originated in 1918 with a report on the machinery of government authored by Lord Haldane, which established a system of research councils, initially confined to the sciences, which were charged with financing what is now called 'research and development' (R&D), mostly at first outside universities but increasingly inside them as well. Recognizing that more direct state investment was needed in academic research – pure as well as applied – than could be generated from their block grants by the universities, Haldane recommended that research councils like the UGC be placed under a neutral minister (in this case, the Lord President of the Council), 'immune from any suspicion of being biased by administrative considerations', advised by an academic council.[5] It was accepted that the research councils – who would make allocations to individual projects as well as institutions, but would also perform commissioned research at the direct behest of government departments – could not be as completely insulated from the demands of the state as the UGC. Nevertheless, what became known (although not until the early 1960s[6]) as the 'Haldane Principle' required an arm's length relationship between government and research councils similar to that between government and the UGC, though perhaps shorter: 'the principle', as the Trend Report of 1963 asserted, 'that the control of research should be separated from the executive function of Government ... which, in our view, has contributed significantly to the councils' ability to promote research and development while simultaneously guaranteeing the independence of the scientific judgments involved.'[7]

Until the time of the Trend Report, only the UGC arm of the dual-funding structure had any impact upon the humanities. Neither the humanities nor the social sciences received much funding from research councils until the Social Science Research Council (SSRC), whose remit included economic and social history, was established in 1965.[8] Indeed, for a long period the humanities and the social sciences preferred the longer arm's length of the UGC to the prospect of the much enhanced funding that research council status might give them.[9] But opinion began to shift in the early 1960s, in large part because the state was then growing more inclined to assert control over both arms of the dual-funding system. The impetus came from the rapid expansion of the whole university system that began under Conservative governments in the late 1950s, and then also from the determination of Labour governments after 1964 to use state investment in science and technology as a motor of economic growth. A key marker of this changing mood came with the creation in 1963 of a new Department of Education and Science (DES), which acquired oversight of the UGC from the Treasury, to which was added in 1965 oversight of the research councils. It was precisely out of concern for such concentration of powers over research in one government department that the Haldane Principle came to be insisted upon, and defined more closely, particularly by Conservatives, who were alarmed at statements, such as that of the Labour Education Secretary Tony Crosland in April 1965, that 'it is desirable in itself that a substantial part of the higher education system should be under social control, directly responsible to social needs'.[10]

In a period of expansion, however, not even a highly interventionist Labour government sought to impinge much on the funding decisions of either the UGC or the research councils. History entered the research council regime in 1965 when the SSRC was set up, and began to make small allocations to projects and postgraduate students in economic and social history; at about the same time, the DES itself began to fund postgraduate students in the humanities on a modest basis. Fears of 'social control' ebbed. The UGC retained its autonomy and its 'predominantly academic membership' under DES, the block-grant principle was 'faithfully maintained', and the Haldane Principle entered bureaucratic argot. Labour's agenda for higher education was shifting by the late 1960s from 'manpower planning' to 'personal development', which favoured the humanities, the link between research and teaching, and university autonomy.[11]

II

The irony is that university autonomy began to be impaired when state aid went into decline. A warning shot was fired across the bows in 1971, when a no-nonsense report by Lord Rothschild of the Central Policy Review Staff recommended that the research council budgets should be slashed and the

172   *Peter Mandler*

savings applied to the relevant government departments to be used for commissioned research on a 'customer–contractor' basis. Still, one of Rothschild's motivations for this recommendation was to preserve the autonomy of 'pure' research – which in 1971 he thought included much scientific and all humanities and social science research – funded by the UGC and the research councils.[12] At this point, already the universities had begun to tailor their own appeals to more stringent times. As the 'unit of resource' (the quantum of funding provided to universities in their block grants for each student) went into decline in the cash-strapped 1970s, both the UGC and the research councils began to talk up 'strategic' research, which was pure research in areas that were more likely to yield practical applications.[13] In the mid-1970s, the government ended the system of quinquennial grants to the UGC, which meant that both the UGC and individual universities had to sing for their supper on an annual basis. At least the government's growing obsession with the unit of resource meant that these negotiations revolved increasingly around student numbers, and government had little time or energy for 'strategic' interventions of any kind in research.

This pattern, already established in the 1970s, intensified in succeeding decades: government was intent on cutting the unit of resource; the universities (and especially the research councils) felt they had increasingly to justify their budgets by recourse to special pleading ('strategic' significance, economic value, 'impact' on society and culture). The arm's length relationship had turned into a clinch, sometimes agonistic, sometimes propitiatory, often very hard to read – were the universities actually offering something that government valued, or were they often making symbolic offerings to the gods that had little effect on the unit of resource, while subtly undermining the block grant and Haldane Principle to which lip service was still paid? The stop–go policies of the Thatcher governments substantially exacerbated this development. In her first government, Thatcher and her Education Secretary Sir Keith Joseph cut the research and teaching budgets not just relative to student numbers but in absolute terms – the famous 'run-down'. Instead of allowing the UGC to manage the run-down on its own, Joseph leaned on them to prioritize 'the needs of industry, commerce, the professions and the public services for manpower, research and other forms of support and assistance'.[14] On the other arm of the dual-funding structure, Joseph leant still harder. Convinced that the SSRC was a waste of public funds, and riddled with socialist bias, Joseph appointed Lord Rothschild to undertake another review, aiming at dissolving and dispersing the SSRC. Much to his surprise, Rothschild repeated and fortified his earlier contention that neither the social sciences nor the humanities ought to be subject to the 'customer–contractor' principle. Furthermore, he gently chided his minister for even suggesting as much, reminding him of the basis on which the arm's length relationship was founded in the first place:

> The need for independence from government departments is particularly important because so much social science research is the stuff of political debate. All such research might prove subversive of government policies

because it attempts to submit such policies to empirical trial, with the risk that the judgment may be averse. It would be too much to expect Ministers to show enthusiasm for research designed to show that their policies were misconceived. But it seems obvious that in many cases the public interest will be served by such research being undertaken.[15]

Joseph retreated, wounded. Only cosmetic changes were made to the SSRC (one of which was to rename it ESRC – Economic and Social Research Council).

In Thatcher's second government, Joseph was replaced by the more emollient and populist Kenneth Baker. The strategy shifted from run-down to expansion, as for electoral and other reasons Thatcher decided to move to mass higher education. The unit of resource now fell precipitously, by 40 per cent from its 1970s peak.[16] Joseph's dirigisme (always odd for an ideologically committed neoliberal) gave way to a fierce economism. The UGC was replaced by funding councils whose job was no longer to plan or strategize for higher education, but only to distribute their block grants to institutions by means of a more transparent funding model. They were no longer principally academic bodies, but more closely resembled corporate boards, with representatives of industry and the professions as well as universities. They put pressure on universities to remodel their own governing bodies on similar lines. Teaching funds were distributed strictly on the basis of student numbers. Research funds were distributed selectively, on the basis of a series of 'research selectivity' or 'research assessment' exercises, which continue to this day. These research assessment exercises were founded on peer review of the academic excellence of research, but also measured other indicators, such as research income, planning and strategy, 'esteem', 'environment', and, from 2014, 'impact'.[17]

The research councils, always closer to government than the block-grant side of the funding structure, benefited from the declining unit of resource allocated to the funding councils. Major cuts in the unit of resource delivered through the block grants could be 'compensated' by increases in the smaller research council budgets, and as a result the total share of research funding deriving from the research councils grew.[18] To encourage this development, the research councils intensified their propitiatory activities. As Lord Rothschild predicted in 1982, the ESRC was most vulnerable to this pressure. An ever larger share of its budget was devoted to 'strategic' priorities aimed at enticing government support. By 1995, 70 per cent even of its postgraduate studentships were awarded on the basis of 'thematic priorities'.[19] The changing managerial structure of universities further fuelled this trend. With the replacement of 'black box' funding models with transparent market-based funding models, universities became much more competitive with each other. As research funding grew in significance, universities competed more vigorously for it at the expense of teaching; as research council funding grew in significance compared to the other arm of the dual support system, universities focused upon it. 'Thematic' or 'strategic' priorities gave their managers something to aim at, which did not require intimate knowledge of the internal structure of an academic discipline.

174 *Peter Mandler*

Anyone who has taught in any British university over the past twenty years will recognize this concatenation of circumstances which has made research councils more responsive to government, and universities more responsive to research councils. The clinch became ever tighter.

III

As we have seen, for a long time the humanities were relatively immune from such pressures, as they were almost entirely funded from the block grant. The Haldane Principle never entered the vocabulary of arts and humanities scholars. From the late 1990s, however, this began to change. As the research councils grew in funding and status, humanities scholars (or at least their managers) began to wonder what they were missing out on. The British Academy had for some years been administering a direct grant from the DES to fund small research projects and postgraduate studentships in the humanities. It set up, first, in 1992, its own Humanities Research Board as a precursor to research council status, and then, in 1998, in partnership with the funding councils (which top-sliced their block-grant allocation for the purpose), an Arts and Humanities Research Board (AHRB). By 2002 it had persuaded the government to give them research council status. The principal motive was to give the humanities 'parity of status' with the other disciplines, to permit them to 'play their proper part in the evolution of research policy and the execution of research goals'. Although it was acknowledged that there was some danger that their 'proper part' would mean the role of 'poorer cousin' to the science councils – their budget would amount to 4 per cent of the total research council budget – these concerns were dismissed as 'overstated'. There was also some appreciation of the risks of courting the closer relationship with government entailed in research council status – the application of 'tests of the national interest' – but consolation was found in 'scope for interesting and excellent research outside the parameters of the national interest ... through a portion of research funds being in "responsive" mode', in the role of the research councils as 'a buffer – though not an altogether impervious one – between government and research funding decisions', and in the Haldane Principle, 'under which day-to-day decisions on the scientific merits of different strategies, programmes and projects are taken by the Research Councils without government involvement'.[20]

No careful cost–benefit analysis was made of this transition. The AHRB, funded as it was largely from the block grant, had been a relatively 'non-strategic' funder. The interesting and excellent research it funded had not had tests of national interest applied, and it was thus almost entirely disbursed in 'responsive mode'. While 'parity of esteem' sounded good, 'poorer cousin' status was always likely – and realized in the event. The New Labour governments that presided over the founding of the Arts and Humanities Research Council (AHRC) first installed it with the other research councils under the aegis of the Office of Science and Technology (OST), then created new business- and science-dominated ministries – the Department for Innovation, Universities and

Skills (DIUS), the Department for Business, Innovation and Skills (BIS) – to hitch all higher education expenditure to its economic growth agenda.

Thus began a series of propitiatory gestures designed both to fit the poorer cousin into the science-dominated research council environment, and to show that the AHRC was just as (possibly more) capable of aligning itself with government's policy priorities as the more established councils. A wave of science-modelled policies swept through the AHRC's subject domain: 'journal metrics', 'team-based research', 'knowledge transfer' (later re-badged as 'knowledge exchange'), 'the e-Science initiative', 'Science in Society', 'Science and Heritage'.

The AHRC first introduced the idea of a compulsory Masters year as 'training' for the PhD, on a science model, and then withdrew it when it decided to cut its own budget for postgraduate support, partly to align with the science councils. It may perhaps have made this decision to transfer funds from postgraduate awards (which were devolved to institutions) to research programmes (which were subject to strategic priorities) without prompting from government, but even as a propitiatory gesture it might be considered 'a breach of the Haldane Principle', which, a Commons Select Committee had recently warned, would occur if 'the Government should direct a Research Council to switch funding from postgraduate awards to programme funding merely on the basis of it being out of step with other research councils, or indeed for any other reason'.[21] It then also reeled in control of its postgraduate awards by requiring that institutions align them more closely with the AHRC's strategy and delivery plan. It signed up to a joint research council initiative on 'Open Access' publishing, driven by science lobbies such as the Wellcome Trust and the Public Library of Science (PLOS), under pressure from the BIS department not to accept that humanities or social science publishing might require a different funding or publication model from the sciences.[22]

As was widely acknowledged by AHRB leaders at the point of transfer, humanities scholars were to have their mouths stuffed with gold – although not that much gold; the final-year grant to the AHRB in 2004 was £77m, the first-year grant to the AHRC was £83m, and the grant (currently subject to year-on-year real-terms cuts) in 2012–13 was £108m (or about £95m in 2004 prices). What did the government get in return for its money? It was able to transfer a further modest sum from the block grant to the research council budget, over which it had tighter control. It was able to rationalize the research council system, so that all academic disciplines were now subject to the same organizational and financial structures. It seems unlikely that government cares nearly as much about projecting its interpretation of 'national needs' through the humanities, as it does through the social or natural sciences, but the propitiatory efforts of the AHRC have aimed to persuade it to do so by means of a series of strategic priorities, which now account for about 30 per cent of the AHRC budget.[23] These have been devised so far as possible to sound like 'national needs' without unnecessarily constraining research on the ground – 'Religion in Society', 'Global Security', 'Digital Economy', 'Connected Communities' – and indeed are often couched in such vacuous terms – 'Care for the Future', 'Beyond Text', 'Translating Cultures' – that it seems hardly conceivable that government would recognize them as strategies.

176   *Peter Mandler*

On one recent occasion, however, the AHRC's propitiatory efforts went too far even for government, requiring exhumation of the Haldane Principle to halt it. This was its decision to align itself with the government's 'Big Society' policy in its 'delivery plan' for 2011–15. The Haldane Principle had been coming under increasing pressure since the research councils were transferred to the business-oriented ministries under New Labour. The oversight of a 'neutral' minister had long been lost; now an aggressively purposeful minister was in charge. As early as 1993, the OST had distinguished between 'day to day decisions' which the research councils could take 'without Government involvement', and 'a preceding level of broad priority setting between general classes of activity', in which government should share – 'a modern rendition of the Haldane Principle in all but name', as a Commons Select Committee observed. Now the minister named it. In a speech in April 2008, John Denham, the DIUS Secretary, redefined the Haldane Principle along similar lines: 'that researchers are best placed to determine detailed priorities', but 'that the Government's role is to set the overarching strategy'. For this he came under a lot of criticism. His Select Committee argued that both the six thematic priorities he had set for the research councils and the specific direction to transfer funds from postgraduate education to research grants violated their own understanding of the Haldane Principle. The minister was perfectly entitled to his understanding, but there should at least be a public debate.[24]

This debate broke out on the terrain of the humanities under the next government, which as part of its austerity campaign put severe pressure on the research councils in the 2010 spending round to give it better value for money. Although the details of these negotiations remain confidential, there is evidence that the government both dictated the forms of research council programmes – insisting, for example, on the elimination of small grants, though they are the lifeblood of the humanities – and at least suggested their content – though there is always the chance that these represented only more earnest acts of propitiation by the councils rather than direct orders from government. BIS announced a 'further clarification' of the Haldane Principle which entitled it to set 'key national strategic priorities' for the research councils, and announced that the highest priorities in arts and humanities had been established as 'communities and big society; civic values and active citizenship, including ethics in public life; creative and digital economy; cultural heritage; language-based disciplines; and interdisciplinary collaborations with a range of [science, technology, engineering and mathematics] (STEM) subjects'. (Interdisciplinary collaboration with humanities subjects was not one of 'the highest priorities' for the sciences.)[25]

The most egregious outcome of this priority setting was evident in the AHRC's 'Delivery Plan' for 2011–15 – itself a novelty indicating the shortening of the leash – which showed how it would meet government's priorities. In addition to aligning itself with all of the government's 'key national strategic priorities', the AHRC went a step further and pledged to 'contribute to the government's initiatives', '[i]n line with the government's "Big Society" agenda'. Now the Big Society had by this point become a rhetorical flashpoint – it stood

The impact of the state 177

for the Conservatives' ambition to shrink down the welfare state and transfer its functions to the voluntary action of civil society. For many academics, and beyond them, the AHRC's kowtowing to the Big Society – it was mentioned five times in the delivery plan, and eight times in some earlier drafts – represented the point-of-no-return at which the 'clarification' of the Haldane Principle had introduced not only 'national needs' but party politics into the work of the research councils. In response to a storm of protest, the AHRC strove mightily to suggest that the 'Big Society' was only another way of saying 'Connected Communities', a pre-existing research council programme, or perhaps a way of selling 'Connected Communities' to Conservative ministers. But in the end, even the Universities Minister, David Willetts, while denying 'any pernicious temptation to steer the money towards ministers' pet priorities', asked the research councils 'to reflect on the hazards of referring at all to current political slogans'.[26]

In its 2010 strategic plan, BIS observed, rather mournfully, that the Further and Higher Education Act 1992 prohibited government from attaching 'terms and conditions' relating to 'programmes of research' to the block grants, in the same way that its 'clarification' of the Haldane Principle had just permitted it to do with the research councils.[27] Nevertheless, the funding councils charged with the block grants have not absolutely exempted themselves from propitiatory gestures either. The chief among these gestures has been the provision for 'impact' in the 2014 Research Excellence Framework (the latest rebadging of the recurrent research assessment exercises), aimed at demonstrating the 'value for money' of university research.

While in keeping with the 1992 Act the definition of impact has been carefully left open and clear of 'national needs' or 'strategic priorities', and remains defined and assessed largely by peer review (by researchers and their 'users'), science models are in evidence here too: in the councils' initial ideas about what impact might mean (principally economic); in the attempts to exclude the impact of research on 'education'; in the successful exclusion of PhD students' research (in the sciences not seen as sufficiently 'independent'); and in the preference for quantitative measures even of those impacts (such as changing 'hearts and minds') that remain defiantly unquantifiable.[28] Similarly, the funding councils initially showed some readiness to follow the research councils' government-dictated Open Access policy, also on a science model, although the differential lengths of the leashes continue to tell in the funding councils' ability, to some extent, to set their own agenda and their own pace. It is not implausible to suspect that some revision of the 1992 Act may be in the offing which will allow a 'clarification' of the block-grant principle similar to government's 2010 'clarification' of the Haldane Principle.

IV

No one would argue that the UGC's definition of 'accountability' in the 1960s is practical in the twenty-first century. Citizens rightly demand more 'value for money', especially as the cost of university research balloons in conditions of

178 *Peter Mandler*

mass education and high technology; they are not content to accept paternal assurances that Whitehall or Westminster (or the Vice-Chancellor's Office) knows best. Nevertheless, the arm's length principle was a coherent strategy to reconcile an interventionist state with a liberal society and culture, and it has more rather than less cogency in a period when the state is retracting rather than growing. Interventionism by selective cuts is less obvious, more insidious, than interventionism by directed initiative. Historically, across the twentieth century, academics accepted limits on their freedom when the public interest had clearly something to gain from a governmental (but non-partisan) assessment of 'national needs'. That worked for scientists because they had big bargaining chips: government needed them (for national prestige, for the health service and defence, for economic growth), as well as vice-versa. The humanities flourished under the more secure protection of the block-grant principle. Assessments of 'national needs' in the humanities, and in the social sciences, were too vulnerable to partisan manipulation and to the illiberal and counter-productive fostering of orthodoxies by funders, as right-of-centre observers from Sir John Clapham to Lord Rothschild argued.

This British story is worth observing closely because it may offer a taste of things to come for the rest of the developed world. Most states seem likely to continue to reduce their relative share of the funding of higher education, even if few have as yet cut that share as drastically as has the British state. Perhaps in the long run universities will free themselves from dependence on the state (although in doing so they are likely to fall into the hands of even less accountable – private, philanthropic – funders, as has happened already to non-governmental organizations (NGOs) involved in health and education policy).

But in the medium term, governments are likely to demand more and more in return for less and less, a 'long goodbye' that can only undermine the academic freedom and independence which enable universities to perform their critical functions in a liberal society. To avert this outcome, there is a pressing need to redefine government's relationship with the universities, and especially with the humanities, in ways that reflect a balanced assessment of what the universities do and what conditions they need to do it in, rather than reflecting only government's immediate needs for 'value' and its increasingly impetuous demands for alignment with its policies. The humanities need this more than most, in part because they bargain with government on more uneven terms than do the scientists. As money talks louder and louder, furthermore, humanities scholars, who need and receive so much less of it, are increasingly at the mercy not only of government, but also of their own managers. The shortened leash throttles, it does not empower them; and it restricts the creativity, and thus the utility, of their research, rather than enhancing it.

There is plenty of evidence that the citizenry still understands, and values, 'arm's length' government when it touches on matters of personal expression and education. Consider the outcry that would ensue if government established 'strategic priorities' for the Arts Council or the BBC, or that did ensue when government sought to implant its own priorities in the national curriculum for

The impact of the state 179

history. Considerable ingenuity has been devoted to devising means of funding arm's length bodies – such as the BBC's licence fee – which give value for money and accountability while protecting autonomy and freedom of expression. The humanities deserve no less.

Suggested further reading

Jonathan Bate (ed.), *The Public Value of the Humanities* (London, Bloomsbury Academic, 2011).

Stefan Collini, *What Are Universities For?* (London, Penguin, 2012).

David Edgerton, 'The "Haldane Principle" and Other Invented Traditions in Science Policy', July 2009, http://www.historyandpolicy.org/papers/policy-paper-88.html, accessed 9 February 2014.

Peter Mandler, 'The Two Cultures Revisited: The Humanities in British Universities since 1945', *Twentieth-Century British History* (forthcoming, 2015).

Notes

1 I am grateful to Stefan Collini and David Edgerton for conversations on these topics and also for specific suggestions on this text; also to my colleagues in the Royal Historical Society for consistent support and constructive criticism along the way.

2 Public expenditure represents 0.7 per cent of GDP, on a par with Chile, Korea and Slovakia, and only Japan (0.5 per cent) spends less. Only in Chile does public expenditure represent a smaller proportion of total expenditure on higher education. These figures pre-date the 2012 upscaling of tuition fees, which has further reduced both absolute levels and share of expenditure. *Education at a Glance 2013: OECD Indicators* (Paris: OECD, 2013), p. 184 (Chart B2.2), p. 193 (Table B2.3), p. 199 (Chart B3.2), p. 200 (Chart B3.3, showing by far the highest shift towards private expenditure in the OECD between 2000 and 2010), p. 202 (Chart B3.4, showing lowest levels of public expenditure per student apart from Chile and Korea), p. 207 (Table B3.2b), p. 208 (Table B3.3, one of only five countries to make absolute cuts since 2008).

3 *Review of the University Grants Committee* (i.e. the Croham Report), Cmd 81 (1987–88), p. 8.

4 University Grants Committee (UGC), *University Development, 1957–62*, Cmd 2267 (1963–64), p. 197.

5 It is an indication of how distant Haldane's time was from ours that the bias he considered likely to arise from 'administrative considerations' was 'against the application of research'. But the exact meaning of this phrase was probably obscure even at the time.

6 See David Edgerton, 'The "Haldane Principle" and Other Invented Traditions in Science Policy', July 2009, http://www.historyandpolicy.org/papers/policy-paper-88.html, accessed 9 February 2014.

7 *Committee of Enquiry into the Organisation of Civil Science* (i.e. the Trend Report), Cmd 2171 (1963–64), pp. 13, 30, 44–5.

8 See Desmond King, 'Creating a Funding Regime for Social Research in Britain: The Heyworth Committee on Social Studies and the Founding of the Social Science Research Council', *Minerva* 35 (1997): 1–26.

9 See the Clapham Report of 1946, which recommended against Research Council status, warning against the 'danger of a premature crystallization of spurious orthodoxies', and plumped for enhanced allocations through the UGC instead. *Report of*

180   *Peter Mandler*

the Committee on the Provision for Social and Economic Research (i.e. the Clapham Report, although Sir John Clapham died before he could sign the report), Cmd 6868 (1945–46), p. 12.

10 John Carswell, *Government and the Universities in Britain: Programme and Performance 1960–1980* (Cambridge: Cambridge University Press, 1985), pp. 72–3; for Conservative evocations of the Haldane Principle against Labour's incursions on academic independence, see e.g. Lord Todd, *Hansard*, 5th ser., 256 (1963–64), 438 (11 Mar. 1964), Quintin Hogg, *Hansard*, 5th ser., 703 (1964–65), 1646–7 (9 Dec. 1964), David Price, *Hansard*, 5th ser., 703 (1964–65), 2053 (11 Dec. 1964).

11 Carswell, *Government and the Universities*, pp. 79–84, pp. 139–40; Jean Bocock, Lewis Baston, Peter Scott and David Smith, 'American Influence on British Higher Education: Science, Technology, and the Problem of University Expansion, 1945–63', *Minerva* 41 (2003): 343–4. I discuss the swing towards the humanities and social sciences in greater detail in Mandler, 'The Two Cultures Revisited: The Humanities in British Universities since 1945', *Twentieth-Century British History* (forthcoming, 2015).

12 Lord Rothschild, 'The Organisation and Management of Government R&D', in *A Framework for Government Research and Development*, Cmd 4814 (1971), pp. 7–8, 10, 17–19.

13 Michael Shattock, *The UGC and the Management of British Universities* (Buckingham: Open University Press, 1994), p. 37.

14 Memorandum submitted by the DES, Mar. 1983: House of Commons. Education, Science and Arts Committee, *Higher Education Funding. Minutes of evidence together with appendices Monday 28 March 1983*, HC 293 (1982–83), pp. 31–2.

15 Rothschild cited approvingly evidence to this effect from the economic historians Peter Mathias and Barry Supple. Rothschild, *An Enquiry into the Social Science Research Council*, Cmd 8554 (1981/82), pp. 11–12, 65–6, 74.

16 Shattock, 'Managing Mass Higher Education in a Period of Austerity', *Arts and Humanities in Higher Education* 9 (2010): 22–3.

17 For a summary of the progress of these exercises, see Valerie Bence and Charles Oppenheim, 'The Evolution of the UK's Research Assessment Exercise: Publications, Performance and Perceptions', *Journal of Educational Administration and History* 37 (2005): 137–55.

18 This long-term tendency was deliberately accelerated by a 'dual support transfer' from 1992, which shifted the balance between block grants and research council grants in favour of the latter.

19 King, 'Creating a Funding Regime', p. 19.

20 'Review of Arts and Humanities Research Funding: Report of the Steering Group to Education Ministers', n.d. (July 2002): dera.ioe.ac.uk/9275/2/SOR_143_1.doc, accessed 17 February 2014. Note that this restatement of the Haldane Principle itself represents a revision, leaving only 'day-to-day decisions' beyond government's remit.

21 House of Commons. Select Committee on Innovation, Universities, Science and Skills, *DIUS's Departmental Report 2008*, vol. I, HC 51 (2008/9), pp. 63–4.

22 I discuss this further in Mandler, 'Open Access for the Humanities: Not for Funders, Scientists or Publishers', *Journal of Victorian Culture* 18 (2013): 551–7. Note that the funding councils, always on a longer leash than the research councils, have been able to negotiate a more flexible Open Access policy which does recognize the distinctive needs and patterns of the humanities and social sciences.

23 'Strategic' programmes grew from 2.5 per cent of the AHRB research budget in its final year (2004–5) to 6 per cent of the AHRC's in its first year (2005–6), at which point it predicted a 25 per cent threshold, to 28 per cent in 2009–10 and about 35 per cent proposed for 2011–15 in the 'delivery plan'; under pressure from its subject communities, AHRC now seems pledged to hold the threshold at 30 per cent.

The impact of the state 181

24 House of Commons. Select Committee on Innovation, Universities, Science and Skills, *DIUS's Departmental Report 2008*, vol. I, HC 51 (2008/9), pp. 63–4; but see House of Commons, *Putting Science and Engineering at the Heart of Government Policy*, vol. I, HC 168–1 (2008–9), pp. 40–4, 49, 55, for a very different spin, advocating 'a much more mission-driven approach' on the part of government. The wording of the latter was based on a misinterpretation of the testimony of the historian David Edgerton, who was sceptical about the Haldane Principle's ability to stop government interference, but not about the principle of non-interference. See Edgerton's letter to *Times Higher Education Supplement*, 30 June 2011, p. 30.
25 Department for Business, Innovation and Skills (BIS), *The Allocation of Science and Research Funding 2011/12 to 2014/15* (Dec. 2010), p. 22, and, on the 'clarification' of the Haldane Principle, pp. 13, 57–8.
26 *Times Higher Education Supplement*, 26 May 2011, p. 36.
27 BIS, *Allocation of Science and Research Funding*, p. 57.
28 For some criticisms of 'impact' so defined, see Jonathan Bate (ed.), *The Public Value of the Humanities* (London: Bloomsbury Academic, 2011), pp. 6–9, and Stefan Collini, *What Are Universities For?* (London: Penguin, 2012), pp. 168–74. Both point out that the greatest impact of humanities research on society lies in the way it informs university teaching, which now reaches nearly 50 per cent of the age cohort, though this has been largely excluded from the Research Excellence Framework (REF) definition of impact.

Index

1900 House 114, 117 (see also experiential history)
Aethelflaed of Mercia 49
Ahmed, Sara 119
Algeria 89, 96, 101–3
Amos, Valerie 157
Anderson, Benedict 7
Annales 2, 86, 141
Anthony, Scott 9
Anthropocene 151
Arrhenius, Svante 147
Arts and Humanities Research Board (AHRB) 174–75
Arts and Humanities Research Council (AHRC) 174–77
The Ascent of Man 47
Ashton, Paul 37, 43–44
Attenborough, David 46

Barbauld, Anna Laetitia 50
Bareh 61
Barnett, Corelli 88
Barnett, Michael 159
Barthes, Roland 48
Beamish 5
BBC 26–27, 46–51, 55, 64, 79, 114, 170, 178; *BBC History* magazine 72
Beckett, Andy 75–76
Benda, Julien 16
Benefits Britain 1949 117
Berger, John 47
Berger, Stefan 8
black history 8, 50; Black History Month 50
Blair, Tony 112
Bloch, Marc 1, 11–14, 16, 91
Boia, Lucian 89
Booth, Charles 118
Borton, John 11, 17
Boucher-Saulnier, Françoise 11

Bourdieu, Pierre 4, 7, 8
Boyle, Danny 8
Braudel, Fernand 1, 3, 11, 49, 55, 76, 86, 96
bricolage 9, 11–13
Brideshead Revisited 23
Bright, Charles 90
Brighton 36, 38
British History Online 38
Bryant, Arthur 87
business studies 4
Butler, Toby 2
Buzatu, Gheorge 85

Caldwell, Lynton 144–45
Callender, G.S. 147
Cameron, David 74, 112
Cannadine, David 71, 88
Carlyle, Thomas 143
celebrities 26–27, 114
Central African Republic 11
Channel 4 (UK) 47, 50, 114, 117
China 21–22, 50, 97, 99, 101; Chinese tourism 22–23
Chartism (social movement) 132
Christian, David 151
Christianity/religion 105, 130–31
Church of Jesus Christ of Latter Day Saints 6, 29
Clark, Chris 75
Clausewitz, Carl von 161
Clegg, Nick 113
climate change 140–42, 145–47, 150–51
Codicote 51
Cok, Christina 49, 51
Colley, Linda 88
Collini, Stefan 15
colonialism 96–101, 105–6; post-colonialism 96–100

Index 183

communism 83–86
commodification 4–17, 22–23, 31–32, 35
comparative history 90–91, 151
Conquistadors 55
Cornwell, Bernard 48
Cowling, Maurice 88
cultural capital 7–8, 28, 31
Cumberbatch, Benedict 79

d'Avenant, Charles 105
The Daily Mail 72, 73–74, 78–79, 115, 117
The Daily Star 75
The Daily Telegraph 79, 116, 132
Davey, Eleanor 11, 17
Davies, Norman 88
De Groot, Jerome 4, 5
democracy: 'cultures of democracy' 71; democratic values 7, 12–15, 32, 74, 78, 131, 134; participatory democracy 113
Der lange Weg nach Westen 87
Dick, Bella 111
Dirlik, Arif 90
Disaster Emergency Committee (DEC) 157
Dorey, Peter 117
Downton Abbey 22–25
Douglas Clark, Jonathan Charles 88
Duffy, Eamon 55–56

Economic and Social Research Council (ESRC) 173
The Economist 147
Edmonds, Brigadier General Sir James 162
education 1, 17, 21, 26, 28, 41, 43, 47, 79, 95–99, 107, 148, 157, 162–63, 169; Haldane principle 170–72, 174–77
Egan, Ronald 50
Eichengreen, Barry 11
Elias, Norbert 16
Elton, Charles 149
Elton, Geoffrey 88
Encyclopaedia Britannica 34
English Heritage 5, 6, 39, 44, 48
environment 41, 51, 124, 127, 131, 133, 140–41, 143–46, 148–52
Evans, Richard 75
experiential history 49, 55

Facebook 30, 123, 125
family history (see genealogy)
Febvre, Lucien 12, 76, 141
Felice, Renzo de 86, 89
Ferguson, Niall 75
field work and field trip 41, 161

The Financial Times 79
Fisher, Mark 21–22
folk music 10, 127, 130, 136
Foyle, Peter 146
France 5, 10–12, 83, 86, 89, 95–104, 106–7, 141
Fraser Darling, Frank 147
French Revolution (1789) 5, 107, 127

Game of Thrones 25, 49
Gandhi 46, 61, 124, 129
Garnaut, Ross 145–46
gender 4, 8, 26, 28, 47, 50, 99–100, 104, 113–14
genealogy 6, 8, 21, 24, 25–32, 35–37, 42, 99, 114, 119; websites 29–30; encoding 29–30
Geographical Information System (GIS) 39, 44
Germany 5, 10, 83, 91; East Germany (GDR) 83; Federal Republic (FRG) 87, 88–89; Nazi past 12, 50, 72, 85–87
Geyer, Michael 90
Gill, Eric 46
Gillard, Julia 146
Gledhill, Jim 134, 136
global history (see world history)
global warming (see climate change)
Gorman, John 126, 135
Gould, Stephen Jay 151
Graham, Alex 26
Grayling, Chris 113
Great Britain 87–88
The Great British Story 50, 55
Great Depression 11, 46
Great War (1914–18) 24, 72, 161
The Great War (TV documentary) 47
Gregory, Ian 39, 42, 44
The Guardian 46, 75, 77, 79, 117, 123

Habermas, Jürgen 87
Hastings, Max 70, 72
heritage 23–25; *The Heritage Industry: Britain in a Climate of Decline* 23; Heritage Lottery Fund 23, 120 (see also English Heritage, National Trust)
Herodotus 141
Hewison, Robert 23
Hildebrand, Klaus 88–89
Hillgruber, Andreas 87–88
Hilton, Rodney 64
History and Policy 79
Historian's Craft 12 (see also Bloch, Marc)
History Workshop Movement 3, 88, 135

184 *Index*

Hobsbawm, Eric 7, 82
Hollywood films 48
Hóman, Bálint 85
Horrible Histories 111
Hoskins, W.G. 38, 43, 64
Howard, Michael 162
Howell, Cicely 64
Humanitarian and Conflict Response
  Institute (HCRI) 164
Hunt, Tristram 49, 110–11

impact 169; 'impact agenda' (UK) 2–17,
  41–42, 79–80, 173
India 61–63, 97, 99, 101, 102, 103, 105
Indian Ocean 97, 99, 101, 153
The Independent 64
industry 3, 22, 111, 172–73
inequality 4, 21–22, 111–19, 123
inheritance 25–32
International Federation of the Red Cross
  and Red Crescent (IFRC) 153, 158
Ireland 55, 89
Italy 5, 86–87, 89
ITV 47, 74

James, Paula 126
Jarausch, Konrad 91
Jenkins, Keith 110
Jenkins, Roy 70
journalism 4, 9, 27, 47 70–80
A Journey Through Ruins 77
Judt, Tony 90

Kean, Hilda 37
Kearney, Hugh 88
Kibworth 64–66
Kraus, Hertha 159

L'Identité de la France 11, 86
Large, Dan 160
Leavis, F.R. 139
Les empires coloniaux, XIXe–XXe siècle
  98
Lewis, David 156
Li Qingzhao 50
liberalism, neo-liberalism 2, 23
Liddington, Jill 37
Lieux de mémoire 5
Light, Alison 23
Lister, Anne 50
local history 26, 36, 38–40, 42–43, 56, 89,
  118, 128
longue durée 4, 14, 49, 55, 100
Lowenthal, David 23, 25

Mad Men 25
Manco Inca 55–56
Mandler, Peter 2, 12, 110
Mansfield, Nick 126
Marr, Andrew 70, 115–17
Marx, Karl 126; Marxism 3, 64, 84, 131
Matheson, Hilda 46–47, 64
Maya Vision 48–63
McKay, George 126
Médecins Sans Frontières (MSF) 11,
  159–60
Michelet, Jules 2
Melman, Billie 111
military 102, 140, 144, 147–48, 161–62, 164
Mills, Robert 113
Morebath, Devon 55
Moore, Charles 116–17
Morris, William 126
museums 41–42, 48, 91, 99, 170; Brighton
  Museum 36; International Museum of
  Slavery, Liverpool 112; Louvre, Paris
  103–5; Museum of London 39–40, 113;
  Museum and Heritage trade show 40;
  People's History Museum, Manchester
  127; Tolpuddle Martyrs Museum,
  Dorset 127; Durham Mining Museum,
  Spennymore 127; Weald and
  Downland Open Air Museum 51
mybrightonandhove.org.uk 36–38

narratives 48–67
National Archives 26–27
national history 82–91
National Trust 5, 48
nationalism 82; historiographic
  nationalism in Eastern Europe 10,
  83–85; historiographic nationalism
  in Western Europe 10, 85–89
New History 2
New Universities Quarterly 77
Newman, John 50
Nolte, Ernst 87
Nora, Pierre 97
Nussbaum, Martha 14

Occupy (social movement) 123, 124–25,
  129–34
Official History Programme (UK) 161–62
Olympic Games (London, 2012) 8
On Living in an Old Country 23, 120
open access 36, 80, 158, 175, 177
oral history 39–40, 163–64
Organisation for Economic Cooperation
  and Development (OECD) 153, 169

Index   185

Osborne, George 21–22
Overseas Development Institute (ODI) 163
Oxford University Press 34

Paine, Thomas 126–28
Parris, Matthew 74
Past & Present 88
The Past is a Foreign Country 25–26,
Pavone, Claudio 89
Paxman, Jeremy 27, 70
Phelan, Peggy 133
Phillips, Mark Salber 14
post-structuralism 13
Profumo affair 71–72
Protocols of the Elders of Zion 10
Public Private Parnership 7

race 6, 8, 10, 98–99, 114, 118, 124, 141;
   racism 101–2, 105–7
Rackham, Oliver 150
Ranger, Terrence 7
Ravenhill-Johnson, Annie 126
Reith, John 46–48, 64
Reunion, Island of 96–97, 99
R&D ('research and development') 3, 170
Robinson, Emily 8
A Room with a View 24
Rosanvallon, Pierre 15
Ross, Kristin 96
Rothschild, Victor – 3rd Baron
   Rothschild 171–73, 178
Royal Geography Society 40

Saint-Pierre, Abbé de 105
Samuel, Raphael 2, 3, 5, 6, 23, 36–37, 43,
   118, 134
Sandbrook, Dominic 73–76
Schama, Simon 5, 23, 67, 75
Schwarz, Bill 98
Sciences: Natural Sciences 98, 139–40,
   170, 174–77; Social Sciences 145,
   172–73, 178
Schmidt, Mária 84
The Secret History of our Streets 118–19
Sen, Amartya 14
Seven Up 47
sexuality 119; gay rights 113; LGBT
   History Month 50, 113
Shakespeare, William 25, 48, 50, 55
Sharp, Cecil 10
Shepard, Todd 96
Singaravélou, Pierre 98
slavery 103–7, 112
Smail, Daniel Lord 151

Smith, Laurajane 112
Snow, C.P. 139, 151
Social Science Research Council 171–72
South America: cultures 55; landscapes 55
Spain 86, 89, 96, 105, 124
Spencer, Herbert 143, 151
Stewart, Frances 8
Starkey, David 23, 75
Stone, Norman 88
The Story of England 64
Stürmer, Michael 87
The Sunday Express 74
Sudan Open Archive 160

Taylor, A.J.P. 74
television 3, 46–69; dramas 22–25, 49;
   history documentaries 5, 47–67, 111,
   114–15, 118
The Times 72; *The Sunday Times* 73
Theatres of Memory 2, 36, 43, 135
Terroirs 10
Thompson, Edward P. 16, 64
Tilly, Charles 132–33
Titanic 24
Tőkéczki, László 84
trade unionism 125–33
transnational history 90, 96–97, 100–103
Trevelyan, G.M. 12, 14, 16
Troebst, Stefan 83
Trouillot, Michel-Ralph 105
The Tudors 24, 25
Twitter 35, 123, 125, 129

UKIP 15
The Undivided Past 71
United Nations (UN) 153, 157, 164;
   United Nations High Commissioner
   for Refugees (UNHCR) 158
University Grants Committee 169–73

Vergès, Françoise 7
Vickery, Amanda 50
Victoria County History 38
Victorian period 115, 124, 131, 149;
   values 5, 87; Victoriana 6–7

Warde, Paul 14
Ways of Seeing 47
Weber, Max 91
White, Hayden 4
White, Jerry 118
Wilson, Harold 73
Who Do You Think You Are? 26–28, 114
Winkler, August 87

186 *Index*

women's history 8, 49–50, 114
Wood, Michael 5, 27
Woolf, Stuart 90
World History 82, 90, 95–96, 99, 101, 103, 105–6
World Wide Web 6, 29–31, 34–44, 47; crowd sourcing 36; genealogy websites 29–30; online publishing 36, 47; privacy on 30; social media of 30, 72

Wright, Patrick 23, 76–79

Yeandle, Peter 15

Zola, Émile 10